A Note to Parents

DK READERS is a compelling program for beginning readers, designed in conjunction with leading literacy experts, including Dr. Linda Gambrell, Professor of Education at Clemson University. Dr. Gambrell has served as President of the National Reading Conference and the College Reading Association, and has recently been elected to serve as President of the International Reading Association.

Beautiful illustrations and superb full-color photographs combine with engaging, easy-to-read stories to offer a fresh approach to each subject in the series. Each DK READER is guaranteed to capture a child's interest while developing his or her reading skills, general knowledge, and love of reading.

The five levels of DK READERS are aimed at different reading abilities, enabling you to choose the books that are exactly right for your child:

Pre-level 1: Learning to read
Level 1: Beginning to read
Level 2: Beginning to read alone
Level 3: Reading alone
Level 4: Proficient readers

The "normal" age at which a child begins to read can be anywhere from three to eight years old, so these levels are only a general guideline.

No matter which level you select, you can be sure that you are helping your child learn to read, then read to learn!

LONDON, NEW YORK, MUNICH,
MELBOURNE, AND DELHI

Series Editor Deborah Lock
Art Editor Clare Shedden
U.S. Editor John Searcy
Picture Researcher Liz Moore
Jacket Designer Emy Manby
Production Angela Graef
DTP Designer Almudena Díaz
Illustrator Peter Dennis
Subject Consultant Peter Bond

Reading Consultant
Linda Gambrell, Ph.D.

First American Edition, 2006
Published in the United States by DK Publishing, Inc.
375 Hudson Street, New York, New York 10014
07 08 09 10 10 9 8 7 6 5 4 3 2

Copyright © 2006 Dorling Kindersley Limited

Published in Great Britain by Dorling Kindersley Limited

DK books are available at special discounts for bulk purchases for
sale promotions, premiums, fundraising, or educational use.
For details, contact:
DK Publishing Special Markets
375 Hudson Street
New York, New York 10014
SpecialSales@dk.com

Library of Congress Cataloging-in-Publication Data
Hayden, Kate.
Starry sky / written by Kate Hayden.-- 1st American ed.
p. cm. -- (DK readers. Level 2, Beginning to read alone)
Includes index.
ISBN-13: 978-0-7566-1959-6 (pb)
ISBN-13: 978-0-7566-1960-2 (hc)
1. Stars--Juvenile literature. 2. Astronomy--Juvenile literature. I. Title.
II. Dorling Kindersley readers. 2, Beginning to read alone.
QB801.7.H395 2006
523.8--dc22
2006006441

Color reproduction by Colourscan, Singapore
Printed and bound in China by L. Rex Printing Co., Ltd.

The publisher would like to thank the following for their kind
permission to reproduce their photographs:
Position key: a-above; b-below/bottom; c-center; l-left; r-right; t-top
Alamy Images: Mary Evans Picture Library 24tl, 25tr; Picture Contact
26b; Royal Geographical Society 7; **Norbert Aujoulat / Centre National
de la Recherche Scientifique / CNP-MCC:** 4; **www.bridgeman.co.uk:**
27t; British Library 17t; **Corbis:** Claudius / Zefa 11b; Stapleton Collection
9; **DK Images:** Anglo Australian Observatory 20; British Museum, London
17b; NASA 1, 30b, 30-31b; NASA / Hubble Heritage Team 21cl; **NASA:**
CXC/SAO 31t; ESA and The Hubble Heritage Team (STScI / AURA)
21cr, 21bl; H. Ford (JHU), G. Ilingworth (UCSC / LO), M. Clampin
(STScI), G. Hartig (STScI), the ACS Science Team, and ESA 21br;
Robert Williams and the Hubble Deep Field Team (STScI) 21t; **Science
Photo Library:** J-C Cuillandre / Canada-France-Hawaii Telescope 3; Dr
Fred Espenak 19b; MPIA-HD, BIRKLE, SLAWIK 12t; NASA 18-19t;
David Nunuk 5b, 32cra; John Sanford 32t; John Sanford & David Parker
11t; Jerry Schad 22b, 24-25b; Dr. Jurgen Scriba 32clb; Eckhard Slawik 5t,
10b, 15, 16, 23, 27b, 29tl, 29tr; Frank Zullo 14br, 28t
All other images © Dorling Kindersley
For more information see: www.dkimages.com

Discover more at
www.dk.com

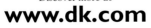

Contents

4 Night sky

6 Constellations

18 The Sun

20 Galaxies

24 Summer Triangle

26 Starry signposts

28 Stargazing

32 Starry facts

DK READERS

BEGINNING TO READ ALONE

2

Starry Sky

Written by Kate Hayden

DK Publishing, Inc.

On a clear, dark night, the sky
sparkles with thousands of stars.
These giant balls of gas make
their own heat and light
just like our closest star, the Sun.

Long ago, when people lived
in caves, they noticed patterns
among the brightest stars.
They made them into pictures.
If you look up into the sky,
you can see star patterns, too.

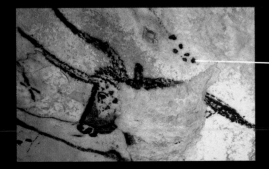

*Stars drawn
onto the wall
of a rock shelter
in France
16,500 years ago*

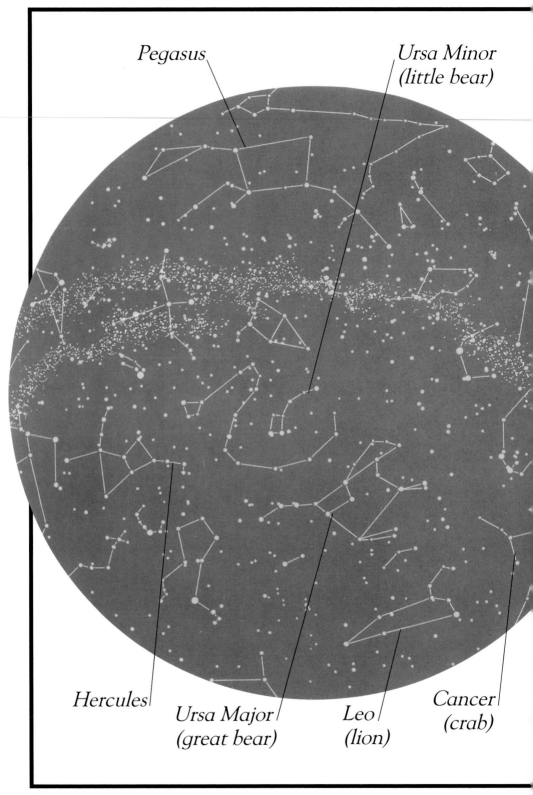

Pegasus

Ursa Minor
(little bear)

Hercules

Ursa Major
(great bear)

Leo
(lion)

Cancer
(crab)

Big star patterns are
called constellations
[KON-stuh-lay-shunz].
Star maps help you find
the constellations.

They tell you what star patterns
you can see at different times
of the year.
Star maps also show you
the different stars you can see
in different parts of the world.

The zodiac
The zodiac is a band of
12 constellations, such
as Leo and Cancer,
that the Sun appears to
pass through in a year.

Cancer the crab

There are 88 named
constellations.
Some are named after animals,
birds, and fish.
Others have the names of people
and creatures from legends.
There are some constellations
named after objects, such as
crowns and cups.
The names help people locate
stars in the night sky.

*Corona
[kuh-ROW-nuh]
the crown*

Ursa Minor

Pegasus

Cancer

Leo

Ursa Major

Hercules

The Big Dipper

The Ursa Major constellation

Many constellations have animal names, such as Ursa Major [ER-suh MAY-jer] the great bear, Leo the lion, and Lupus the wolf. The constellation Taurus [TOR-us] shows the front of a bull. Bulls were important symbols for people in ancient times.

The Big Dipper
A star pattern called the Big Dipper, or the Plow, links seven bright stars in Ursa Major.

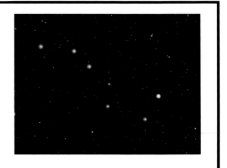

The Taurus constellation

*Apis [AY-pus],
the Ancient Egyptian
bull god*

They made statues of them
and worshipped them as gods.

*The Pleiades
star cluster on
the shoulder of
Taurus*

*The seven sisters
called the Pleiades*

Different cultures tell different
star stories.

In a Greek legend, the hunter
Orion chased seven sisters called
the Pleiades [PLEE-uh-deez].

The girls escaped from him
by turning into doves.
Finally, they became stars.

Navajo [NA-vuh-ho] Indians
call these seven stars
the Flint Boys.
Their sky god, Black God,
wore them on his ankle.
When he stamped
his foot, they bounced
onto his forehead
and stayed there.

The Flint Boys

*Navajo drawing
of Black God*

Orion [oh-RYE-un] the hunter is another well-known constellation. He carries a club, and a sword hangs from his belt.
Nearby is his hunting dog—the constellation Canis Major [KAY-nus MAY-jer] the great dog. The brightest star Sirius [SEER-ee-us], or the Dog Star, is found in this constellation.

Sirius

The Canis Major constellation

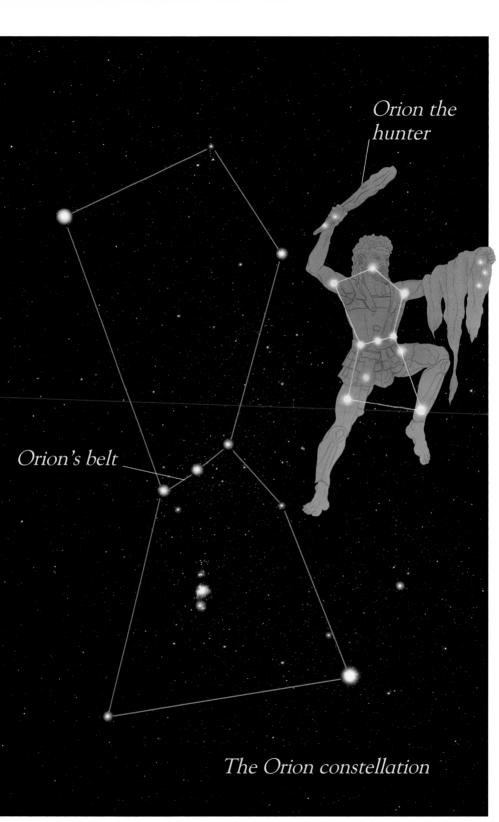

Orion the
hunter

Orion's belt

The Orion constellation

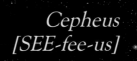

Cepheus
[SEE-fee-us]

Cassiopeia
[kass-ee-oh-PEE-uh]

Perseus
[PURR-see-us]

Andromeda
[an-DRAH-muh-duh]

The W-shaped constellation is called Cassiopeia.

In a Greek story, she is the wife of King Cepheus and they have a daughter named Andromeda.

*Perseus killing
the sea monster Cetus*

Andromeda was chained to
a rock, waiting to be eaten by
the sea monster Cetus [SEE-tus].
The Greek hero Perseus flew down
on the winged horse, Pegasus, and
saved Andromeda.

Pegasus [PEG-uh-sus]
The winged horse, Pegasus,
appears in many Greek
stories. He was shown
on Ancient Greek coins,
vases, and other objects.

Earth is more than one million times smaller than the Sun.

Faraway stars look small
and vary in brightness.
Close-up, they are enormous,
fiery balls of gas.
The Sun is our nearest star.
Explosions in the Sun's scorching
core make it shine.

Huge flares jumping into space from the Sun

Star colors

The hottest stars are blue and the coolest are red. In between are white, yellow, and orange stars.

The sizzling surface simmers like milk bubbling in a saucepan. Heat and light escape into space from the surface.

A spiral galaxy

In our galaxy, the Sun is in one of the spiral arms.

Most stars belong to giant
star groups called galaxies.
The Sun is one of at least
100 billion stars in
the Milky Way galaxy.
This galaxy has a spiral shape.

There are many
other galaxies
in the universe.
Some are spiral
with a bar of stars across the middle.
Others are shaped like tadpoles,
rings, or even Mexican hats!

Sombrero (Mexican
hat) galaxy

Barred-spiral galaxy

Ring galaxy

Tadpole galaxy

A Chinese story says that the star Vega [VEE-guh] was Chih Nu, the gods' weaving girl, and the star Altair was Niu Lang, a cowherd. When Chih Nu married Niu Lang, the angry gods separated them with a river, the Milky Way.

The Milky Way
From Earth, our galaxy is seen on its side. The light from the distant stars looks like a river of milk.

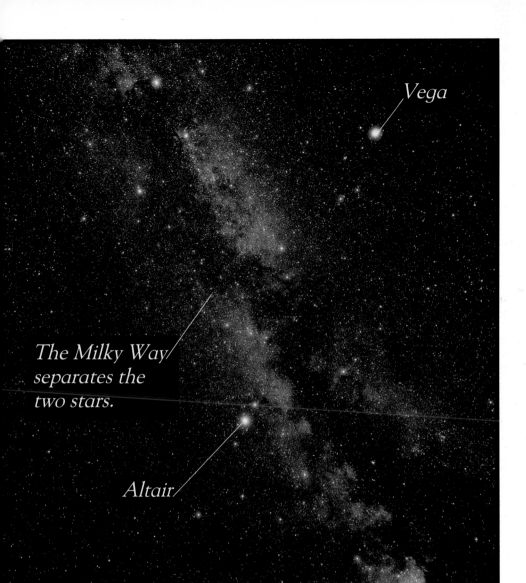

Vega

The Milky Way separates the two stars.

Altair

On Chinese Valentine's Day,
the Milky Way appears dimmer.
On this one day, Chih Nu
and Niu Lang are not separated.

The Eagle

Altair is found in the constellation of Aquila [A-kwuh-luh] the eagle. This bird belonged to the Greek god Zeus.

Altair

Altair, Vega, and a star called Deneb form the Summer Triangle. Deneb is 25 times larger and shines 60,000 times stronger than the Sun.

Vega

Deneb means "tail" in Arabic.
This distant star can be seen
on the tail of the constellation
Cygnus [SIG-nus] the swan.

Stars have often helped people
in their daily lives.
In Egypt, people realized that
when the star Sirius rose before
the Sun in summer, the Nile River
would soon flood.
They needed the flood for growing
healthy crops in their fields.

A traveler finding his position from a star

In the past, sailors and other travelers used special tools to look at stars so they could check their position and find their way.

Starry signposts

Two stars in the Southern Cross point to the South Pole. The North Star is seen above the North Pole.

Sirius, the
brightest star
in the night sky

On a clear night we can see
thousands of stars, and with
special equipment we can see
even more.

Sirius seen through binoculars

Sirius seen through a strong telescope

With binoculars, we can see
tens of thousands of stars.
With a small telescope,
we can see millions of stars.
Astronomers—people
who study the stars—
use powerful telescopes.

Powerful telescopes have been put into space to discover more about the universe. The Hubble Space Telescope orbits the Earth. It provides very detailed images of faraway galaxies.

Hubble Space Telescope

Chandra X-ray
Observatory

The Chandra X-ray Observatory
picks up X-rays—light that is
invisible to us—from the stars.

In the future, who knows
what else we will discover in
the mysterious starry sky. . .

Starry facts

There are more stars in the universe than grains of sand on all of the beaches on Earth.

Astronomers measure how far away stars are in light-years. A light-year is the distance light can travel in a year—about 5.88 trillion miles (9 trillion km). The star Sirius is eight and a half light-years away.

A shooting star is not really a star. It is actually a meteor, a piece of comet dust falling from space.

An observatory is where astronomers observe the night sky. In the mountains of Chile, where the skies are very clear, four separate telescopes work together to get amazing images of the universe.

A planisphere is a star map that has a rotating window. The window is lined up with the date and time of night to show the stars that can be seen.

Also by Will Thomas

Some Danger Involved
To Kingdom Come
The Limehouse Text
The Hellfire Conspiracy

THE BLACK HAND

A Barker & Llewelyn Novel

Will Thomas

A Touchstone Book
Published by Simon & Schuster
New York   London   Toronto   Sydney

TOUCHSTONE
A Division of Simon & Schuster, Inc.
1230 Avenue of the Americas
New York, NY 10020

First Touchstone trade paperback edition July 2008

Library of Congress Cataloging-in-Publication Data

Thomas, Will, 1958–
The black hand : a Barker & Llewelyn novel / Will Thomas.
        p. cm.
    "A Touchstone Book."
1. Barker, Cyrus (Fictitious character)—Fiction. 2. Private investigators—England—London—Fiction. 3. Great Britain—History—Victoria, 1837–1901—Fiction. 4. London (England)—Fiction. I. Title.

PS3620.H644B56 2008
813'.6—dc22   2008013980

ISBN-13: 978-1-4165-5895-8
ISBN-10:   1-4165-5895-0

THE BLACK HAND

I'm not interested in the status quo;
I want to overthrow it.

—Machiavelli

be at that time of night—in bed and thankful for a sturdy roof over my head. Why are leaves from foreign plants always thin and spiky, a danger to one's eyes? Why can't they be round and safe like English leaves?

"Step forward," I muttered to myself. "Step forward. Blast! Where is he?"

Overhead, above the outstretched palm trees and the glass and ironwork canopy, the roiling heavens suddenly released a bolt of lightning that branched across the leaden sky, accompanied by a crash of thunder that rivaled in loudness the explosives I've worked with in the past. All the blackness to which I'd become accustomed was replaced in a heartbeat with whiteness, a polar scene that flashed for a brief second before darkness enveloped us again. That instant revealed the location of the intruder, and I didn't hesitate. My pistol barked, but he was no longer where he'd been.

Reaching a corner, I headed off in a new direction. The rain began in earnest then, beating overhead like grapeshot. Neither of us could rely on sight or sound anymore; we would keep going until we blundered into each other and one of us died. It came sooner than I expected. A splash of lightning revealed an outstretched arm; and before I could move, a blade sliced across my knuckles, causing me to drop my pistol, which skittered across the concrete paving stones to some unknown position. My assailant pressed his advantage, attacking again with an overhand motion, ready to bury a dagger in my chest for decoration, if I had no objections.

I rather thought I had. I raised my left arm to block the stabbing motion; and his blade made a grating, metallic sound against my forearm. Another bolt illuminated us briefly, re-

Prologue

I STEPPED ACROSS THE SILL OF THE CONSERVATORY, glass crunching under the heels of my boots, and steadied my Webley pistol with both hands, reluctant to step inside. It was black as pitch in there, so unlike the safe, comfortable, gas-lit room I was leaving. I could see the palm trees silhouetted against the gray night sky, writhing like demons. The glass had been broken at both ends, affording someone easy access to the house we were supposedly guarding; and the plants brought here from five continents were being buffeted by a gale coming from the Channel. Under such conditions, I'd generally tell the estate owner to go hang himself, but this wasn't just any estate owner. It was *her* estate we were guarding, the Widow's, the lady love of my employer, Cyrus Barker; and I would have done anything to protect her.

The low-lying plants clawed at my trouser legs as I shuffled down the narrow aisle in a fencing stance, leading with my right foot and drawing up my left before stepping out again. I had reason to suspect there was someone in that hothouse jungle, or I'd have been where any sane person would vealing that we were both small and swarthy and armed with the same weapon, as I slid a ten-inch dagger out of my sleeve. My brief scrutiny revealed that my adversary wore the flat black cap of the Sicilians. The sky went black again, and the intruder melted away among the waving fronds.

I backed away until I felt the cold comfort of a glass wall behind me and sidled along it, knowing I'd either circumvent him or meet him coming from the other side. The manor house seemed remote just then, surrounded by this artificial forest created at a rich woman's whim. Pushing through the growth underfoot, I waited for another bolt of lightning to provide a glimpse of my attacker.

Suddenly, the glass behind me shattered as he burst through in a hail of shards. We stabbed at each other back and forth, blocking inexpertly in the semidarkness. I was thinking that I'd had a single lesson in the Sicilian blade, while this lad had likely been indoctrinated in it since youth, when his blade finally found purchase, entering the skin just below my left eye and plowing a furrow almost to my ear. Hot blood spilled down my cheek, and I lurched away into the fury of the gale he had brought with him, a voice in my head telling me I was disfigured for life.

What were professional criminals doing here in the gentle slopes of the Sussex Downs? I asked myself, as I gripped my dagger and tried to ignore the searing pain in my cheek. I should be having tea and trying to winkle secrets of Barker's past from our beautiful hostess. Why had the Mafia chosen now to leave their sun-bleached isle for our northern clime, and how did Barker and I find ourselves the only ones to oppose them? Was it really only a few days since this had all begun?

1

I WAS COMING DOWN THE STAIRS ON THE MORNING of the twenty-second of August 1885, when there came a knock upon Cyrus Barker's front door. Now, I don't function well, as a rule, until coffee is singing freely in my veins, and that day was no exception. I'd applied a naked blade to my throat in two dozen strokes, and handled the task successfully, so my brain and nerves were ready for a rest; and yet there was that irritating knock. I could have answered it, of course, but getting the door was one of our butler's duties. In fact, Jacob Maccabee insisted upon it, as if opening a door was an art requiring years of rigorous discipline and study. I vacillated between the front door, Mac's private domain, and the back hallway. It was like being onstage when an actor misses his cue. I had taken two steps in the direction of the sound when the back door burst open and Mac came in at a trot, muttering under his breath in Yiddish. He brushed past me, giving me a look of minor annoyance— probably for taking up space in his hallway—and continued toward the front door. Freed from the responsibility and the taxing conundrum, I shambled off to the kitchen in search of sustenance.

"*Bonjour,* Etienne," I said to Barker's chef, though I managed to yawn through half of it.

Etienne Dummolard took the cigarette from his mouth long enough to spit upon the slate flagstones in greeting before replacing it again. In a bachelor household such as ours, words are measured slowly in the mornings. Sometimes it is quite eight o'clock before anyone risks a full sentence. I poured my coffee and sat at the table in front of the large window that faced my employer's garden.

Barker was outside, enjoying his potted Eden. He had his jacket off and was practicing one of the longer fighting forms he had learned in China while around him, Asian gardeners raked stones and pushed barrows containing new cuttings. As I watched, Mac came into view from the back door and I followed his progress over the bridge and along the crooked path to our employer. There was a yellow slip of paper in the butler's hand, a telegram. *Thus endeth the mystery of the knock at the door,* I thought, sucking down more coffee. I reached for the marmalade jar and a slice of toast from the rack.

A telegram is generally of interest, most people feeling that sixpence warranted information of some import, but Mac stopped at the edge of the gravel. The form was not to be interrupted. As a play, this was all mildly entertaining, but I'd almost run out of coffee. I got up and poured another cup, noting that Dummolard was making beef and mushroom pie, one of my favorites. When I returned to my seat, Barker had finished the form and was reading the telegram with one hand on his hip.

The Guv nodded and handed it to Mac, who turned back to the house. I opened the Dundee jar and began spreading marmalade onto my toast, noting that Barker was slipping on his jacket. The toast was halfway to my mouth when Mac slapped the telegram against the glass in front of me and I dropped it. According to some inevitable law of physics, the toast fell jam-side down onto my plate. Behind me, Etienne erupted in laughter. He has a rather infantile sense of humor, I've had occasion to notice.

The telegram read:

> SOMETHING HERE POOLE SAYS
> YOU'LL WANT TO SEE STOP
> COME QUICKLY STOP WON'T
> KEEP IT HERE LONG STOP
> DUNHAM

Mac snatched it away and returned to his duties. Barker was just coming over the bridge. There was no time to attempt another slice of toast. I poured the rest of the scalding coffee down my throat and stood.

"No time for breakfast this morning, Etienne," I said, turning to leave.

"*Imbécile,*" Dummolard responded. It's the same word in French and English. His free and caustic opinions would not have been tolerated in any other house in London, but, then, he did not receive any actual pay. He used our kitchen to experiment with new recipes for his Soho restaurant, Le Toison d'Or, claiming he came here out of a sense of gratitude for his former captain in the China Seas—meaning Barker, of course. I thought it more likely he preferred to get away from his wife, Mireille, a six-foot-tall French Valkyrie with whom he had a most volatile relationship.

Once in the hall, I ran to the front door, jammed my straw boater onto my head, and retrieved my malacca stick from the stand. When Barker came through the back door, I was waiting as if I'd been there for some time.

"Good morning, Thomas," he said.

"Morning, sir," I replied. He lifted his own stick from the hall stand and we stepped out the front door into Brook Street. It was a warm morning; summer was keeping its grip on London, refusing to surrender. The houses across the street were painted in sunlight, and the birds in Newington were in full throat. It seemed a shame to bring up the subject of work.

"What do you suppose Dunham wants now?" I asked. A few months earlier we had worked on a case with Inspector Albert Dunham of the Thames Police involving missing children.

"You read the same words I did, lad," he said patiently, as a hansom eased up to the curb and we clambered aboard. We bowled off and were soon clattering down Newington Causeway on our way to London Bridge and Wapping, where the Thames Police station is situated.

Barker lit his pipe and ruminated. Any attempt on my part to instigate polite conversation would have been met with stern resistance—and, at any rate, what would we have discussed? He attended no theater, was tone-deaf, and read few novels. I had not had time to look at the morning's newspapers; and it was too early to discuss ethics, religion, or politics. I had left without eating my toast merely to sit in a cab for forty-five minutes with nothing to do.

Eons later we arrived at the curious vertical building that housed the Thames Police and were directed around to the back to where the steam launches bobbed gently like tin boats in a bath. In the center of the dock, a large tarpaulin had been thrown over an object roughly the size of a chest of drawers. Whatever it was, the object was sodden, probably having been fished from the river. It had also been doused in carbolic, but the constables who manned the dock had managed to use both too much and not enough. It stung the nostrils but did not sufficiently cloak the reek that emanated from it.

"Hello, Barker," Dunham said, coming out of the station with Inspector Poole of the Yard. Dunham was short, barrel-chested, and bandy-legged; while Poole was tall and thin. Dunham had white hair like a wad of cotton, with brows and a mustache as black as shoe polish; whereas Poole was going bald with his long, sandy side-whiskers that swagged to his mustache like curtains. One worked for the Thames Police, the other Scotland Yard; and though the two organizations claimed to cooperate, they were as jealous of each other as a pair of opera sopranos. "Poole here said you might be interested."

"You're working with Scotland Yard on this?" Barker asked.

"I ain't decided yet," Dunham admitted, glancing at his tall companion. "It's river police business so far, but Inspector Poole has been gracious enough to contribute information. He recognized the body and suggested I telegraph you."

"Hello, Cyrus," Poole finally said. He had his hands in his pockets, as if to say he was present merely to give support and would let Dunham handle the actual investigation.

"Terry." My employer nodded.

Poole was one of Barker's friends and a seasoned member of the Criminal Investigation Department. He was also a former student, when the Guv taught a class in antagonistics in the C.I.D. building at Scotland Yard. Unlike my employer, who preferred his independence, Poole functioned well within the hierarchical confines of the Metropolitan Police. He'd need all his tact to deal with the prickly Thames Police inspector.

"Well, show us what you brought us here for," Barker said in his Lowland Scots accent.

"Very well," Dunham replied. "Mind the reek." He took a deep breath, like a diver, and crossed over to the tarpaulin, than whipped the canvas away.

Perhaps it was a trick of my mind, but it seemed as if a brown miasma rose from the horrid spectacle that the sunlight revealed to us without mercy. It was a hogshead whose top had been opened and the hoop dislodged, splaying the staves out on one side like jagged teeth. A very large man filled the barrel the way a cork does the neck of a wine bottle. He wore a checked suit of bilious green, making me think of a giant bullfrog. His face was mottled in death, a waxy yellow like cheese rind above, and rusty purple below. I was suddenly glad I'd only had coffee that morning. We all reached for our handkerchiefs and stuffed them under our noses.

Cyrus Barker moved forward and crouched, resting easily on the balls of his feet, eye to eye with the corpse. Absently, he stuffed his handkerchief in his pocket and examined the face.

"I know this man," he said. "This is Giorgio Serafini. He

was an assassin, the best north of Naples. I would not have believed this without seeing it with my own eyes."

I recalled Serafini, whom Barker had questioned during our first case together. He'd worn a checked suit then as yellow as Coleman's mustard, and had a high-pitched voice with no trace of an Italian accent. He'd tried to intimidate Barker and ended up flat on his stomach in front of his employer. The meeting had taken place in a restaurant called the Neapolitan, owned by Victor Gigliotti, leader of an Italian criminal organization called the Camorra.

Barker stood again and circled the barrel. He completely removed the top hoop and jumped back as the rest of the staves fanned out. He is fastidious about his clothing. Serafini's rigid body sat upright in the center, like a stamen surrounded by petals. The effluvia began to work its way around the edges of my handkerchief. Barker coughed once into the back of his hand.

"Get that bloody carboy out here again!" Dunham barked.

One of the constables ran into the station and trotted back a minute later with a large glass container of disinfectant to pour over the head of the late Giorgio Serafini. Of the two—the stench of decay or the burning carbolic—I could not say which was worse.

Barker had stepped out of the way and was now staring down the river. His hand came up and he scratched under his chin, as he often did when he was thinking.

"Are there many Italians working on the river?" he asked. "Dockworkers, stevedores, and so forth?"

"You're asking me?" Dunham replied, breaking into a grin. "I thought you knew everything. Yes, as a matter of fact, there are. Hundreds of 'em. Mostly casual laborers."

"Are many of them Sicilian?"

"Sicilian?" Dunham asked, as if it were a new word to his vocabulary. "Dunno 'bout that. One I-talian's pretty much like another, I reckon."

"Oh, no," I put in. "They're all different. Italy's only been unified in recent times, and even now, the country is in discord. Most of the south is full of secret criminal societies. What are their names, sir?"

"The 'ndrangheta," Barker supplied. "The Mafia—"

"I've heard of the Mafia," Poole said, looking up. "They're the Sicilians, right? An inspector from Palermo is at the Yard this week. He spoke of the troubles they have down there."

"This kind of trouble," Barker said, tapping the barrel with the head of his stick.

"You think the Sicilians are behind this?" Dunham asked.

Barker shrugged. "They export olive oil in Sicily, and they use a lot of barrels. This sort of thing is common there."

"Well, it ain't here," Dunham stated. "The only thing we store in barrels is good English ale, which is as it should be."

"Any sign of how he died, Cyrus?" Poole asked.

Barker nodded. "Shotgun wounds, close up. One here in the right breast, you see, and the other in the back. It scorched the clothing, and the pellet pattern is very tight. I'd say the shooter got him in the back at point-blank range and, when he was down, administered the coup de grâce."

"I wonder how long he's been in the river," Poole said.

"A week or more, I'd say," Dunham answered, being the expert on anything pertaining to the water. "They shot your boy here and bunged him in the barrel, then tossed it

off a dock somewheres. The air in his lungs couldn't coun-
teract the weight of the barrel and the flesh and bone. It
sank to the bottom, probably not more than ten or fifteen
feet, and stayed there for several days, putrefying. Then the
body filled with enough gases to lift the barrel off the bottom again. I reckon a fellow as big as this one coulda done
that. The barrel eventually came to the surface and was spotted by pedestrians on London Bridge. Some fishermen tried
to pull it in, but it was too heavy without a winch. We was
called in, and don't even ask me what it was like when we
pried off the lid. Made me wonder how much pension I'd
have if I resigned this morning."

"Have you sent word to the Poplar Morgue?" my employer asked.

"We have," Dunham said. "They are taking their time
getting here with their barrow. So you think this is some sort
of feud among the I-talians?"

"It would appear so. They have elevated opinions of
honor and are often involved in acts of retribution such as
this."

"So this fat fellow was an assassin," Poole said. "I've
heard his name before but never actually laid eyes upon him.
To tell the truth, for a professional killer, he doesn't look like
much."

"Don't let his girth fool you; he could move very quickly
and shoot with unerring accuracy. On a dare, he once shot
down the barrel of another rifle at fifty yards, bursting the
shell in the chamber, or so I've heard." Barker began pushing
on one of the lower staves with his stick. It was not going to
be an easy thing to get this huge, bloated body onto the barrow when it arrived.

"Sir," I said, as a thought occurred to me. "What about Serafini's wife? The two were inseparable."

"Very good, lad," Barker said. "You remembered."

"It's difficult to forget the first woman who throws a dagger at you."

"Well," Barker said, peering into the barrel with a sigh. "They are inseparable still. She's here at the bottom. I'm afraid the morgue may need to send another barrow."

2

THERE IS NOTHING AN EAST-ENDER LIKES TO DO more than gawk; and if the sight is gruesome, so much the better. The Thames constables, with the peculiar water-spider insignias on their uniforms, kept the crowd pressed behind a barrier; but still every man, woman, and child was afforded a clear view of the late Mr. and Mrs. Serafini being extracted from the barrel. One of the constables even set up a tripod and camera to record the victims in situ, but whether it was for official purposes or a personal souvenir I could not say.

Theoretically, we were gawking with the rest of them, though we had been given a closer view. So far our agency was without a client, though I was certain Victor Gigliotti would be interested in hiring our services. However, if I knew Cyrus Barker, he would refuse such an offer, since the Camorran would undoubtedly set his men loose upon Serafini's killer like a pack of hounds. Beneath his rough-hewn exterior, the Guv's scruples grind exceedingly fine.

We departed ahead of the barrow, bound for the Poplar Morgue, a ten-minute walk. Barker knew the way better than I, for I had not yet developed the mastery of London streets that he has, being content with a skeletal knowledge of the main thoroughfares and the use of the odd map. Barker's method involved tacking an ordnance map to the wall at knee level, sitting on the floor cross-legged, memorizing street by street for an hour, as if the map were a Tibetan mandala. The position gives me leg cramp.

When we arrived, the coroner for the East End, Edward Vandeleur, was occupied with another postmortem. We cooled our heels in the main corridor, while the assistants, in gutta-percha aprons, brought in the bodies and washed them down with more carbolic. I sat and pondered the fact that there was at least one occupation worse than mine to be had in London.

One of the doors in the hall opened suddenly and Vandeleur appeared, his long laboratory coat heavily stained with gore. His appearance always reminded me of Franz Liszt, with his sharp features and shoulder-length white hair combed severely back. Vandeleur was a perfect choice for an East End coroner, having both a law and a medical degree, no small feat. The latter is not a requirement for the position, and most coroners depend on hired surgeons to do their postmortems for them, at two pounds apiece. By doing them himself, Vandeleur was not only saving the government two quid, but also was able to draw his own conclusions, which was far more important.

"Barker!" he said, when he'd noticed us sitting on the bench. "What are you doing here already?"

The Guv frowned. "I came to see about a postmortem."

"I've just finished it. Come have a look."

Confused, we stood and followed him into the room, to the spattered table where a corpse lay. I had reached that state in my experience as an enquiry agent where the sight of a body no longer made me ill. On the marble slab, its fluids draining into the troughs on the sides, was the body of a man in his early sixties. His nude form had been savaged by the examination process, and the top of his skull lay in a pan. The neatly trimmed gray beard and the state of the nails and hands informed me that this was no common East-ender but a man of substance, a merchant, perhaps, or a banker.

"What have we here?" Barker asked, looking at the corpse.

"Don't you recognize him?" Vandeleur asked. "It's Sir Alan Bledsoe."

"Director of the East and West India Docks? He's one of the most powerful men in the East End. What's his body doing here?"

I concurred with my employer that the sight of a man so important to Her Majesty's government lying here in the Poplar Mortuary was unexpected. Men like Bledsoe died in their Pall Mall clubs or their manors in Hampshire. This corpse was on the wrong side of town.

"His body was found yesterday afternoon in Victoria Park. He went there every day after lunch to read the newspaper. In fact, *The Times* was still open in his hands when he was found. All factors point to heart failure. He'd already had one a year ago, and was taking digitalis for it. Since the death occurred nearby, the body was brought here, but I've had a devil of a time getting permission to do the postmortem. The examination itself was rather routine until about fifteen minutes ago, when I discovered the actual cause of his death."

"What caused you to doubt it was heart failure?" the Guv asked.

"I found ash on the man's lips. As luck would have it, I'd seen that sort of thing before. I inserted a long forceps into the throat, and what do you suppose I found? The fag end of a cheroot."

"He'd swallowed it?" I asked. Sometimes I speak before I think. "Was it lit?"

"It was. Singed his throat, though he was beyond caring by that time. With an infarction of the heart, there is often a constriction of the chest cavity, producing a cough. But if the victim is shot or stabbed, there is an involuntary, sharp intake of breath, and the jaw unclamps. The result is that the cheroot or cigarette may be swallowed. It happens more often than one might think. It's not conclusive in a court of law, of course, but it was enough to send me looking for an alternative means of death. I methodically examined the body from scalp to sole but found no external wound. I thought perhaps my hunch was wrong."

"You're rarely wrong, Dr. Vandeleur. What was the actual cause of death?" Barker asked.

"Something had been inserted into his ear, penetrating the brain; some kind of stout wire perhaps, or an ice pick. Killed him instantly."

"Wouldn't that result in an issue of blood?"

"It did. There was a small amount in the ear canal, but the outer ear appears to have been wiped clean. Someone came up behind him while he was reading and killed him so quickly he never even had time to drop his newspaper."

"The thing that strikes me," the Guv said, "is the only person I know in London capable of such a subtle method of killing is in the other room there, being disinfected at this very moment, an Italian assassin named Serafini. In fact, it was Serafini's postmortem I was coming here to speak with you about."

"That's more than a coincidence," Vandeleur said. "Was he killed the same way?"

"No, but he was definitely murdered."

"Let's take a look. I don't suppose Sir Alan will mind if I sew him up later."

The doctor led us across the hall. If possible, the odor of the corpses was even stronger in the confines of the examination room. Serafini's form lay stretched on the table, a mountain of mottled flesh. Beside it, the coroner's assistants bent over a second table.

"What's going on here?" Vandeleur asked curiously, looking over their shoulders before stepping back with a start. "Ye gods! What is it?"

"It's a woman, sir," the first assistant said. The man's name, I knew, was Trent, and he had helped us on a previous case. Medical students were always queuing up to work under Vandeleur. He was the best coroner in London. "Most of the bones have been crushed. There's no way we'll ever get her stretched out, I'm afraid."

"It's Serafini's wife," Barker supplied. "He never went anywhere without her, not even into the afterlife."

"It's obvious both were dispatched by shotguns, though it won't be official until I file my report. Your Italian assassin took a gun blast to the chest."

There was no doubting it, for a purplish wound cratered

his left breast and another was found among the ribs on his right side.

"I beg your pardon, Dr. Vandeleur," Trent put in, "but there's another in his back and two in the woman's as well."

"His flesh is all churned up," the coroner said. Pulling the forceps from his pocket again, he began poking about the wounds. In a moment, he held up a round, metal ball.

"Lead shot," he pronounced. "His internal organs are peppered with it."

Barker crossed his arms. "Two blasts; four, if you count his wife. Even if one were to discharge one barrel at a time, it would require reloading."

"I cannot imagine either one of them giving someone sufficient time to reload," I hazarded.

"Very true, Thomas," my employer said. "This was done by two men, then, who would have to be professional killers. For all his girth, Serafini was quick and deadly, and his wife every bit as dangerous as he. Only professionals could have killed him."

"Three assassinations in London in a day?" Vandeleur remarked. "What is the city coming to?"

"I don't know, but I intend to find out. So, shall you give a verdict of willful murder regarding Sir Alan?"

Vandeleur stepped into the corridor, and my employer and I followed him, leaving his assistants to their grisly task.

"I am not in the habit of sharing my conclusions before rendering a verdict, Mr. Barker," he said cautiously, putting the forceps back in his pocket, "but the evidence seems conclusive enough."

"Is there no possible way that he could have had a seizure which produced bleeding in the brain?"

"Keep to your own field, Barker, and leave the diagnoses to a trained pathologist," Vandeleur snapped. He could be quite waspish at times.

My employer hesitated. "I was merely thinking of your reputation. In your shoes, I would not wish to render a verdict based upon a wound so small it is barely visible. I wonder how you even spotted it, despite the convolutions of the brain."

"It was the blood in the ear canal. What are you getting at?"

"I'm afraid no good can come of declaring it a murder. Sir Alan was a very important man. Is there proof it will hold up in court? Most likely, the government shall think you mad despite your reputation, and your position will be in jeopardy."

"Are you suggesting I render a false verdict?" Vandeleur snapped. "I have never done so in my life and shall certainly not start now."

"I was thinking of Sir Alan's wife and Scotland Yard. They will wish to avoid a scandal at all costs. The wound is too small to appear in any photograph. As far as I can see, you won't have enough proof to convince your peers."

"For once, I don't require it. A half hour ago, a representative of Her Majesty's government arrived informing me that Sir Alan's death was now a government matter. I don't know how he knew the man had been murdered. He said he sent for you, as well. That's what I thought you were here about when I saw you in the corridor."

"I'd like to speak with this gentleman," my employer said. "Where is he now?"

Vandeleur led us out of the room and down the main

corridor, while I contemplated what it would be like to work all day in a place that smelled of carbolic and moldering bodies. Just before we reached the desk, where an orderly watched like a sentinel, Vandeleur turned and opened a door on the left.

A man stood up in the room beyond, but I could not see him. Barker is over six feet, and Vandeleur approaches it. As unobtrusively as possible, I tried to peer over their shoulders. I was expecting a stranger, but in fact I knew the man. Coupled with what I had seen so far that day, I rather wished I didn't.

3

"GOOD MORNING, MR. ANDERSON," BARKER SAID.

The official was Robert Anderson of the Home Office, a man with a most intriguing title, that of Spymaster General. He had employed us a year before in an action against a group of Irish dynamiters. At the time, he had attempted to recruit my employer, saying he had more than enough work for him, but Barker had turned him down. It didn't take a private enquiry agent to see that he was about to ask him again.

"You look fit," Anderson said. "Are you still causing trouble?"

"I'm still setting all the government lads straight, if that is what you mean."

"You know how it is, Mr. Barker. Too much to keep up with, too little payroll for overworked men. Why don't we take a walk? The smell in here is giving me a headache."

Anderson passed between us. He was a man in his mid-fifties, his hair and beard just starting to gray. Barker had told me once that Anderson was a devout Evangelical who

spent his nights studying biblical numerology. The spymaster walked to the door and opened it, saying, "Are you coming?" He was unaccustomed to being refused. With a nod at
Vandeleur, Cyrus Barker followed Anderson, with me making a trio.

"Is he coming, too?"

"He is," the Guv said. "Anything you wish to say can be
said in his presence. It won't be repeated."

I'm grateful for whatever praise Barker throws my way.
Like most Scotsmen, he's frugal with it. In fact, I'd say a dog
would starve on it, but perhaps I exaggerate.

"Very well. He was present at our last encounter, I suppose. Come."

The attendant generally has visitors sign in and out, but
he did not come forward as the three of us left the morgue
and began walking down Poplar's High Street, a downtrod-
den street like a thousand others in the East End.

"Sir Alan was murdered by men from Sicily, who are
part of a criminal society that calls itself the Mafia," the
Home Office man said.

"I am familiar with the Mafia," Barker rumbled.

"I assumed you would be. Your file says you are informed on the workings of most secret societies. That's why
I need your help."

"Oh, come, the information I have could be memorized
by the average constable in an hour or so. There's more to
your being here than that."

"There is," Anderson admitted. "There has been a sharp
rise in crime all over London in the last month or so, particularly among the criminal class. Close to a dozen have crawled
or been carried into local hospitals with stab wounds. Mer-

chants have been harassed, young women interfered with, and fights broken out along the river under the slightest provocation. It's as if London has gone back to the days of Marlowe, where the slightest brush against a fellow would cause a duel."

"Surely you know who is responsible," Barker said.

"Yes. It's a group of dockworkers from Sicily, perhaps a hundred or more, mostly casual labor. They go where the work is, and right now, they're needed to unload cargo from the Indies and America. They live with the other Italians in Clerkenwell."

"You know who they are and where they are. Why not simply arrest them?"

"It's like trying to pick up sand with your hands. Most of it escapes. We've deported a few dozen to the Continent, only to find them back in London within a week, even more determined to cause trouble."

"They are playing by Palermo rules," Barker explained. "Justice is swift and punishment severe. London must seem like a holiday to them. Have there been any known incidents of one Sicilian group attacking another?"

"Not to my knowledge."

"Then I would hazard a guess that it's being planned by a single man, an organizer recently arrived, someone the Sicilian dockworkers look up to and will follow who can keep them from fighting among themselves. It would have to be someone highly placed in their organization. Find him, and you'll bust his ring of criminals."

"We're not total dolts at the Home Office, Mr. Barker. We understand that, but no one has come forward with reliable information, not even for money. There's a rumor of one or more caped figures moving about London, but who they are is still unknown, and it may be a hoax." We passed a closed vehicle at the curb and Anderson spoke to the driver. "Follow at a discreet distance. Keep your eyes and ears open."

"Yes, sir," the driver said, a young man who looked too well-groomed to be a common cabbie. He must be another Home Office man.

"This way, gentlemen," Robert Anderson coaxed. "There is still much to talk about."

"Aye, there is," Barker said. "Why isn't the Yard being brought in on this matter?"

"They're working on it already, but we'd rather keep our oars in."

"You make it sound like the annual boat races on the Thames, Oxford versus Cambridge. Anyone I personally bring in to help will find his life in danger. I'm loath to allow that to happen merely so that the Home Office can put one over on the Yard—or the Foreign Office, for that matter."

"Your point is well taken," Anderson said, not insulted, "but I feel that for once, it will take a combined effort to stop this organization. Once these people are established, they are like rats, nearly impossible to drive out. However, my staff is still occupied with the Fenian crisis. Frankly, we're spread too thin to handle both situations. That's why I thought of you."

"So, you're throwing it all in my lap, to handle as I choose?"

"Within reason. I don't want anything on the front page of *The Times*. Under normal conditions, I would be concerned that you are something of a law unto yourself."

"What concerns me," Barker said, stopping to pull his

tobacco and pipe from his pocket, "is that I'm but one man—two if you count Llewelyn here. If pressed, I could collect a handful, but it sounds to me as if you require an army. I've tried the army life and have no taste for it."

"Are you turning me down?"

Barker paused to light his pipe, taking his time about it. The spymaster huffed impatiently.

"I am considering it," the Guv said, blowing out his vesta. "Do you wish to deport only the Mafia, or do you also include the Sicilians or even the Italians? That's a tall order."

"I'm not one of these 'England for the English' chaps," Anderson stated. "If the Italians and Sicilians wish to come here and succeed through hard work and obeying the laws, they are welcome. But if I have to deport a hundred unlawful immigrants in order to stop a handful of Mafia criminals knowledgeable about making bombs and killing people, I won't lose any sleep over it. I have public safety to consider and I can't afford to be subtle."

Just then it began to rain, and we took shelter under a butcher's awning, trying to ignore the hanging ducks and pig carcasses on the other side of the glass. My mind tried not to connect the sight to our recent viewing of the late Sir Alan Bledsoe of the East and West India Docks, tried and failed in the attempt. The bile rose in my throat.

Barker spoke. "I may be able to assemble some men because they are opportunistic and others because they owe me a debt, but if I need to pay for the services of others, will funds be available?"

"Very little, I'm afraid, beyond your two salaries. You know how tightfisted my superiors can be."

Our remuneration for the last case we took from the

Home Office had barely covered expenses. It was a wonder to me how anything in the Empire was accomplished if every department ran on so tight a budget.

"We shall simply have to make do. I'm owed certain favors here and there. Perhaps I'll call in my debts."

"You do that," Anderson said, as I wondered just what sort of debts he would call in.

"Just how much autonomy would I have?" my employer asked, watching the rain puddling on the pavement while puffing meditatively on his pipe.

"How much autonomy do you need?"

"Carte blanche."

"Impossible," the Home Office man said, crossing his arms. "My superiors would never allow it. That's the complaint the Foreign Office has with you. You always want things your way."

We waited for Barker's response. And waited. He seemed in no hurry to give one, safe from the downpour, with the pipe stem between his square white teeth. Give the man a book and he could stand there all day.

Robert Anderson could not. He had neither the time nor the patience. "Well?"

We stepped back as a gust of wind sprayed rain across our shoes.

"Mr. Anderson, I understand how important this matter is. I don't want the Mafia working in London. It would change the game completely. If I had wanted to open my agency in Palermo, I'd have stopped there instead of coming all the way to London."

"I'm sure the climate is better," I remarked, looking at the sky.

"This is nothing, lad," Barker said to me. "Someday, I'll show you a Chinese monsoon. A man could drown standing in the middle of the street. Very well, Mr. Anderson. I'll accept the case as we've discussed it."

"You're certain you can complete it successfully? We are taking a very large chance," Anderson said, as if my remark had not reached his ear. A man single-handedly saving the British Empire does not have time for the flippant remarks of a private enquiry agent's assistant.

"No less so than in most of my cases. If I thought otherwise, I wouldn't accept the offer."

"Understand that the Home Office might find the subject too volatile to handle publicly."

"I'm not concerned," the Guv replied. "It will be in my hands to bring the work within the perimeters of governmental requirements."

"Very well," Anderson said, offering his hand. "Consider yourself working for the Home Office again." Barker seized Anderson's hand and shook it in his manner—two pumps that almost pull one's arm from the shoulder socket.

"Good, then," my employer said. "Who is in charge of the investigation at Scotland Yard? Please tell me it is not Munro."

Inspector James Munro was one of the few men at Scotland Yard with whom Barker did not get along. It might be closer to the mark to say they despised each other.

"No. I understand the C.I.D. is handling the case. I believe an Inspector Poole is coordinating the effort."

"Poole?" Barker murmured.

"You know him?"

"I know him well. You said it is permissible to coordinate with Scotland Yard at some point?"

"It would be in your best interests not to tell Poole you're working for the Home Office, politics being what they are, but I suppose you are bound to run into the C.I.D. eventually. If you succeed, those to whom it matters will know whose operation it was. You have permission to work with the Yard if you find it necessary. Have you got a plan in mind?"

"Not yet," Barker admitted. "I'll come up with one in a few days. If you receive any pertinent information, send it directly to my office."

"Very well," Anderson said. "I suppose there'll be no going undercover on this one."

He was referring to our Irish case, in which we'd posed as a German bomb maker and his protégé.

"No," he said. "The best plan when facing the Mafia is to be as mobile as possible and to gather about one men as vicious and cunning as any they can produce. To beat a Sicilian, one must think like a Sicilian."

"And can you?"

"I believe I can. It's necessary in my work to know my adversaries."

Anderson nodded. "Good. I'll leave you to your plans. I need to get back to Whitehall. I'll await word from you."

He stepped out into the downpour as his cab came up the street to meet him. His driver was now sodden and looked in need of a restorative cup of tea, if nothing stronger. Barker put away his pipe and we stepped out from under the awning, the rain drumming on the brims of our bowlers, not an unpleasant sound.

"Are you sure you can find enough men to take on the Mafia, sir?" I asked, struggling to keep up with his long strides while skipping around puddles.

"We shall see, lad."

"You seemed very accommodating," I continued. "I rather thought you might turn him down."

"Someone has to get involved, Thomas, and if the Home Office's hands are tied at the moment, I'd rather it was me. Scotland Yard is excellent at what it does, but this sort of thing is beyond its scope."

"Anderson must trust you implicitly to ask you to take over what the Home Office can't do itself."

"Perhaps," Barker admitted, raising his stick to hail a cab while the rain poured off the brims of our bowlers, "but on the other hand, I've put him into my debt, which is a very important thing if we are going into debt ourselves."

"Debt?" I asked, thinking of his account at the Bank of England.

"Aye. Oh, not money, lad. Favors. Don't think anyone is going to help us merely out of the goodness of his heart."

4

FOR ONCE I HAD SOME IDEA WHERE WE WERE
going as we clattered along Aldgate High Street, heading
toward the West End. Our destination was the Neapolitan,
a restaurant in Westminster run by Serafini's former employer, Victor Gigliotti, leader of the English branch of the
Camorra. Gigliotti's bodyguard and his wife were now dead,
leaving me to assume Gigliotti must have done something
to warrant the attack on his people.

In Marsham Street, we pulled up to the curb and
alighted. Passing beneath the metal red, white, and green
flags of unified Italy that adorned the exterior of the restaurant, we stepped inside. A large portrait of Giuseppi
Garibaldi, the Italian patriot, hung on one wall. Not as
welcoming perhaps were the steely stares of several hard-
looking men in the room, including the owner, who sat at
a table near the back. The bodyguards moved their hands
nearer to where their guns were secreted as we entered, but
Gigliotti held up a hand to them.

"Victor," my employer said, coming to a stop in front of

his table and offering a slight bow of respect as he removed his bowler.

"Cyrus," the man replied with a smile, revealing a wide mouth with sharp canines. He was about thirty, thin but well built, with pomaded black hair. His jawline was so dark it looked as if gunpowder had been discharged into it. He spoke with only a slight accent. "How have I offended you that you have not honored my establishment with your presence in over a year? Rafael! A bottle of Gallo Nero and some antipasto."

Barker pulled out a chair and sat close to him, speaking in a low voice. Gigliotti looked around, as if he did not even trust his own employees, and waved Barker even closer. The Guv spoke for almost a minute in his ear. As he listened, the Camorran smoothed a hand across his hair, though it was as flawless as if it had been shellacked. Eventually he nodded and sighed.

"Forgive my manners in not coming sooner, Victor," Barker said, sitting back. "My only excuse is that I go where my work takes me, and there is no crime in Westminster to speak of, largely due to your presence."

The table was suddenly surrounded by a gaggle of mustached waiters in long white aprons, setting down bottles and glasses and plates. A basket of fragrant, hot bread wrapped in linen appeared and then a cold platter of rolled meats and cheeses with olives. We helped ourselves. Perhaps it seems strange dining after the morning's tragedy, but it is the Italian habit to punctuate everything, especially death, with food.

Gigliotti unstopped the basket-covered bottle of Chianti and poured three glasses with polished ease. He gave us each one and then raised his own.

"To Giorgio and Isabella, may they rest in such peace as God will allow them. They were cold-blooded killers and mad as hatters, but they celebrated life better than any Englishman."

We drank. The Chianti was strong and sour, but it went well with the food. Gigliotti allowed us to eat for another minute or two, though I knew he must have questions about the fate of the Serafinis. An unwritten protocol demanded that everything occur in precise order, a play in which I alone seemed to be without a script.

"Barreled," the Camorran finally said. "You know what that means."

Barker nodded. "Sicilians, unless you have internal troubles of your own."

"We don't," Gigliotti insisted, "and if we did, we would not be so ignorant as to float them in barrels. One might as well paint an Italian flag upon the lid for all London to see. Our community will be blamed for this. Giorgio, Giorgio! Who would have thought you'd be caught out in this manner?"

"It appeared to be the work of two men," the Guv went on. "Serafini and his wife were gunned down together."

"No one ever thought Isabella would die in bed."

"There was another murder yesterday."

Gigliotti gave him a sharp stare. "Who was killed?"

"Sir Alan Bledsoe, director of the East and West India Docks."

"Bledsoe, is it?" Gigliotti asked. "My supplies for this restaurant, the ice warehouse, and my other businesses all arrive at those docks."

"Bledsoe was stabbed in the ear with a sharp instrument,

perhaps an ice pick. His death was made to look like heart failure, but something was driven into his brain."

"Ice pick? I own the largest ice warehouse in London. It looks as if the Sicilians are trying to implicate me in Bledsoe's murder. It is an old Sicilian murder method, used to get rid of judges and witnesses." He snorted in anger. "I liked Sir Alan. We had a good working relationship. Now the position shall probably fall to Dalton Green, who is a martinet and far less willing to listen to reason."

"Has there been any friction on the docks between the Italians and Sicilians?" Barker asked.

"Several of my people have approached me about the Sicilian riffraff. There have been fights, robberies, and men demanding money from merchants for protection. The English don't know the difference between an Italian and a Sicilian, and we all get blamed. I have never interfered in Sir Alan's work, though the docks are a necessary part of my business, because I felt he ran a tight ship; but recently, I spoke to him myself and expressed my concerns. He told me he would consider excluding the Sicilians from the docks permanently."

"Who is the leader of the Sicilians?" my employer asked. "You are head of the Italian community. Surely you must have heard."

"There isn't one that I know of," Gigliotti replied with a shrug. "Until now it has been individuals, doing in London as they did in Palermo. Such small crimes are not worth my attention."

"Until now, as you say. Someone hired professionals to kill the Serafinis and Sir Alan. What was Serafini doing when he disappeared?" the Guv asked.

Gigliotti shook his head. "I have had few assignments for him. He and Isabella discussed going to Naples, despite a warrant there for their arrest. Looking back, I would say Giorgio had grown out of touch with the dangers he faced. I fear we have all become Anglicized."

"Might it be possible to insinuate someone among the Sicilians and pick up information?" my employer asked.

"No," Gigliotti said, dismissing the idea out of hand. "They trust no one but Sicilians. Even then, they are always feuding with one another. It is said that a Sicilian hates everyone but his own brothers, and those he merely distrusts. Sicily is a crucible of poison. What it knows, how it acts, will infect your own native criminal classes in London. They will find this new group has something to teach them about ruthlessness and will admire the way these men do business with heavy arms and cold eyes. Even if they are deported, London may never return to the way it was."

Gigliotti drained the rest of his wine in one gulp. "So," he said, pouring another glass, "would you consider helping me put the Mafia in its place? It is the Mafia we are speaking of, you know. No one else would dare come against me."

"I did not intend to get involved," Barker replied.

"The Sicilians are a plague, Cyrus, and not even you will be immune to it."

"Going up against the Sicilian Mafia is not something one undertakes lightly, Victor," Barker said.

"You need not get involved. Your honor was not besmirched. It is a matter for my people."

Barker stood. I wondered if he was going to tell Gigliotti that he had already been recruited by the Home Office. "One need not be a member of the Honored Society to have honor.

However, going up against the Sicilians would take a great deal of planning. This must be thought out thoroughly."

"You have lived among the English too long, Cyrus. You have become phlegmatic. Don't expect me to sit on my hands and wait for you. Good day."

We had been dismissed. Barker stood and nodded, then we left the restaurant. Outside, he strode off in the direction of Whitehall, deep in thought, but I wasn't about to let him walk in silence.

"Would you really consider working with Gigliotti? He's a criminal."

"There aren't many choices. We should at least keep the Camorrans in reserve."

"Wouldn't it be best if Scotland Yard had all the Sicilians arrested and deported?"

"Not every Sicilian is a *mafiusu,* any more than every Irishman is a terrorist. Some have come here to escape the violence."

There was no doubt in my mind that the Guv had agreed to a task of Herculean proportions and volunteered my services without so much as a by-your-leave. How could he possibly assemble a group that could stop someone of Serafini's caliber? I badgered him with questions all the way to Craig's Court, where I suddenly slipped on the pavement and almost fell. Barker put a steady hand on my shoulder and pointed to the paving stones with his stick.

"Blood," he uttered.

There was a puddle of it just inside the narrow entrance to Craig's Court.

"There's another," I said, pointing a few yards closer to our office door.

We hurried up the steps and went inside, where we found our clerk, Jenkins, kneeling in the middle of the waiting room. He was unhurt, but a man lay prone in front of him in a pool of dark blood, a man I knew quite well.

"Etienne!" I cried.

Then, as Barker dropped to his knees to check the pulse of his old friend, my eyes focused on a sheet of paper that lay beside the Guv's cook, a sheet with a black hand inked in the very center of it. *This has struck too close to home,* I thought. There would be no talking Barker out of it now.

5

———⁓⁓⁓———

IS HE ALIVE?" I ASKED. SURELY DUMMOLARD COULD not be dead, my mind told me. I'd spoken to him but a few hours before.

"Yes," Barker said, "but his pulse is weak."

"He tumbled in not a minute ago, sir, all covered in blood!" Jenkins blurted.

"Turn him over gently," Barker ordered. "Very, very gently."

We did so, laying him supine on our entranceway carpet, my mind registering the fact that the bloodstains might never come out. Dummolard's shirt was slick with crimson from chest to waist, but whether he'd been shot or stabbed we could not tell. He groaned suddenly. He was alive, at least for the present.

"The ewer, lad," Barker said. "Bring it quickly."

I ran through our chambers to the table behind his desk where Barker kept a full pitcher of water and brought it back to him. My employer had reached into the sleeve of his coat where he kept his dagger and cut open Etienne's shirt, revealing our cook's thick pelt of chest hair matted with blood. The Guv is a believer in expediency. I would have wiped gingerly until the wound was exposed, but he emptied the pitcher onto the man's chest.

"Blade wound to the stomach," he pronounced. "Looks deep."

As we watched, blood seeped from the wound, and Etienne gave another groan. His pale lips were moving, but no sound came out. I bent forward and listened closely.

"Front and back," I said, after finally making sense of what he had murmured. "He's been stabbed twice, sir."

"You had better run over to Charing Cross Hospital for a barrow, lad. I don't believe he'd survive a cab journey."

There was no horse ambulance system in London at that time. Everyone, be it His Lordship with an acute case of gout or Old Sal, knocked down the tenement stairs by her fella, had to go to hospital on one of the public hand barrows, the only manner of conveyance. The lack of ambulances was a public disgrace, and there was much discussion of it in the newspapers. The Metropolitan Police had wheeled over fifteen hundred people to hospital the year before, and it was a strain on their resources, not to mention an embarrassment to the patient, who suffered public display and exposure to comment. Paris, Vienna, and even New York were already experimenting with ambulance systems and they had been successful; but something in the English character instinctively cringes at new ideas. It wasn't likely that we would be getting such a modern convenience any time before the next century.

When I arrived at the hospital in Agar Street, I explained in words and gestures that one would reserve for a simpleton that a man was bleeding to death a few streets away, but they made me feel as if I were imposing on their time, as if I myself had stabbed someone merely in order to upset their schedules. As I waited, pulling my hair, an orderly attempted to convince various doctors to step down the road and see to the dying man, but they could not be bothered. I finally hit upon the realization that if I spoke as loudly and forcibly as possible, I would either attract someone to help or get myself chucked out. I surrendered my dignity in hope of saving Etienne's life, not that he would appreciate it. Finally, the orderly came out with a hand cart, followed by a physician just putting on his topper. I'd have felt better if the barrow was not in every way the twin of the one I'd seen bearing Giorgio Serafini's corpse off to the Poplar Morgue.

There was a logistical problem as soon as we arrived. The cart would not fit through the door. I went inside while the orderly stood at the curb watchfully, as if the whole of Whitehall had come there that day with the express purpose of stealing his cart.

Etienne was awake, or nearly. His eyes opened and closed now and then. He gestured, ever so slightly, and the physician bent down to listen, then shook his head dismissively.

"Stabbed twice, and the man wants a cigarette," the doctor said, disapprovingly. He probed the wound, producing a faint curse from the Frenchman.

"There is no way to know immediately how deep the wounds are or how much damage has been done to the organs. If the smallest scrap of cloth has gone into the wound, it shall quickly fester. We must get him to the hospital immediately. May we use the rug to transport him to the cart?"

"Of course," Barker said, though I knew he must have spent a good deal for it. Together the five of us lifted Etienne by the ends of the carpet and carried him down to the cart, while our cook cursed in his native tongue.

I walk the streets of London every day, arguably the most civilized spot on earth, especially in Whitehall where all is marble, but just put an injured friend in a hand litter and try wheeling him a few blocks and one shall see that the streets are not as smooth as one might think. They rise and fall like waves, and there are cracks and broken paving stones even in the seat of government. We left Jenkins to mind the office and mop the floor, and led the grim procession all the way to Agar Street.

Private enquiry agents or no, there was a point beyond which we could not pass. Dummolard was wheeled through a set of doors, and when we tried to enter, the orderly at the desk cleared his throat, as if issuing a warning. At loose ends, we found a couple of chairs in the hall and fell into them.

"Do you think this is related to Sir Alan and the Serafinis?" I asked the Guv.

Barker nodded grimly. "Etienne has complained about the Sicilian coffee shops opening up in Soho near his restaurant," he stated, turning his bowler in his hands. "The Sicilians hate the French, of course."

"The French? Why?"

"Sicily was ruled by the Bourbons for decades. The Mafia was formed to combat them. The word *Mafia* is an acronym for 'Kill the French is Italy's cry.' Something was brewing, and I should have realized it before now."

Barker spends his evenings in his garret aerie, poring over newspapers and pasting articles into oversized notebooks. Then he broods and prays over them, sometimes late into the night. He tracked civilization's progress, or, rather, its descent, through the chronicling of its events. Many times I'd seen him solve a case based upon a seemingly unrelated event in *The Times*—an exhibition, perhaps, or the arrival of a foreign dignitary. But no man is omniscient. It is impossible to stuff one's brain with thousands of facts, adding a hundred or more daily, and expect it to automatically produce all possible connections. My employer's reliance upon such a method, as far as I'm concerned, is a recipe for an attack of brain fever. A brain is a human organ, not a machine.

Barker pulled the paper with the black hand from his pocket and glanced at it again while I looked over his shoulder. The writing was in English: *You are a swine gorging at the trough,* it read. *Now you must give way so that others may get to the husks. If not, it shall go ill with you. This is your only warning.*

"I imagine this came from Clerkenwell," he noted, tapping the letter.

"The Italian quarter," I replied. We were suddenly interrupted when Inspector Poole came in the front entrance and spotted us.

"How is he?" the C.I.D. man asked, putting a foot up on one of the empty chairs.

"We don't know yet."

"Your clerk said he was stabbed in the street somewhere and must have staggered to your door. I find it hard to believe a man can be stabbed in broad daylight a street away from Scotland Yard."

"I slipped in the blood going into Craig's Court," I said, bristling. "That was real enough."

"Stabbed twice, your clerk told me," he went on, ignoring me as Anderson had. "I suppose someone crept up and stabbed him from behind, then when he turned, they got him a second time in the stomach."

Poole acted out the motions, and being cursed with a vivid imagination, I clothed them with accompanying images.

Barker shook his head. "No, we have a pattern here. Serafini was murdered with two shots, one to the front and one to the back. His wife was probably killed in the same manner. Etienne is a savateur, a seasoned fighter. Being stabbed in the back would not stop him from defending himself. I think it more likely he was stabbed simultaneously in a surprise attack. It was why he said 'front and back' to us. He was defending his reputation as well as warning us to expect such an attack ourselves."

"Hold on. You're going too fast," said Poole, who was scribbling in his notebook.

"You need lessons in Pitman's shorthand," I recommended, but all I received for my solicitous advice was a rude stare.

"You think Gigliotti is mixed up in this?" Poole went on.

"Not yet, but he knows about the Serafinis."

"Oh, that's just what we need," Poole said. "An Italian gang war. At least they only kill one another."

"Terence," my employer pointed out, as if he were a child, "the fact that we are here now proves they've gone beyond killing one another. Bledsoe was a member of the gentry."

"Blast. I suppose you're right, but they're all Latins, hot-blooded."

"Gigliotti called the Sicilians a plague," Barker said. "I'm afraid I concur with that assessment. Right now, the English gangs content themselves with sticks and coshes, but what if the Sicilian gangs arrive with daggers? All the English lads will want them in order to survive. Daggers will be smuggled across the Channel from the Continent, and soon every criminal in London will have one. Violent crimes and robberies at knifepoint shall rise. But the Sicilians will want to have the upper hand, so they'll begin smuggling in pistols and carbines. The violence escalates, you see."

"Meanwhile," Poole noted, "London's Finest are still patrolling the streets with truncheons and whistles. I'll have to convince my superiors such is the case, if what you say is true."

"Ask them how they'll feel about the Thames being choked with barrels like the one this morning," Barker said.

"I don't know as the Yard can do a lot, however, until the Sicilians visibly break the law," Poole went on. "We can't arrest them for simply coming into the country or for congregating."

"We must discourage them somehow—not the Sicilians as a whole but the criminal element."

"Men armed with knives and the wherewithal to use them might be difficult to discourage," I pointed out.

Cyrus Barker reached into his pocket and retrieved his old repeater. "Thomas, I've been remiss. Go to Le Toison d'Or and inform Madame Dummolard of her husband's injury."

"Me, sir?"

"Yes. I must stay to hear of Etienne's condition when he gets out of surgery, and it would frighten Madame to death

if Inspector Poole arrived in the restaurant. Bring her," he
ordered, "though God help us all."

It's easier to stand on the tracks and argue with the approaching express train from Brighton than with Barker once
his mind is made up. Not finding a cab, I walked to Soho, a
matter of ten minutes. It was still too early for the restaurant
to open, so I entered through the back door. Before I even
knew what happened, Madame Dummolard had me by the
shoulders and was shaking me.

"Thomas, *où est* Etienne? What has happened?"

Madame, a blond woman in her mid-thirties, is a true
beauty, but she towers over most men. As she shook me, I
clutched my hat to keep it out of the potage cooking nearby
on one of the stoves and had to extricate myself from her
clutches before I could speak.

"Etienne has been attacked. Stabbed. He stumbled into
our offices half an hour ago. He is in surgery now."

"He is not dead. Tell me he is not!"

"He was awake when I last saw him. He spoke to us."

"Where is he?"

"Charing Cross Hospital."

"Take me to him at once, Thomas. *Vite!*" She pushed me
out the door again. There was no question of her walking
the distance I had just come, but cabs congregate in Soho,
even at that early hour. I hailed a hansom and told the driver
to take us to Charing Cross Hospital.

"No!" Madame cried. "Clothilde! His stepdaughter must
be by his side. It is but three streets south of here. Go!"

Madame can be difficult enough, but the thought of sharing a cab with her sharp-tongued daughter was even more
daunting.

"Where was he stabbed?" Madame Dummolard continued, once we were safely ensconced in the cab and on our way.

"In the stomach and the back."

"*Ma pauvre!*" she cried. "Did he have the note with him?"

"The Black Hand note? Yes, Mr. Barker has it."

"It was shoved under our door yesterday morning. It was from the Sicilians, I know it. They are trying to take over Soho," she cried. "They want to shut down Le Toison d'Or and fill the district with cheap little coffee shops."

There wasn't much use arguing with her. The cab pulled to the curb in front of a row of town houses on the south edge of Soho in Old Compton Street. The Dummolards were doing well for themselves, I noted. They lived in a sand-colored three-story building with window boxes full of bougainvilleas. We sprang from the cab and I followed Madame into the hall.

Clothilde Dummolard is a miniature version of her mother. She's the kind of girl that could swoop down upon one like an eagle, and suddenly one wakes up with three daughters, a position in the city, a house in the country full of furniture one wouldn't sit on, and a mortgage it would take two lifetimes to pay. Luckily, I didn't have an earldom to attract her, but I saw through her schemes and she found that vexing.

"Injured, you say?" she demanded. "How badly?"

"He's been stabbed," Madame cried. "Stabbed in the street, and is now in the hospital!"

"Don't stand there like an idiot, Thomas," Clothilde said, pushing me out the door. "Take us to him at once!"

I ushered the ladies into the waiting cab.

"Now, tell me everything from the beginning," the girl ordered, once we were in the cab and on our way again. "How did Papa get stabbed?"

I explained in as much detail as I could what had occurred, but it only took up half the brief journey, leaving her plenty of time to sum up for the jury.

"If he wasn't involved with Mr. Barker, this wouldn't have happened," she insisted. "He would not have been hurt if he just came straight to the restaurant in the mornings."

"Madame, I deeply regret Etienne's injury. Mr. Barker is anxiously waiting for him to get out of surgery."

"We'se here, miss," the cabman announced, pulling up to the curb, putting an end to my misery.

"Pay the man," Madame replied, and the pair of them alighted from the vehicle. Clothilde stopped to fix me with a look of pure loathing. I sighed and reached into my pockets.

"Is she the missus?" the cabman asked when she was out of earshot.

"No, thank the Lord."

"She's a stunner, no mistake, but if I was you, I'd run in the uvver direction."

"That remark," I answered coldly, "is uncalled for. However, it has just earned you a tip."

When I arrived inside, the Dummolards, *mère et fille,* were speaking in a mixture of voluble French and English to a doctor while Barker made his way around to me as warily as a man walking through a swamp infested with crocodiles.

"We've just been informed that Etienne's out of surgery," he said, as we watched the women remonstrate with the staff. "The wounds were deeper than I had suspected. I believe his attackers were armed with swords instead of daggers. The doctor says the operation was successful, but Etienne has not yet awakened."

"Should we leave Madame to look after her husband? I could use a cup of coffee after that cab ride. Perhaps there is a café in the area."

"Good thinking, lad. A café is a perfect idea, but not in Charing Cross. Let us find one in Soho instead."

6

THE CAFÉ ROYAL IS THE UNOFFICIAL HEADQUARTERS of Bohemia in the heart of London. Men such as James Whistler and Oscar Wilde ate there while plotting how next to amuse society. People came for reasons other than dining, although both the food and the cellars were considered the best in London. They came to be seen and to further their careers. Artists pushed themselves upon playwrights, who fawned over aristocrats, who collected intellectuals, who hoped to meet famous beauties.

The man we were coming to see fit none of these categories. If pressed, I'm sure he would say he was of no fixed occupation, though I understand he had read for the bar, as if that were some trifling thing he picked up in passing. The Honorable Pollock Forbes was a gentleman, son of a Scottish laird. That was more and less than what he actually was. If there was a scandal brewing, Forbes would be summoned. If some great man threatened to throw over his wife for a dancer, Forbes would discreetly talk him out of it. If a criminal attempted to blackmail an earl, Forbes would buy him off or warn him off or, for all I know, kill him off. The dandified silk gloves he wore belied the chain mail underneath, and mail there was. His people had fought at Culloden and Bannockburn, but before that they had fought in Jerusalem. Forbes was a Freemason and the only man in London who I felt carried as many secrets as Cyrus Barker, which is saying something. I'd heard them joke about splitting the town between them, East End and West End. And yet there was a finiteness to this young man's abilities. Forbes, I knew, was fighting tuberculosis. He only had so long to live, and every time I saw him I was cognizant of the fact that one day I might come into the Royal and he would not be there.

Barker and I slid between the Regent Street doors of the establishment. It was easier to slip in here than into the Neapolitan, but, then, there was far less danger of someone entering armed. I'm not slighting the service, which is impeccable, but the Royal was not the place for an overattentive waiter. People came here to mingle and chat and sometimes disappear into various discreet rooms, or so I've heard. It would not do to be inquisitive, or rather to seem so. Any information is funneled into the ears of one of two people: the first is Monsieur Daniel Nicols, a French exile, owner of the place, the second Forbes, who makes it his pied-à-terre.

Had I known we were going to visit the Café Royal that day, I wouldn't have eaten so much of the antipasto at the Neapolitan. I had made several attempts to cadge a meal there in Barker's presence but had never had anything more substantial than the mocha coffee they served. We were always too busy or had just eaten a meal or were on our way to one. I had to content myself with coffee once again, not that the mocha is anything of which to complain. I suppose it would have been churlish to eat at Dummolard's chief rival in London, while he was under the scalpel. One of these days, I promised myself, the meek will inherit the earth.

After the coffee arrived, Pollock Forbes dropped into the chair beside us as if out of a skylight. Forbes's pale, foppish appearance contradicted his clandestine credentials. An amiable-looking fellow, young and urbane, with little trace of a Scots accent, he dressed in the latest aesthetic fashion: light-colored suit, soft collar, and fresh boutonniere in his lapel. He favored waistcoats by Liberty.

"Carlos!" he called to a waiter, in a tone that seemed bland and bored. "Champagne over here and none of that seltzer water you brought me the last time! Hello, chaps. So, Cyrus, what has happened? You're not exactly in the habit of indulging your assistants."

"Dummolard was stabbed today," the Guv said flatly. The day's events had scraped off his veneer of civility and left the more elemental Barker showing.

"Who was it? Any idea?"

"It was the Sicilians. Etienne received a Black Hand letter."

"Is there any chance it is the Camorra instead of *mafiusi?*"

"None," Barker said. "The Serafinis have been assassinated also. Gigliotti is considering retribution."

"Is that all?"

"No, actually. Sir Alan Bledsoe, director of the East and West India Docks, was murdered, in what Gigliotti claims is a Sicilian method. The initial signs seem to point toward a group of *mafiusi* moving into the area."

"Do you have any idea who is in charge?"

"Not yet."

"Oh, come now, Cyrus," Forbes said. "You know how Black Hand notes work. Sometimes it is a Camorra gang, sometimes Sicilian or some other Italian secret society. Sometimes it's not even Italian in origin. It could be Irish or even English. We have our own underworld. I work with a delicate system of checks and balances. I cannot move without certainty."

Barker lifted his glass of champagne and downed it without savoring it. He wiped his mustache with a thumb and shook his head. "It's the Sicilians, I'm sure of it."

"What if you're wrong?"

"If I'm wrong, a few Sicilians will be sent back to Palermo needlessly. But if I'm right and we do nothing, more people will die."

"It's all circumstantial," Forbes said guardedly.

"You're speaking like a solicitor, Pollock. This is not like you. I'm going to track down these Sicilians. Will you assist me?"

"I'm sorry, but I cannot."

"Cannot or will not?"

"It amounts to the same thing, doesn't it?"

"Can you give me a reason why you should not help bring down a gang that is a danger to our way of life?" my employer said coolly.

"You're the professional reasoner here. I'm certain you can work it through yourself."

"You will not help me?" the Guv repeated.

"I'm afraid my hands are tied," Forbes answered.

"What about Nicols? He is a Frenchman in Soho, like

Etienne. His life could be in danger, as well. Don't you see that?"

"He is a lodge brother, and under our protection, but thank you for the warning."

Barker sat immobile for a moment, puzzling it out. Obviously, he'd come expecting support. "You're leaving me to fall back upon my own resources," he said sternly.

"I wish there was another way. I'm sorry, Cyrus."

"Very well, if you won't help, I'll do it my way. You leave me no alternative."

"You're going to cut up rough about this, aren't you?" Forbes asked.

Barker stood. "As rough as it takes. If I'm left out in the cold on my own, then I needn't take anyone's feelings into consideration. Also, if I end up dead over this, it won't be because of anything I've left undone. Come, Thomas."

The Guv stalked out, leaving me to follow. These were matters too deep for me. It was all insinuation and vague pronouns. "We." "They." I didn't care for the talk about ending up dead. Surely it wouldn't come to that.

Coming to Glasshouse Street, the Guv headed south, striding purposefully but to no apparent end. I'm not even certain he knew where he was going, like an engine off its tracks, barreling ahead until it ran out of steam. Eventually he came to a stop at a park in Leicester Square. He sat down with his long limbs stretched out in front of him, crossed at the ankle, a hazard to passing pedestrians, and did not move for a quarter hour.

As I said, I knew Barker better now, after nearly a year and a half in his employ, and I understood that there was nothing to do but to leave him alone. I crossed the street and looked through the windows of a shop that was to let. Poole and a few others of his former students had been after the Guv to rent a gymnasium and start teaching physical culture classes again. More correctly, Poole had spoken to me, wishing that I would make the proposition to Barker, as if somehow I could convince him to do anything. So far I hadn't got up the nerve.

He was smoking his pipe when I returned, which was a good sign. He had unbent. I sat down and waited for him to speak first.

"Mazzini," he growled.

"I beg your pardon?"

"Giuseppe Mazzini. He was a political refugee in London who joined the Freemasons and conceived of an organization along the same lines, called Young Italy, that would grow until it overthrew the Bourbon government. Later, after Sicily won its independence, the organization there gained power but began to factionalize."

"Wait, wait," I said, holding up a hand. "Are you trying to tell me the Mafia was conceived in London and is a Freemason organization and that's why Forbes won't help us?"

"Mazzini is the father of Italian Freemasonry, and he is also called the founder of the Mafia, but in his defense, he didn't live to see it become a criminal organization. That only occurred with the chaos engendered after the Bourbons had been driven out."

"And Forbes? How is he connected to them?"

"The Masons straddle international borders. In Italy's case, lodges such as the Grande Oriente d'Italia and the Propaganda Due include members of the Camorra and the Mafia, but they are a small part of the general membership.

I suspect Forbes thinks it politic not to stand against them, at least until he has more information. He and his little star chamber may lend us aid eventually, but there's no saying what situation we shall be in by then."

"Star chamber?"

"A metaphor. Cabal, if you prefer."

"Ah." I nodded. When in doubt, I say, best to act as if one knows what's going on and hope not to be caught out by a question.

Behind our bench, swallows were flitting in and out of the shrubbery. It was remarkably warm and I felt almost too drowsy to think. It was difficult to imagine that nearby a secret, foreign organization was plotting who knew what form of devilry.

"So," I said, going on, "Nicols has joined the English Freemasons and has its protection. He even has a lodge at the Royal."

"Aye."

"But Etienne has no such protection, since he's not a Mason."

"Oh, he's a Mason, all right, but not a member of the English order. He's a member of an ancient French lodge from Dijon called the Order of the Golden Fleece."

"Golden Fleece," I repeated. *"Toisin d'or."*

"Exactly."

"I believe I am getting a headache. So why would they help the Mafia but not Etienne?"

"They're not. Pollock is saying they won't choose sides."

"Excuse me, sir, but are you prepared to face the Sicilians alone?"

"Not completely alone, I trust, but I must do something. We are obligated to the Home Office now."

"Or is it because of Etienne?"

"No. I know that as soon as he can crawl out of his hospital bed, he shall go after his attackers and, in his weakened state, give them the opportunity to finish what they started, but, believe me, Etienne would be the very worst of clients."

"So, are you a Freemason, sir?" I dared ask.

"No," he replied. The word was accompanied by a plume of smoke from his mouth.

"But if you were, you would not be permitted to tell me, correct?"

"Correct."

"So, either you are not a member, or you are a member. Which is it?"

"You tell me—you're the detective."

"Private enquiry agent," I corrected.

"Not yet, rascal." Barker finished his pipe and knocked out the ash against the bench, scattering it in the light breeze. "You're still an apprentice."

7

I CANNOT HELP BUT AGREE WITH DICKENS, WHO said in *The Mystery of Edwin Drood,* "I don't love doctors, or doctor's stuff." Now I have no wish to slight the medical profession, great men all, but I have a little trouble with those who will cheerily offer promises of a healthy recovery based solely upon a spirit of optimism. I wouldn't go so far as to call Dummolard a friend—our relationship was rather as it was that morning multiplied by three hundred and sixty-five—however, I was relieved when we returned to Charing Cross Hospital to find that the Frenchman had awakened from surgery and the doctor assured us that, barring the unforeseen, he would pull through. I wanted to know the exact amount the unforeseen represented in his mind; but the doctor, all smiles, amiably brushed off my concerns. He had managed, at least, to pacify the two-headed hydra, *mère et fille,* and they were in the room with the patient now. We sat down again, and I felt vaguely concerned that there was now a chair I considered mine in this hospital.

"Now that we know he's safely out of surgery," Barker

said to me, "let's go over to Scotland Yard. I want to speak with this Palermo inspector Poole mentioned. Perhaps he can shed some light on what's going on."

There was a time, and recently it was, too, when walking into the Criminal Investigation Department made me go clammy all over. It felt as if all I had to do was answer one question wrong and I'd be on my way back to prison. The fear had passed now; and I saw the building as it was, slightly damp and seedy, in need of a fresh coat of paint, and full of people milling about who looked bored or upset.

Cyrus Barker stopped and looked at some offices on the first floor. This was where he had taught his physical culture classes before a bomb left by the Irish Republican Brotherhood had rent it asunder. He sniffed dismissively and walked on.

When we found Poole's office, he had a small crate open on his desk and was looking through it.

"What have you got, Terry?"

"More work," Poole grumbled. "Commissioner Henderson has chosen me to try out the new Bertillon system of detection from Paris."

"Does it work?" my employer asked.

"I have no idea as yet. It's scientific enough, I'll grant you that. I can see the importance of photographing criminals as they are booked in and taking down their vitals, I suppose, but Inspector Pettigrilli's taking it much too far. Why measure a man's forearms or the circumference of his head, I ask you? What's that going to accomplish? It's a waste of our valuable time. It takes a good half hour to fill out each card, and someone walking in the door every five minutes. It will turn us all into clerks."

"What card?" I asked. "What exactly is the Bertillon system?"

"It's a scientific method created to identify criminals," Barker explained. "It was invented by Alphonse Bertillon, chief of criminal identification for the Paris police. It involves a careful measurement and indexing of dozens of parts of the body, parts that cannot change over time and that no criminal can disguise, such as the shape of his ears or the length of his feet. It's more complicated than that, of course; and, as I recall, it's tied up with the so-called science of eugenics. If one has the wrong ear shape, for example, it proves somehow one is racially inferior."

"I haven't read that far," Poole admitted. "I just got the instructions today. Look at all these instruments!"

He lifted a pair of calipers and mockingly measured the diameter of his own head. Then he brought out a set of rulers, measuring tapes, special tools for measuring parts of the body, and finally a small wooden bench with centimeters marked upon it.

"So this Sicilian inspector Pettigrilli is in the country to teach the latest police methods," Barker stated.

"Yes. It's a cooperative effort between the French, English, and Italian governments."

"Europe's once again bringing enlightenment to benighted England," I put in.

"Something like that—though if you ask me, it's more a way to put money in Monsieur Bertillon's pocket."

"What's your impression of Pettigrilli?" Barker asked.

"He's all right, for an Italian. He's the first one trained by the Sûreté."

"I thought the Sicilians hate the French," I said.

"Pettigrilli says it is important to make alliances; and if the French are willing to extend an olive branch and allow him to study the latest methods, he would be a fool not to do so. Claims it will r-revolutionize the world."

"I'd like to meet him," Barker said.

"He's giving a lecture now for the benefit of the Special Branch, not that they'll appreciate it." Poole pulled out his watch and consulted it. "He should be done soon."

"How much practical use do you think the Bertillon system will be?"

Poole ran his fingers through his long, drooping whiskers. "It would require retraining every officer in the country and getting them to agree on the same procedures. Then thousands of these kits must be sent out everywhere and a working camera given to every constabulary, with training in photography and developing. Records would have to be filled out after each arrest and an officer hired and trained to do naught else but keep them. You're talking about thousands of pounds there. Plus, it's all theory. Only a few arrests have occurred in France because of the new records, and those were due more to the photographs than the measurements, I'm thinking. It's all good intentioned, but I'd have to be convinced of its reliability."

"You're skeptical," Barker concluded.

"I am, but then, the commissioner doesn't lose any sleep at night wondering whether the Yard is being run to my satisfaction. It's more 'go and make it work, or feel my boot hard against your backside.'"

There was a clamor of stout shoes in the hall and men began filing past Poole's door.

"The meeting must have adjourned," Poole said. He

came quickly around the desk and stepped out into the corridor. "Mr. Pettigrilli!" he called out. "Could I speak with you for a moment?"

A squarely built man stepped into the room, dressed in a European-looking suit and an alpine-style hat. He had good features—dark eyes and a thin mustache that made him look refined. He seemed vigorous, a dynamo running on some internal source of energy.

"Yes, Inspector. What can I do for you?" he asked.

"May I present Mr. Barker and his assistant, Mr. Llewelyn? They are private enquiry agents."

"Ah!" The Sicilian's face lit up and he pumped Barker's hand soundly, as if he were drawing water from a pump. "Umberto Pettigrilli. So good to meet a representative of the private fraternity. The methods I teach, they will change the way we do everything. Science is the way of the world now, and it is only a matter of time before it r-revolutionizes detective work."

I could see now that when Poole said "revolutionized" he had been mimicking Pettigrilli's rolling *r*'s. The Sicilian seized my hand in his firm grip, shaking it with enthusiasm.

"How long has it been since you were in Palermo, Inspector?" Barker asked.

"Six months, sir. The Sûreté keeps me to a very strict schedule. I shall be traveling around England for the next two weeks, and after that I go to Scotland and Ireland. My schedule was put together by a madman, sir, a madman."

"Mr. Pettigrilli, there have been three murders and one attempt on another's life here in London by what I believe to be members of the Sicilian group that calls itself the Mafia."

The Sicilian inspector frowned a moment in puzzlement,

then suddenly threw his head back and laughed. "This is a joke, is it not? This group you mentioned—it does not exist outside Sicily."

"Not even in a city like London where there are hundreds of Sicilians?" Barker asked. "Or where the Camorra is already well settled? At least one of them received a Black Hand note."

"Just that? No request for money? That is—" Here he snapped his fingers impatiently until the English word finally came to him. "Atypical. It is *atypical.* The reason for a Black Hand note is generally to extort money. I'm afraid also that few such notes come from the actual group that uses that name. Often it is another group or individual posing as *mafiusi* hoping to scare someone out of a few liras by it."

"They are not merely posing," Barker rumbled in a harsh voice. "The first two victims were shot and barreled. Another, who is a friend of mine, was stabbed twice and was barely able to crawl to my door. A third was killed with some sort of thrust in the ear."

Pettigrilli rubbed his mustache in thought. "I admit, sir, that those are all genuine methods used in Palermo."

"I assure you, Mr. Pettigrilli, that they are without precedent in London. Four attacks in just a few days . . . We generally don't see that many in a season. It is, as you say, atypical. Also, all the crimes have had some connection to the Italian community here. One of the victims is a friend of mine who owns a French restaurant in Soho. He gave me this note but a few hours ago." Barker pulled the paper from his pocket and handed it to the inspector, who read it intently.

"Pardon, signor," the Sicilian said gravely. "I have misspoken. It would appear that either you do indeed have some *mafiusi* here, attempting to take control, or someone who has adopted their tactics to discredit them; though personally I don't think it possible to black their name any further. That is good English, isn't it? To black their name?"

"Er, yes," Barker said. "I assume you have intimate knowledge of the Mafia, sir, having worked as a police inspector?"

"You cannot know what that word does to me. It chills the spine. It is not spoken openly in my country. Politicians use it in our newspapers, until inevitably they are mown down, like so much hay. Mr. Barker, you must not put yourself in the path of the Mafia. I was once vain and stupid enough to do it myself, and I am a marked man. It's why I left Sicily. I survived two attempts on my life while in Paris, and am exiled from my homeland and my family. I fear for the lives of my fellow officers, my friends, anyone whose death could be used as a warning to me."

"How came you to be under the Mafia's wrath, sir?" I asked.

"I was naïve and ambitious once, gentlemen. There was a *mafiusu* who was gaining great power in Palermo, by the name of Marco Faldo. I received information from an informer that he would be in a certain restaurant at a certain time, and when he arrived my detectives overwhelmed him as well as his men and arrested them all. We had what we believed was a case watertight; but as Faldo sat in jail awaiting trial, being cosseted with free wine and food provided by the very restaurant from which we took him, our case began to fall apart. Some witnesses disappeared or experienced sudden, fatal accidents. Others recanted their testimony.

Rumors came to my ear that the judge hearing the case had been threatened. It came as no shock when Faldo was found innocent of murder and extortion, but I had become a marked man and put myself and my family in danger.

"As I said, I was naïve. Two days later, I found the freshly stripped pelt of my daughter's kitten tacked to our front door. It was a warning from Faldo. Immediately I packed up my family and sent them to Corsica, where my wife has an aunt. My commissioner showed me a letter from the Sûreté, offering training in the new Bertillon system of criminal identification, and suggested I accept the offer. Normally we scoff at the Sûreté. We have no respect for it as we do the Scotland Yard. However, it seemed a way to both spare my life and to continue working. Reluctantly I left for Paris. On the day I left, I was shot at in the harbor; but the assassin's *lupara*, his shotgun, was far enough away to merely pepper me with stinging shot. Later, in Nantes, I was set upon and stabbed, but the blade point went into a leather wallet inside my coat pocket. I have been very fortunate." He looked away for a few moments, shaking his head. "So you say they are here now. But I suppose it cannot be Faldo if all these other people you mention are being killed. The families are in constant competition with one another, and they kill for many reasons. I shall be on my guard all the same."

"Does it look like a genuine Black Hand note?" Barker pursued.

"It looks genuine enough, though it would not be difficult to duplicate. It is in English, of course. I don't know that Faldo speaks English. I regret I cannot be more help to you in this matter, since your friend was killed."

"Not killed," Barker corrected. "In fact, he survived."

Pettigrilli smiled. "I am glad to hear it. Perhaps I will survive as well. I have given thought to emigrating to America, somewhere safe where my family can live."

"I suppose," Poole said in the silence afterward, "that it would be prudent to send a telegram to Palermo to ascertain if Faldo is still there."

"What will you do if he is actually here, Inspector?" Barker asked.

Pettigrilli shrugged as if to say it made no difference to him. "What can I do? Their tentacles, they reach everywhere. I have Scotland Yard to protect me. I shall continue my scheduled course. Perhaps Faldo will consider a Sicilian going to Manchester to be punishment enough." The inspector laughed at his own joke, but it was a hollow laugh. "If you are planning to pursue this case, have a care, Signor Barker. Watch over your shoulder and test the locks of your house. Are you married?"

"No, sir."

"Good! And no children?"

"I have a ward, but she does not live with me."

"Better still. My advice to you, sir, is not to take this case. And if you receive a Black Hand note of your own, take it seriously." He handed the note back to Barker. "Your friend didn't, and see what happened to him."

"Have you heard of the Mafia working outside Sicily before, Inspector?"

"There has been some action in Italy, but never in England. And, yet, why should they not come here? You make it very easy for criminals in this country. They come and go quite freely, if I may say it. England is very indulgent."

The Sicilian looked down at the instruments on the desk.

"So, Inspector Poole. How did you find your new Bertillon kit?" he asked.

"Delightful," Poole remarked, but the sarcasm was lost on Pettigrilli.

"You fellows here at Scotland Yard, you will take to this new method the way a fish takes to water. It is orderly, and so should appeal to an English mind such as yours. The only mystery is how it was originally conceived by a Frenchman."

Dummolard was awake when we returned to the hospital, but he'd been so sedated with morphine his mind wandered. He'd been moved to a ward and given a cot, while his wife and daughter fluttered about demanding better conditions. For once, he was too weak to bawl French curses at us all.

"Etienne, do you recall who attacked you?" Barker asked, lowering his large frame gently down onto the bedcovers.

"*Oignons,*" he replied. "I was not satisfied with the *oignons* at the restaurant this morning. I was going to Tottenham Court Road for fresh ones. The market was crowded. There was a man in a cloak in front of me. Suddenly, he stopped too quickly. I knocked into him, and the man behind, he knocked into me. Then I felt pain. Very bad pain. I thought I was having heart failure. Then I saw the blood and realized I had been stabbed. I thought perhaps they would try to finish me, so I came as fast as I could to see you, *Capitaine.*"

"Monsieur," Mireille Dummolard implored, "he cannot speak. He must conserve his strength for recovery."

"A cloak, you say," the Guv went on, ignoring the woman. "Did you see his face?"

"*Non,*" Etienne stated. "He had a broad-brimmed hat, all in black."

"All in black?" my employer repeated. "Hat, cloak, and everything?"

"*Oui.*"

"And the fellow behind?"

"I didn't see him."

"Very well. Thank you, Etienne. We'll stop by tomorrow. Come, Thomas."

Outside in the street, Barker turned in the direction of Whitehall, his stick swinging, leaving me scurrying to keep up.

"Assassins," he growled.

"Professional, do you think?" I asked.

"Only skilled and dangerous men dress all in black as a rule, though I knew one in Kyoto who wore white, which amounts to the same thing. Black is a symbol among the underworld. It must be earned. If a minor criminal wishing to build a reputation were to attend certain places in full black, he would have to fight for the right to wear it."

"What places?" I asked, noting to myself that my employer generally wore black himself, save for his crimson tie and white Windsor collar.

"Gang meetings, clandestine prizefights, pubs known to attract a certain type of fellow. These men that Etienne stumbled into, they killed Serafini and his wife, quite a brace of feathers for their caps, I'm sure. Then they killed Sir Alan and made the attempt on Etienne. The only thing all these individuals have in common is that they stood in opposition to the Sicilians. It's highly possible that there is a pair of professional assassins walking the streets of London today; and sooner or later, we shall have to face them."

"Sir," I said, wishing he would stop at an outdoor café and sit down so we could talk properly. "I admit I know next to nothing about professional assassins, but don't they generally work under contract? They wouldn't do something like this on their own."

"As I said before, lad," he replied, "there must be a leader, someone they're working for, the way the Serafinis worked for Victor Gigliotti. I think that is a reasonable possibility."

"Three of them, then."

"Let us say two, at least. We don't yet know if Faldo does his own work."

"Faldo? Do you really think it is he that followed Inspector Pettigrilli here all the way from Sicily?"

"Men that ruthless and skilled at murder and intimidation are rare, Thomas. I'll take it as a probability that Marco Faldo is somewhere in London this minute, considering his next Black Hand note. If that doesn't concern you, it should."

8

⁓⁓⁓

THE NEXT MORNING, CYRUS BARKER AND I AT-
tended service as usual at the Baptist Tabernacle, while Mac
crept surreptitiously across the street to that den of iniquity,
the Elephant and Castle public house, for our Sunday lunch.
The Reverend Spurgeon's sermon was up to its usual standard, but the meal in no way made up for the loss of our
cook.

"What are you doing today, lad?" Barker asked over his
bowl of tepid brown Windsor soup.

"I need to write a letter, sir, but I had no further plans
beyond that. What about you?"

"I've got to think this problem through. Would you
mind doing a favor for me today? I need you to take Juno to
Victoria Station and put her in a horse carriage. I'm sending
her south, out of harm's way. She'd make a large target for
the Mafia's wrath."

"How far south?" I asked.

"All the way to the coast, a town called Seaford. I've already made arrangements for her to be picked up there."

"I'll take care of it as soon as my letter is done."

"Good. Cusp, is it?" the Guv asked.

"Yes, sir." Thad Cusp was our solicitor. He was Barker's until recently, but now he worked for me as well. Recently I had hired my employer to find the grave of my late wife, who had died of consumption while I was still in prison. Her mother, the most disagreeable specimen of womanhood I'd ever met, had buried her in an unmarked grave and packed up for parts unknown. Once I was freed, I tried to locate Jenny's grave to no avail. Now, with more than a year's salary in my bank account, I had turned to my employer. It took him little more than a day to find it, going from constabulary to mortuary to church. It was difficult for me to be in Oxford again, the site of my former disgrace, but finally I stood over the grave of my dear girl and could begin the task of having her buried properly. To do so required the services of Mr. Cusp. Jenny's mother had put her in the ground and I could not move her without the woman's consent, which meant a settlement of some sort, much as it galled me. Thad Cusp, a man as sharp as his name sounds, was now in the process of scouring the country for my former mother-in-law. I began to fear the case would end up in Chancery before it was finished.

Having sent off my letter with the inevitable accompanying bank draft, I made my way to the stable and saddled Juno. As we trotted through the streets, I wondered who would pick her up at the end of the line and what sort of treatment she would receive there. The south coast is full of racing stables, any one of which was capable of looking after the mare, but I'm rather particular about her care and wished I could have seen her settled in. I led her into the horsebox myself and watched as the express pulled out of sight, gathering speed as she steamed away. At loose ends, and feeling rather unsettled, I admit, I took a hansom back to Newington.

On the ride back, I began to fret. Together, Barker and I had taken on terrorists and murderers, but facing organized criminals was another matter. From where would Barker recruit enough men to face these *mafiusi* who traveled about armed with shotguns and swords? Matters were clearly coming to a head if Barker felt it necessary to send his horse out of town. I began to wish he'd sent his assistant along with it.

When I arrived at the house, Mac met me in the hallway, giving me a look that said I'd been dawdling and wasting his time. He held a paper in his hand.

"Mr. Barker has asked that you go to this address in Soho," he said. "You are to meet a Mr. Antonio Gallenga there."

"Gallenga?" I asked, taking the slip of paper that held the address in Barker's illegible scrawl. "Did he— No, I know. You wouldn't presume to say."

"Exactly, sir."

"A font of information, a regular oracle of Delphi you are, Mac."

"I endeavor to give satisfaction, sir."

"Yes, but to whom?"

He ignored the gibe. "Mr. Barker has asked not to be disturbed for the next few hours."

So that was that. I wouldn't be getting any more information out of Mac. Grumbling to myself, I turned and went in search of another cab. It took half a mile before my brain, like a cog, engaged and began to turn. Where was Barker sending me? It couldn't be an interview, for I had no knowledge of what to say. I had no message to deliver. *No, I thought with a groan, it could only mean more blasted training.*

My employer is of the opinion that everyone—man, woman, or child—should be able to protect themselves, at least to the point that they can break away and run. As his assistant, he expected a good deal more of me than that. So far, I had endured lessons in both English and Chinese boxing, Japanese wrestling in canvas jackets on mats, stick fighting of various sorts, and techniques from a dozen other defensive arts that the Guv found useful. Barker may well have been the most highly trained fighter in Europe, which was why Poole and others were eager for him to teach them. It was difficult enough being trained in all these arts, often by cramming courses, and going to bed with bruises and sore muscles. I wasn't anxious to add another dangerous art to the list.

The address was a comfortable little semidetached villa, a trifle overgrown with browning wisteria, but pleasant enough in its aspect. It seemed to be drowsing in the late summer sun. I might almost have been standing in front of a villa in Palermo itself.

I rang the doorbell and was greeted by a stark, old Italian woman in a jet-black dress, with unnaturally black hair and an even blacker mood. I explained what little I knew about why I was there, while she frowned at me, debating whether or not to let me in. Finally I heard a man behind her speaking in Italian; and she left with a sigh, like a guard dog that had missed the chance to bite an intruder.

"Come in," the man said, pulling me inside. I would have called him an old man, but then I was not much more than twenty at the time. He was in his seventies, of that type of hale, masterful men one sometimes meets whose years rest lightly. His hair was iron gray, shot with white at the temples, and he wore a short beard shaven from his lower lip to the point of his chin. I'd never seen whiskers carved in such a fashion, but then I'd never met Antonio Gallenga before.

"So, you're Mr. Llewelyn, eh?" he asked with no trace of an accent.

I always came up short in these visual evaluations, be they work related or personal. Just once, I would have liked to impress someone.

"Barker vouches for you, anyway. Just what have you studied?"

"Boxing, Japanese wrestling, and stick fighting, sir. Oh, and explosives."

Gallenga made a sour face and shook his head. I'd failed again. You'd think I'd eventually get used to it.

"Nothing practical, then?"

"Practical?"

"Save perhaps the bomb making, they are all sports. You have had no training in actual combat."

"No, sir."

"It's a wonder you're still alive then, working with a man like *Il Brutto.*"

"The ugly one," I translated, with what smattering of Italian and Latin I have. "Do you really call him that?" Barker was weather-beaten, I'll admit, but "ugly" was going a bit far.

"Many Italians in London call Barker that. I don't know who first gave him the name." The old man shrugged. "So, I am to train you. How do you feel about that?"

"I'd be more assured if I knew what I was actually to be trained in."

"Good point," he said, smiling. "Let me enlighten you. For the most part, I shall teach you the use of the Sicilian blade, that is, the Italian dagger. This is no sport. It is to be used solely to kill another human being or to save yourself from being killed, which amounts to the same thing. This is a practical education. You should be very grateful to your employer, for the art is normally passed down from father to son among the Sicilians. To not be an Italian and yet receive this instruction is rare indeed."

"Why are you willing to teach me, then, if I may ask?"

"I owe your employer a debt of honor. Beyond that I will not say."

I absorbed that, or tried to, and found I couldn't, so I set it aside. "Er, what other instruction am I to receive?"

"*L'occhio,* signor," he said, drawing down the skin of his lower eyelid. "I am to 'give you the eye.'"

"I don't understand."

"Of course you don't. You know nothing. You are a mere babe in the woods, but you will learn. When I am done with you, Mr. Thomas Llewelyn, you will be a different man. Oh, you may look the same, but you will be changed in here." To demonstrate, he thumped his chest with a fist. "I will make a man of you."

"I can hardly wait," I responded. He didn't react to sarcasm any more than Barker.

"Come then, sir. Let us take a short walk. Just a simple walk in the street."

He led me out the back door of his house, which was furnished in an overdecorated European fashion—full of ornate, overstuffed chairs—through a garden in full bloom and down an alleyway into a busy street.

"Stop here, signor. Now tell me, if you were in fear for your life right now, how would you proceed down this street?"

"What do you mean? How should I walk down the street?"

"Would it be safer to walk there—close to the buildings, near the entrances—or out here, near the curb?"

I mulled this over for a moment.

"Near the curb," I pronounced.

"And why?"

"Because one could be seized from an alleyway or doorway."

"Very good."

"But what if I'm going the opposite direction and can't walk on the outside?"

"Then you cross the street. Do not put yourself in a position where a man can reach out and seize you or, worse, stab you. A practiced rampsman can seize a cuff and pull a man into an alley the way a fisherman draws in his catch before gutting it."

"But being near the curb is so . . . open. One might be attacked from a vehicle or shot at from a window."

"Of course, the curb is not without its dangers. That is why it is important to look for open windows or vehicles slowing near you. One grows accustomed to looking for movement in upper windows. As for vehicles, they are difficult to get out of. It is a true dullard who cannot get away from a man in a cab. Come."

He led me briskly down the street. Gallenga moved easily for an old man, and he walked without a stick or hat. The sunlight glistened on his pink scalp beneath a thin layer of hair.

"At night," he continued, "it is necessary to move even farther out. It is best to walk in the street if possible, but avoid standing under gas lamps and making oneself a target for an enemy's bullet. Now tell me, you are walking down the street. What are you looking at?"

"The windows above?"

"Yes, but I mean the people. Are you looking at the women?"

"Well, yes, actually."

He gave a low chuckle. "So am I. Unfortunately, at my age, all I can do is look. But you must study the men as well. Any one of them, even a group, could be a grave danger to you. What kind of men would you need to keep an eye out for?"

"Bigger men," I hazarded.

"Which in your case is most of them. Yes, bigger men, stronger men. What else?"

"Armed men?"

"Very good. Look at their hands or even their pockets, if their hands hover near them. What else?"

"I scarce can say."

"What of trained men? Would you avoid a man with the cauliflower ears and heavy brow of a fighter? Of course you would. If you did not know him, would you avoid a man like your employer?"

"Yes, sir. Definitely."

"Good. You are tethered to a hard man. What other kind of man should you avoid?"

"I'm afraid I don't know."

"A mad one, sir. Watch carefully those who mutter in the street or who look worried and disturbed. Very well, Mr.

Llewelyn, now suppose a man seizes you, despite all your carefulness. What do you do?"

"Order him to let go."

"And if he won't?"

"Take a swing at him, I suppose."

Gallenga opened his hand and fluttered it in a very Italian gesture.

"Eh, sometimes that might work. It would get you arrested in London, but that is not a bad thing if you suspect the man has a gun or knife. Better arrested than dead, don't you think? But the best thing to do is to simply break the hold. I assume your employer has shown you how to do that?"

"Oh, yes. Dozens of ways," I told him.

"Good. So you break his hold. What then?"

"Run."

"Yes, run. Or shout your head off. Cry 'murder' if you like. Anything. Above all, do not allow yourself to be trapped again. What else should you look for?"

Again, I had to admit I didn't know.

"Accomplices. Look for the man with a cosh or a life preserver. Yes, a smack behind the ear and down you go, maybe forever. Watch out for the second fellow. They often work in pairs, you know." He stopped in front of a café and looked inside. "Do you like coffee?"

"I love coffee," I admitted.

"Step in here, then. This is a Sicilian café."

Gallenga led me into the small establishment, tastefully set up with mahogany tables and white linen. I thought it looked new and wondered if its owner might have anything to do with Etienne's attack. Le Toison d'Or was but a few streets away.

"Where would you suggest we sit?" the old man asked in my ear.

"That's a fair question," I replied. "If I'm by the window, I risk being shot at from the street. If I'm in the corner there, I shall be trapped like a rat, but if I'm by the kitchen, I'm at the mercy of someone coming through the back door. My word, it seems as though no place is safe."

"No place *is* safe, my friend. In fact, safety is an illusion, and the safest looking place may be the most dangerous. You were acquainted with the late Mr. Serafini? He was not always the large man you knew. Once, he hid inside a small chest through an entire ball and a political meeting afterward. Several hours later, when his target, a general, was seated and going over plans for a political coup, Serafini jumped up like a jack-in-the-box and shot him dead. The man had thought he was safe, and it cost him his life. Eventually Serafini himself let down his guard. As far as this café is concerned, I believe I would choose a table near the kitchen. One could always fight one's way out the back door."

We sat down at a table and Gallenga ordered two coffees from a waiter who appeared to know him well.

"Excuse me, sir," I asked after the waiter left, "but how do you know all these things? Are they common knowledge among the Sicilians or do you have some connection to . . . to any organization involved in this case? How did you learn how to use a dagger?"

"Once, I was a student agitator, when the Bourbons ruled Sicily," Gallenga said, "then a political prisoner, and then I met the man, Giuseppe Mazzini himself, and became an assassin."

There was a time when I would have blurted out "assassin!" and attracted attention throughout the café. Now I merely said, "Really?"

"Yes, but I was not very good at it, I admit. After a failed attempt, I became a fugitive, eventually coming to England. *The Times* required someone knowledgeable about Italian affairs and I needed work. I've been doing it now for twenty-five years and have written several books."

"Do you have any connection to the Mafia?"

"I am a member, Mr. Llewelyn. I took a blood oath, one I can never forswear."

I thought about that as the coffee arrived, small porcelain cups of espresso with rusty cream on top.

"Oh, my word," I said, after I'd taken a sip. "I believe that's the best cup of coffee I've ever tasted."

"I will not doubt your word, sir."

"So, Mr. Barker says the Camorran organization is older than the Mafia."

"Far older. It goes back a century or two when Naples was ruled by Spain and a criminal organization known as the Garduna sent exiles to Italy."

"So, in order to escape prosecution in Spain, they went to Naples, just as you came to England in order to prevent your arrest in Italy."

"Yes, and as Victor Gigliotti did. You did not think he came to England to sell tutti-frutti, did you? He is wanted in Naples."

I put down my empty cup and hesitated. "That's cracking good coffee. Might I have another cup?"

Gallenga shook his head. "Better not. Sicilian coffee is very strong. Another cup and you won't sleep tonight."

"I'm not certain I'll sleep anyway now, not without checking every closet and chest in the house for assassins."

"That is the 'eye' I was telling you about. From now on, if you enter a room without asking yourself what is the safest way to escape, it shall not be my fault."

"It looks like some trouble is brewing between these two rival organizations. Mr. Barker seems determined to stop a war from breaking out in London, but, if I may say it, you appear to be in the enemy camp."

"After twenty-five years, I consider myself a Londoner, and believe me when I say that I do not want to see it turned into another Palermo with a list of assassinations in the Sunday edition of *The Times*. I am willing to help your employer up to a point. I will teach you to fight with a dagger, for instance. However, I want you to understand I'm doing this to repay a debt."

Gallenga paid the bill with a few brief words to the owner and went out the door with his hands in his pockets, hunched over as if he'd forgotten I was there. I followed along behind him back to his garden.

"Have you ever seen a dagger?" he asked, turning back to me suddenly. "Do you know the difference between a dagger and a knife?"

"Yes, sir," I responded. "Mr. Barker owns a few. A dagger has two symmetrical blades and is weighted for throwing."

"Not always," the journalist said, holding up a finger, "but most of the time, I'll grant you. Have you ever held one?"

"Yes, but only to open a letter."

"Open a letter!" he roared in my face. "You use an Italian dagger to open a common letter? Why do you tell such things to an old man? Are you trying to give me a heart attack?"

"No, sir. I'm sorry."

"Open a letter," he muttered to himself, rubbing his chest. "*Mia madre.*"

He opened a garden shed and reached down by the door, pulling a dagger out of a bucket that was full of sawdust. "The old woman will not let me keep my blades in the house," he explained. "If they are not kept in oiled sawdust, they will rust. It is important to take care of one's weapons."

He wiped the dagger and handed it to me hilt first.

"Here is a proper dagger. The point, for thrusting forward, an edge on either side for cutting, a hilt for stopping another weapon, and a ball at the other end for breaking a bone or punching a hole in someone's skull. In a city such as London, it is the most important defense one can own."

"What about a walking stick?" I asked, holding up my malacca.

"Pfui. A wand. A stick of wood. A splinter. Try putting that through a man's intestines. It's impossible."

"Well, I can't argue with that," I admitted.

"Put your stick down," Gallenga ordered.

I put it down beside a bench in the garden, then came forward at his bidding and reached for the dagger he presented.

"Ow!" I cried, as the point entered the fleshy webbing between my thumb and forefinger. He'd done it on purpose.

Gallenga raised the blade he still held in his hand and watched as the drop of blood slicked the blade and puddled at the hilt.

"This is your blade now, Thomas Llewelyn. It has tasted your blood and now it knows its master. I make it a gift to you, for I cannot stand between you now."

"Thank you, sir."

Gallenga cut his own hand in the same place with his personal blade, then reached out to me. We shook hands and in so doing, a blood covenant was made between us.

"You must promise not to teach what you learn here to anyone save your own son, when the time is right. I assume you have none at the moment."

"No, sir. I promise."

He raised his hand like a soothsayer. "A benediction from an old man, then. May you have a houseful of sons."

I had not asked for a houseful. In fact, I hadn't asked for any, but I knew sons were important in Italian culture, and so I merely thanked him.

"And now, let the lesson begin. This is how to hold a Sicilian dagger."

9

BARKER DECIDED THAT BEFORE THE DAY ENDED he must stop and see how Etienne was progressing. It was perhaps coincidental that he chose an hour at which Le Toison d'Or was just opening its doors for the dinner crowds and Madame Dummolard was occupied.

When we arrived at Charing Cross Hospital, we buttonholed the admitting orderly to see about Dummolard's condition.

"He's not allowed visitors, sir," the young man told us.

"What? Is he still gravely ill?"

"No, sir, but he boxed the ear of the last doctor what got near him. The hospital cannot be liable for your safety, I'm afraid."

"I know his temper," Barker said with a chuckle. "I've been acquainted with it for many years. I'll take my chances. Come, lad."

When we entered Etienne's room, we narrowly missed the chamber pot shied at our heads.

"Good afternoon, Etienne," Barker replied, as if flying pots were our cook's standard form of greeting.

"*Mon capitaine!*" Dummolard roared from his bed. "Get me out of here. These *cochons* don't realize I have a restaurant to run. London must have a choice beside le Yorkshire pud."

"You stay until the doctor says you can leave," the Guv ordered. "I won't have you collapsing over your roux."

Dummolard crossed his bare arms and cursed, but it was obvious he would comply. He was used to taking orders from his former captain, if no one else.

"Are you feeling any better?"

"*Comme ci, comme ça,*" Dummolard replied. "Mireille made such a nuisance of herself that they have restricted her visits to two hours a day. I have not had so much rest since before my wedding day. I must warn you my brothers came to pay a visit."

"Your brothers?" Barker asked, frowning.

"*Oui.* All five of them: Robert, Thierry, François, Martin, and Jean. The family honor has been bes-, bes-, oh, damn, what is the word?"

"Besmirched?" I offered.

"Besmirched! *Merci.*"

"They are apache, as I recall," Barker said. "Is that not so?"

"*Oui.*"

"Apache?" I queried.

"Not Indians, lad," Barker explained. "French gang members. Good fighters, savateurs, for the most part. Normally I'd chase them back across the Channel, but I might have use for them now. You say there are only five?"

"*Oui*, but they despise Sicilians. They would cross a desert to fight them."

"Do you know where they are staying?"

Dummolard picked up a slip of paper from a table beside his bed and gave it to Barker.

"How long have they been here?"

"They arrived this morning. Smuggled themselves in from Dieppe."

My employer sighed and put his hands on his hips. "And how much trouble have they gotten into since then?"

"Not much, not for them, anyway. They broke up one of the Sicilian cafés in Soho and had a good fight with the Irish in Seven Dials. They say this London of mine is very tame and that I was more likely attacked by a child in a perambulator armed with a rattle. They said I am getting old. I intend to thrash them all when I get out of here."

"When will you be released? Have they said?"

"Two days if I agree to stay in bed at home for a while. Two weeks if I intend to go back to work."

"They know you too well, Etienne," I couldn't help but say. "Are you eating the food they serve you here?"

"Of course not. Are you mad? Mireille brings me lunch and dinner from Le Toisin d'Or, so I can be certain they don't make a shambles of the meals in my absence. You think I would eat the poison they serve in this place? I have no wish for the suicide."

"So I take it Robert is the next eldest brother, and in charge of the others?" our employer asked, changing the subject.

"He is. You will find him in front of this hospital somewhere. He has convinced himself that the Sicilians intend to finish the work they started."

"Has he reason to be convinced?"

Dummolard shrugged and then winced in pain. Being stabbed twice seriously impedes a Frenchman's ability to express himself. "Some fellows resembling Sicilians attempted to enter the hospital yesterday but left when my brothers made a show of strength."

"And you considered this not noteworthy enough to mention until now?"

"I was hoping for a chance at them myself, if you must know. They caught me unawares once. I will not let them do so again."

"You'd fight them with a chamber pot?" I couldn't help but ask. Dummolard was fearless, but that was going too far, even for him.

"No, you idiot," he replied, reaching behind his pillow and pulling out a wicked-looking pistol.

"A gift from one of your brothers," my employer commented.

"A man has a right to defend himself, *non?*"

"It's a wonder you merely boxed the doctor's ear," I commented.

"I'll leave you to your convalescence, Etienne," Barker said drily. "Try not to shoot anyone."

As soon as we came out of Charing Cross Hospital, Cyrus Baker came to the curb and stopped, his hand resting on the head of his stick. He stood immobile among the stream of citizens passing by and I was reminded of an old motto of one of the Scottish clans: Stand Fast. The nation to our north produces rough men like my employer; it was no wonder Hadrian tried to keep them out with a wall from sea to sea.

The Guv's head turned as he scanned the crowd. He hadn't bothered to ask what Robert Dummolard looked like. It was something of an intellectual exercise, picking Etienne's brother out of a crowd, so I attempted to find him as well. It was a variation on Mr. Gallenga's "eye." I glanced from face to face, looking for similar features to our cook, similar build, wondering if there was a way to recognize Frenchness in a person.

"I don't see him, I'm afraid."

"Look lower," Barker said, then gave a short summons with his hand before turning and moving south. I had just enough time to see a fellow stand before I followed my employer. Dummolard's brother had been seated on some steps going down to a basement across the street, and smoking a cigarette.

There is an unwritten code of behavior that goes with being an enquiry agent. I knew I would show myself to be a rank amateur were I to turn my head to see if the Frenchman was following us. The mere act of looking back might raise his scorn and we'd lose him, so I forced myself to keep looking forward.

Barker unlocked our chambers and we crossed to our desks, where I pulled out my ledger book, as if being followed by a French apache was such a common occurrence it was not worth a change in routine.

I blinked and he was there. Very well, perhaps it wasn't that fast, but nearly so. I looked down at the ledger, and soundlessly he slipped past me and sat in the visitor's chair. Robert Dummolard was tall and swarthy with black hair and a mustache. He looked nothing like his elder brother, save for the misshapen nose. I could tell he was dangerous. The nose had been broken before, and there was a vertical scar creasing his jawline. He wore a tan overcoat and carried a bowler.

"You wish to avenge your brother against the assassins who almost killed him," Barker stated, his elbows resting on the arms of his green leather chair with his fingertips pressed together.

In answer, the Frenchman gave the very briefest of nods.

"So do I. In fact, I wish to completely discourage the Mafia from settling in London, though I won't molest the Sicilians unconnected with it. If we both go after the same individuals we might get in each other's way. I am considering a confrontation in a few days' time, and I require skilled fighters. Would you and your brothers be interested?"

"*C'est possible,*" Robert Dummolard muttered. He had a harsh voice, the kind one gets from smoking too many cigarettes.

"Are you able to speak for your brothers? No pistols. You may bring a knife, but I would prefer sticks at first. I want no fatalities."

"I cannot promise," he pronounced slowly.

"We shall cross that bridge when we come to it, then."

"*Comment?*"

"We will decide then."

"*D'accord.*"

"I would reach you in plenty of time to get you to the skirmish. I may set up a meeting beforehand. Until then, consider that you'll be of no use to your brother if you end up in jail."

Robert gave a low chuckle and stood. He moved quickly past me and was gone, on his way back to his post in front of Charing Cross Hospital.

I looked at my employer. "Are you really planning to have a confrontation with the Mafia with the two of us and Etienne's five brothers?"

"What? You don't approve of my plan?" the Guv asked, leaning back in his chair. "If it makes you feel any better, I do plan to recruit others to help."

"But, sir, what if the Sicilians arrive armed with pistols and shotguns? It could be a bloodbath, and you'd be responsible. We don't know how many men the Sicilians can muster," I continued. "It could be two or three hundred. There are too many variables. Is there any other way? Obviously, you intend to flush out the Mafia fellow Marco Faldo and his assassin and force them out of London, but will it work?"

"I cannot give you a guarantee, lad, if that is what you want. The head of the Sicilians is bound by honor to appear with his men. Once I see him, I'll figure out how to bring him down."

"If you see him first!"

"Oh, I'll see him, all right. I don't believe he's that resourceful. He's a traditionalist. Look at the methods he's used already: the barreling, the ice pick, and the Black Hand note. They are classic Sicilian tactics."

"I'm for more men," I said. "As many as possible. Where do we find them?"

"We'll go to the source, lad. First thing in the morning, we'll go down to the docks."

10

We were coming out of our door the next morning when we heard the loud, braying voice of a street vendor a few streets away. We did not get many out here in Newington. I would not have noted it in passing, but Barker's ears are more acute than mine, or perhaps he was listening for it. It made him turn and follow the voice to its source. At the corner of Brook Street, there stood a hokeypokey man with his cart.

There were two of them, to be precise, a man in his fifties and a boy no more than twelve. The man was alternating between offering his wares and singing snatches of Verdi. He was talented enough to have attracted a handful of people so early in the morning.

"He is too well dressed to be a hokeypokey man," Barker commented.

The man had a heavy mustache, black hair going gray at the temples, and wore an elegant frock coat. He did not touch the ice cream at all but left the messy work to the boy, a cheerful lad with a halo of black curls and sleeves rolled to the elbows.

"Could he be training the boy?" I ventured.

"It is rather early in the day for ice cream and too much of a coincidence that he should appear on a corner so close to our home."

"Tutti-frutti!" the man bawled. "Italian ices. *Ecco poco,* only a little!"

"Gigliotti runs most of the ice cream vendors in London, because he holds a monopoly in the ice trade here. The Neapolitan is only one of his enterprises."

"What sort of criminal activities is he involved with?" I asked.

"Merely those that ensure his monopoly stays a monopoly. Any attempt to start a rival business is run off."

"Are you going to speak to this fellow?"

"He's not breaking the law, Thomas."

"Gentlemen!" the man called out to us from across the street. "May I interest you in a bowl of cold ice cream on this warm morning?"

"Not at the moment, thank you, sir," Barker answered, raising his hat.

The Italian broke into song again, while my employer turned into Newington Causeway. The incident left me with an unsettled feeling. It seemed to me that the man had sinister intentions, but then it's easy to feel that way in the middle of a case. The pair could be no more than they appeared, ice cream vendors, but, in my opinion, the Italian looked just like the sort of man who could plan and operate a Sicilian takeover.

"Is he one of Gigliotti's men, perhaps?" I asked.

"I find it no more comforting to think he's a Camorran than a Sicilian. Let us be cautious, lad, and keep an eye on this corner either way."

"What if the Serafinis had become a hindrance to Gigliotti and he has bigger plans?" I asked. "What if we can't find the Sicilian leader because he does not, in fact, exist?"

Barker looked at me for a moment or two. "Now you're thinking like an enquiry agent, Thomas."

"Is it possible?"

"Aye, 'tis. But there are other scenarios that are equally possible."

"For example?" I challenged.

"Suppose the Sicilians were actually hired by Mr. K'ing or the Irish criminal Seamus O'Muircheartaigh, who has a good quarter of the East End in his pocket. This may all be an attempt to wrest control from Gigliotti's grasp."

"My word," I said. "I hadn't thought of that."

"And it could just as easily be something else we haven't thought of."

"That's comforting," I replied.

"Come, lad, we have an appointment," Barker said.

"With whom, sir?"

"Mr. Dalton Green. He is in charge of the East and West India docks until a successor for Sir Alan is found."

My employer hailed a cab with one of those piercing whistles of his. We were taking quite a number of hansoms, I noted, wondering if the Home Office could afford such extravagances.

"So has Dr. Vandeleur ruled that Sir Alan was murdered or not?" I asked once we were seated and rolling through Lambeth.

"Lad," he replied solemnly, "you really need to read the newspapers every morning, rather than mooning about, ingesting coffee by the bucketful. There is a world out there with events of more than passing interest."

"Sorry, sir."

"If you had, you would have already discovered that he ruled that the death was due to natural causes. It was his only option, really. Claiming that Sir Alan was murdered without ironclad proof would create a scandal that would have certainly cost Vandeleur his position. The gentry doesn't like unwelcome news. All the same, Vandeleur takes his work very seriously and must have hated to bring a false report."

"So he did the next best thing," I said. "He told you. This is just the sort of bee Vandeleur knew would get in your bonnet. He could soothe his conscience by knowing that you'd taken over the case."

"Unfortunately, he has given me little to work with. Pray give me some quiet to come up with an appropriate ruse."

Neither of us spoke for the rest of the journey. I wondered if the hokeypokey man had concerned him more than he let on.

One smells the West India Docks before one sees them. The smell is not salt water or seaweed or damp, it is rum. The sweet odor pervades everything, so that one expects to see barrels broken on the quayside, instead of lined up neatly and sealed tight. We made our way to the dock offices, where Barker presented his card; and after a twenty-minute wait, we were shown in to Dalton Green. He was a corpulent, jowly man, as if he had been designed with a French curve. The windows were open, admitting a heady breeze, but there was a sheen of perspiration across the man's brow.

"What can I do for you, Mr. Barker?" he said a trifle testily. "I can spare you but a few minutes."

"Sir, I am investigating a case for a barrister whose client claims he was assaulted by a gang of Italian dockworkers."

"Did the incident occur on the docks or out beyond the gate there?" Green nodded his head toward the stone gates separating the docks from the rest of Poplar.

"Just outside them, sir, in Bridge Road."

"I don't see that it is any of my concern, then," he replied, waving a dimpled hand in dismissal.

"The District Council and the Tower Hamlets have received complaints of disruptions by Italian stevedores from these docks as far as Clerkenwell."

"This is the first I've heard of it," Green declared, as if information that didn't reach his ear was either unimportant or downright erroneous. In this case, I knew it to be a total fabrication. "Were the men drunken?"

"No, sir. Organized. I understand it is either some sort of labor dispute or a matter between the various Italians. Had Sir Alan some trouble with them before he died?"

"He did, and now his problems have fallen into my lap. The Italians are willing to work for a wage that, frankly, the English workers won't accept, but they have begun to demand a minimum number of working hours per day, which is madness, because we can't guarantee the work. Ships arrive at their own pace. Some days they come in all day long, and other days the docks are empty for hours. I understand that they don't like spending the entire day hoping work will pull up to the dock, but that's the nature of maritime casual work. If we agreed to pay them for even three hours per day, it could ruin us if the freight doesn't arrive."

"Has there been some problem with the Sicilians?"

"Bloody dagos," Green replied, loosening his collar in irritation. "They're always at each other's throats. The Sicilians think themselves a cut above the rest. They swagger about like they own the docks and are too concerned about slights upon their honor, as if wharf rats had any. Was it the Sicilians who attacked your barrister's client?"

"There was that indication. Were there any reprisals being considered against the Sicilians in particular?"

"As a matter of fact, there was. Bledsoe was going to ban them from the docks entirely. He said the labor issues began when the Sicilians arrived. He thought them natural-born troublemakers and said as far as he was concerned, we could do without them altogether."

"Do you know if he said so in front of them, or if he kept his opinions to himself?"

"Bledsoe was a very forthright man, Mr. Barker. It was his way to throw it back in their court, so to speak. 'You shape up and quit causing trouble, or you can work elsewhere,' he told them."

Barker tented his fingers in front of him in thought. "Did he receive any threatening notes? They are generally stamped with a black hand."

"I believe he did," Green said. "He said the Italians were trying to frighten him, but that he 'wunt be druv,' as the Sussex folk say."

"Might the note still be among his effects?"

"No. I watched him crumple it up in anger and throw it to the floor. I'm sure it was thrown away days ago."

"Was there anything in his death," Barker asked casually, "that might make you think it was not an accident?"

Green sat up. "Here now, what's all this about? You're the second chap to ask me that. The first was the coroner at the inquest. Is this something to do with Sir Alan's assurance claim? Do they plan to contest it? His heart failed, and there's an end to it. What does this have to do with a client getting coshed by a gang of dagos?"

Barker put up his hands. "I don't work for an assurance company, sir. I'm merely trying to determine the size of the Italian presence on the docks and in particular the Sicilians among them."

Green pulled back his chair and crossed to the open window. The rum-scented wind was pushing in the curtains on either side, and from where he stood he could survey the unloading of the ship. "I wish they were lazy workers, these Sicilians. Then I could sack them; but they are hard workers, even if they give themselves airs. Sometimes I wish we had all good, honest Englishmen on these docks like in the old days, but we can't afford them anymore. The Poles, the Jews, the Chinese, the dagos—they get the work done faster and at less cost. They bring in profit, and when it comes to it, the numbers on the ledger sheet are what really matters. Are we done here?"

"Just one more question, sir. Is it possible I could speak to your foreman who works day to day with the Sicilians?"

"I suppose so. His name's Ben Tillett. He's a good man, though I don't care for his politics. He should be around the docks somewhere."

"Thank you for your time, Mr. Green. Come, Thomas."

Outside, Barker passed through the gates and then

stopped. He put his hands on top of the ball of his stick and inhaled slowly. I'd seen him do it before in our garden, while he was beginning his exercises. He was shaking off whatever he had been doing and preparing to take new impressions.

We watched the unloading of vessels in hope of seeing the Sicilians who had been causing so much trouble. They were not difficult to spot, for they all sported black cloth caps with short peaks. I also noticed that when compared with the Italians, the Sicilians looked thinner and harder, as if they'd seen more trials on that Mediterranean island than their brethren on the mainland. They seemed to have a preference for putting things in their mouths when not actually working, whether cigars, cigarettes, short pipes, or toothpicks. Somehow it made them look foreign and insolent. The Italians were trying to fit in with the other dockworkers, while the Sicilians stood out.

Most of the Sicilians were young, I had noticed, about my age. They could not work without making chafing remarks to their companions, even to ones across the dock. They had not come here to join a criminal organization, I thought, which they could have done in Sicily. No, they'd come because the opportunity to work and the living conditions were better in London than in Palermo. Working as casual labor was hardly ideal, however, if one was forced to wait all day and the work never arrived at the docks. In order to survive, some may have reluctantly stepped under the umbrella the Mafia offered. It was that or starve. For all of their bravado, none of the Sicilians looked well nourished, and I doubted anyone on our little island ever gave them a warm greeting or a full belly. Gallenga had said once one took the blood oath, one was bound for life, which meant forty or fifty more years of being indentured. That is, if they lived that long. To men like Faldo, I thought, these were the yeomen guard, the least trained, the most expendable, the first to be mown down in battle.

11

We stood on the West India Dock, out of the way of the watermen unloading a ship full of cotton from America. The sun was hot, beating down unmercifully, melting tar and bringing a sheen to every man's face, but Barker did not remove his hat or coat. I assumed we were watching only the Sicilians, but when an English worker passed by, Barker plucked his sleeve and murmured a name.

"Mr. Tillett?"

The man Green had recommended was a young fellow with a fawn-colored mustache. He seemed too young to be a foreman, but as usual the Guv was correct.

"Who are you?" he asked guardedly.

"Cyrus Barker. I'm a private enquiry agent. Might we have a few moments of your time?"

"I'm busy at the moment, as you can see. What is this in regard to?"

"I'd prefer to speak privately," Barker insisted. "I believe there is a public house nearby called the Drake."

"I am temperate," Tillett replied. "And, anyway, I cannot simply leave. I still have two more vessels to unload."

"Where, then, and when?" Barker pressed, as if to say *You cannot avoid me.* Tillett sighed and stood, arms akimbo for a moment.

"Oh, very well. There's a tearoom called the Brown Betty in the next street. I'll meet you there in an hour."

"Done."

Tillett moved off, and it was as if neither of them had spoken. I looked at the Sicilians bringing large bundles of cotton wrapped in burlap down the gangplank. No one openly looked our way, but then they would no more draw attention to their actions than we. I thought we would be forced to wait another hour in the heat, when at the far end of the docks there was a commotion.

A group of men parted, and Victor Gigliotti stalked across the dock. He shouted in Italian, and I could tell by the inflection that he was cursing. He buttonholed a young Sicilian and started yelling at him. I thought it a dangerous thing to do, knowing how they carry knives, but the young man merely shrugged as if to say whatever had upset the Italian wasn't his affair. Gigliotti argued with a second man, who pointed to a third, who shrugged in exactly the same way as the first. No one took responsibility for whatever had enraged Gigliotti. He turned to the first man again, the closest to him, and gave him a strong shove, knocking him off his feet. The young fellow hissed a curse of his own around the now broken cigarette in his mouth and pulled a dagger. The phalanx of men Gigliotti had brought with him would not stand for that; to a man, they ripped pistols from their pockets. Faced with a half dozen armed bodyguards, the young

Sicilian dropped his blade and went back to shrugging, all innocence. This incident, I realized, had become a powder keg that could blow up very quickly.

"What is the trouble?" Barker called out. He has no qualms about inserting himself—or me, for that matter—into a dangerous situation.

"Barker!" Gigliotti cried, and suddenly all six pistol barrels pointed at us simultaneously. He waved impatiently at his men and they stood down, returning their weapons to pockets, waistbands, or hidden holsters. "Come look at this! You won't believe what they have done!" He led us across to the warehouses. The dock here was wet; and in front of one of the warehouses, large blocks of ice were melting.

"They have deliberately unloaded my ice this morning and put it in the smallest warehouse, allowing half of it to melt out here! And look! They have scraped off most of the sawdust. The sawdust insulates the ice. And they used the warehouse on the end, facing east. This was deliberate! My ice—it came all the way from Greenland, merely to melt on these God-rotting docks! I will kill the man who did this to me!"

I stepped into the entrance of the building beside my employer. Inside, it was cool, but the floor was a mash of sawdust and water. The ice in tall, concave blocks had washed away the shavings until one could nearly see right through them. He was right: they were ruined. If he and his men hurried now, perhaps they could save half the shipment.

Cyrus Barker passed to the ship unloading cotton and came over with Ben Tillett. The Englishman gave a low whistle.

"What happened here, then?" he asked. "Who unloaded this?"

"That's what I'd like to know," Gigliotti said.

Tillett checked the schedule. "This wasn't meant to be unloaded until tonight."

"I just said that!" the livid Italian cried.

"I'm not doubting your word, sir," the foreman said diplomatically. "Let me go into the office and see what has happened." He trotted off toward the East India Docks office while Gigliotti fumed and muttered to himself.

"There is not a moment to lose if I am to save what is left of this ice. I must have all my vehicles brought here immediately!" He turned and hurried off after Tillett.

I shook my head, looking at the melting ice, but I couldn't help enjoying the cool air and shade. I glanced at my employer. "Do you think this was deliberate?"

"Of course it was," Barker said.

"They are trying to rattle him."

"They're succeeding," my employer growled. "In that note they said he's had things too much his way, and they are right. No one here has dared try this sort of thing with him before. They're scrappy, I'll say that for these Sicilians. One has to earn their respect."

"By that, you mean *we'll* have to," I muttered.

"Aye, lad, and it won't be easy."

A few minutes later, Tillett trotted back, full of news. "What a to-do," he said. "Apparently, one of the Sicilians— and, of course, we don't know which one—got the dock guard drunk early this morning and the ice was unloaded under cover of darkness. The sailors aboard ship said that the paperwork looked to be in order, but the waterman took it away when he was finished. He was Sicilian by the cap he wore, but he knew how to use the dock hoist. These blocks weigh a ton or more."

"I suppose, if one were to question these dockworkers, they would say they were all snug in their beds this morning in Clerkenwell, and each could vouch for the presence of the others the entire night," my employer said.

"Shall we report it, anyway?" I asked.

"Wasted breath. This was just a feint at Gigliotti's head."

Victor Gigliotti returned from the offices looking even less satisfied than he was when he left.

"Green will do nothing!" the Camorran cried, throwing his hands in the air. "Sir Alan would not have allowed such a thing to happen. He would have run off every Sicilian on these docks. My ice, my beautiful ice, all the way from Greenland. 'Nobody saw anything, Mr. Gigliotti.' 'We cannot blame the Sicilians without proof, Mr. Gigliotti.' Pfuh!" Here he gave an Italian gesture, a raking of his chin with the back of his fingers in the direction of the offices. "If he cannot even stand up to a few low-browed Sicilians, he is half a man!"

Gigliotti's first wagon arrived about a quarter hour later. He moaned at the state of his ice all the while. The slush had crossed the threshold and seeped out across the docks toward the harbor. Finally, Gigliotti could take no more and charged toward the Sicilians, who were now done with the cotton and waiting for the next ship to arrive. The Sicilians united were not as docile as before. They charged back, breaking into a shouting match in Italian in the center of the dock with Gigliotti and his men.

"Wait for it," Cyrus Barker said casually, pushing at a shell on the ground with the tip of his stick.

The shouting escalated. As a Briton, I had to marvel at the way these men argued: with expansive gestures and deep passion. It was like watching an impromptu opera. Gigliotti raised a finger and started to declaim something. I didn't understand what he was saying until he got to the final word. That at least was one I'd heard before. It was "vendetta." At once, Gigliotti turned, and with his entire entourage, stalked off, leaving the Sicilians jeering at his retreating form.

"There it is," Barker said. "The Camorrans and the Mafia are officially at war."

An hour later, Ben Tillett sat across from us at the Brown Betty having tea. He ate the cucumber and cress sandwiches but eschewed the sliced ham. Apparently, he was a vegetarian as well as a teetotaler.

"Mr. Green mentioned your politics," Barker commented. "Are you a Fabian?"

"I am," Tillett admitted, wiping crumbs from his mustache. "Do you consider that relevant?"

"Indirectly. The East End seems to be full of socialists these days."

My understanding of my employer is based upon the slightest changes of his expression. In this case he turned his rough-hewn face a half inch toward me, which meant he was regarding me from behind his smoky black lenses. It was true that my best friend, Israel Zangwill, was a member of the Fabians, and he had been quietly agitating for me to join. Cyrus Barker was a staunch conservative and would have no use for a radical reformer in his household. Everywhere I turn it seems I'm stuck between Scylla and Charybdis.

"Our membership is expanding," Tillett said with enthusiasm, "but there is a lot of work to be done in the East End."

'   "I understand there is a problem at the dock regarding a promise of hours?" the Guv asked.

"Yes. We're trying to get Mr. Green to agree to pay every laborer for at least three hours a day. The men have to stay whether or not a ship arrives in port, or the work goes to someone else. It only makes sense that they get paid for it."

"I wish you luck convincing the dock owners of the need to pay idle men."

"Something has to be done," Tillett explained. "These men have families, mouths to feed. Green needs to bring an end to the casual labor system."

"I understand the Sicilian workers have added to the trouble."

"Yes, they have," the young man said, pouring himself a second cup of tea. He had decimated his plate of cucumber sandwiches. "Their numbers have trebled in the last year or more, and they've become a force to be reckoned with on the docks. The long periods of inactivity while waiting for a new boat to arrive often lead to fights and drunkenness. They've taken up the issue of paid hours as well but are rather heavy-handed in their methods. Sometimes I wonder if there's going to be a fight between the Sicilians and the rest of us."

"Are all the Sicilians involved?" I asked.

"No. Perhaps I should have made that clear. Some of them are good family men, but pressure is being put on them to conform. I wouldn't be surprised if their families were threatened."

"Have you ever heard of an organization called the Mafia?" the Guv asked.

"I can't say that I have. What is it?"

"It is a secret criminal organization centered in Palermo. I believe the leader of your dockworkers is a member. Have you seen a recognizable leader among them?"

"I haven't," Tillett replied. "But that's just the thing. They seem to arrive each morning with a planned agenda. For example, the Sicilians will save space for one another, allowing their members to go off and cause trouble in Poplar, and then they'll alert each other when a ship's arriving. Frankly, we don't know whether to disallow the practice or adopt it ourselves. It flies in the face of several centuries of tradition."

"But then, so do socialism and paid hours," Barker said.

"Touché, Mr. Barker," the young man admitted. "You've got me there."

"How do the Italians stand in this situation?"

"They're getting fed up," Tillett replied. "The English confuse them with the Sicilians, and the Sicilians consider them rubbish. They nudge them in passing while unloading, knocking them off balance. One even fell off the gangplank the other day, breaking his elbow. Frankly, we've never cared for the Italians, but we prefer them to the Sicilians by a long chalk."

"Do you take this morning's situation with the ice to be a continuation of the problem?"

"Definitely. Gigliotti's the most successful Italian in London. Until now, even the Sicilians have bowed to his demands. I'm sure this will cause ripples from here to Clerkenwell."

"Let me put two questions to you, if I may. Do you think a battle planned by the Sicilians would be straightforward and on the level?"

"No, I do not."

"Nor do I. Do you think if the confrontation does not come to pass that the Sicilian element will settle in quietly and merge with the general population of London?"

"The only way they'll merge with the population," Tillett admitted, "is if they are at the head of it."

"Aye," Barker said. "I agree. So do you intend to sit on your hands and let the thing wash over you? There's going to be a dock fight with belaying pins and marlin spikes and whatever comes to hand."

"You sound as if you've been in this sort of scuffle before."

"I was a ship's captain before I was a private enquiry agent, and an able seaman before that."

"What do you want of me, Mr. Barker?" Ben Tillett asked. He was an educated man of the middle class as far as I could tell, but one does not last among the Fabians without being able to ask a blunt question when necessary.

"If I were a Sicilian leader and I knew a dock fight were in the offing, I would start making alliances among my fellow Sicilians, as well as with anyone else I could coerce into joining. If I were working for the welfare of the docks, I would expect the English watermen to stand with the Italians, and I would want you to organize them."

"Me?" Ben Tillett asked.

"Aye. You've got a good head on your shoulders and refuse to be intimidated the way Mr. Green is. If you agree, your dockworkers would follow."

Tillett gently set his cup down in his saucer, but I noticed his cheeks suddenly flushed.

"Who are you, Mr. Barker?"

"As I said, I am a private enquiry agent. At present, I'm working for Her Majesty's government. It might interest you to know that your late employer did not die of a heart attack. He was assassinated by a method perfected in Sicily."

"I have only your word for that."

"That is correct, Mr. Tillett. If I or anyone else handed you a letter claiming to prove themselves an agent working secretly for the government, that letter would be false. I could give you the names of five men who could provide references, but that would depend on whether you trusted those five men, and frankly, I don't have the time. I have learned enough about you in the last half hour to trust you to gather a force to combat the threat of Sicilians taking over the docks. I ask you to trust me to lead it."

"Based solely upon your word?" Tillett asked, a trifle desperately.

"No," I put in. "Based upon mine, as well. I've seen three people killed by this Sicilian, whoever he is, and a fourth is in the hospital. I was present when Mr. Barker was hired, and there are very definite signs that Sicilian criminals are trying to take over the London underworld. The docks are the one place where there is open conflict, and he has chosen you because he believes you're capable and honest. He makes snap judgments like that sometimes. Now you can have a controlled conflict organized by Mr. Barker, or you can have open warfare whenever it erupts, and people will probably be killed. That's all I have to say."

"I'll be frank with you, gentlemen. I'll have to think

about it and talk with a few watermen I know and trust about whether it is in our best interests and also whether they trust me to lead them. There might be one among them more fit to lead than I."

"Find out what information you can, then, Mr. Tillett," he said, as if the young man were another assistant to be ordered about. "And speak to your men. Give me an idea of how many you can recruit. Here is my card."

"Very well, Mr. Barker," he said, taking the card and studying it. "I'll do my best. Now I must get back to the dock and see what's happened to Mr. Gigliotti's ice."

We watched him exit the tearoom. Barker pushed his cup away from him with one of his thick fingers.

"You really think we can do it, sir?" I asked.

"As you so ably put it, lad, the fight is inevitable. Our only hope is to turn it to our advantage."

12

COMING OUT OF THE BROWN BETTY, BARKER headed north into Poplar following the bend around Limehouse Reach. There was no need to wonder where we were going. He was headed for a tearoom of his own choosing, a clandestine one, run by his closest friend, Ho. Once we'd reached the establishment, we walked down the dark stairs that led along the tunnel under the river. After an inspector had been shot in the darkened tunnel, lamps were placed and lit permanently at either end, though Ho complained about the price of naphtha. There was to be no more walking in complete darkness, which had once been the sign that one was a regular. However, in my opinion, the gloom and odd shadows cast by the flickering lamps were more eerie than mere darkness.

Inside the restaurant, Barker skirted our usual table and made his way to a door on the other side of the room that led to a banquet hall. I followed him through it. Ho was already inside. He is a squat Chinaman with weighted earlobes, a braid of hair, and heavily tattooed arms. In his hands was a long length of rope with a metal spike on the end that he twirled about the room. He dropped it to his feet, kicked it across the empty space, and then snapped it back again. At the other side of the room lay a row of shattered clay vessels, and as I watched he shot the dart forward with a kick and broke the least damaged of the lot. Some might have called it a child's game, but the pointed dart made it look far more dangerous to me.

"We're going against the Sicilians," Barker stated, crossing his arms. Ho continued spinning the rope, wrapping it and unwrapping it around his arms again and even whipping it around his head close enough to ricochet off one of the gold earrings he wears. He gave no sign of hearing what Barker had said.

"We're gathering a ragtag army against them, since the government cannot supply us with any assistance. I was wondering if you might help us."

"I can feed your troops if you wish it," Ho said, launching the dart at the row of pots again.

"I don't need cooks," Barker said, clearly irritated. "I need soldiers."

"I have no concern about the Sicilians," the Chinaman finally remarked.

"You should. They will be taking over London before you know it."

"Mr. K'ing has reached an agreement with a representative. He will not go against them. Bad for business."

"What about you, then? You must have a dozen cooks here."

"Cooks, not soldiers," Ho continued, winding his rope

dart back again. "Cannot run a restaurant with dead cooks and waiters."

"Not if you're there, too," Barker pointed out.

Ho shook his head. "Mr. K'ing would be displeased."

"Are you his lackey now?" my employer asked. "Is this the same man I fought alongside against the Heavenly Kingdom?"

Ho shrugged one of his brawny shoulders. "If I can help, I will help."

Barker tossed one of the sharpened pennies he always kept in his pocket at his friend. It could sever a jugular. Without breaking stride, Ho sent the dart after it, deflecting the coin into one of the beams overhead.

"You are slowing down," Ho commented.

"Come, lad," the Guv said to me. "Apparently no one in town has the pluck to take on the Sicilians save us."

Barker walked past me and was gone. I turned and followed. In the tunnel, I caught up with him.

"That's it?" I asked. "What are we going to do now?"

"We'll go back to our chambers and see if any new information has surfaced."

An hour later, we heard a voice in the outer office.

"Is your boss on the premises?"

I recognized it instantly, though on previous occasions it had been heralded by the sound of hobnailed boots. Patrick Hooligan was a gang leader in Southwark, who had crossed our path before. He had a gift for listening closely to the word on the street and brokering his services quickly. Had he a proper education, I'm sure he would have done well as a businessman, not that he was doing badly now.

When last I'd seen him, Hooligan had a donkey-fringe haircut and bell-bottom trousers. Now his hair was shorn close, little more than stubble, and he wore a long black coat over a shirt, whose collar and tie were held in place by a diamond-studded pin in the shape of a horseshoe. One thing hadn't changed, however; his boots still had brass caps on the toes, all the better to kick agreement out of certain persons.

"'Lo, Push," he greeted, coming into the office with his usual swagger. "May I?"

"Help yourself," Barker said, waving to the cigar case on his desk.

"Fanks. You allus 'as the real goods, not the stuff that passes for a proper cigar these days."

"You're quite the Brummell today, Patrick," the Guv noted.

Hooligan opened his coat and turned around slowly, allowing us a view of his sartorial splendor. His waistcoat looked as if it had been cut from a Persian carpet, but of course, I wouldn't tell him that.

"I'm movin' up in the world," he announced. "A man of business like you yourself, Push. A little bit of advertisement for me services, a little word of mouf, a kick to the jaw for them what deserves it, and me and the lads are doing well for ourselves. Expandin' is what we are. 'Member the Ratcliff Highway Boys?"

"Of course."

"Brought 'em down Friday. Nobbled 'em proper. Them not willin' to join my lot were ducked in Limehouse Basin, they was. I gave 'em the choice. Almost got ol' Kingy hemmed in now."

"Kingy" stood for Mr. K'ing, head of the Chinese Blue Dragon Triad, Hooligan's personal nemesis, though Mr. K'ing never acknowledged his presence. Hooligan wanted to take over the East End but was not as powerful as K'ing. Still, Hooligan was young; and if hunger and drive were enough, he might make a name for himself in the underworld.

"So, what can I do for you?" asked Barker.

"Word is you're recruitin'."

"What word?"

Hooligan shrugged and dropped into the visitor's chair. He never explained where he got the information that brought him to our door. "Word."

"I might be recruiting," the Guv admitted. "It's all in the planning stage, contingent upon certain conditions. I may require your services at the last minute."

"Last minute will cost you double. What 'zactly do you need?"

"A handful of your best men, and you yourself, of course."

Hooligan frowned, considering the request. "Do you want the ones that look dangerous or that are dangerous?"

"A compromise between the two. I'm hoping to scare them off, if possible."

"Scare who off?" Hooligan cut the end of the cigar with a small jackknife he'd pulled from his boot and lit a vesta against the ceramic striker on Barker's desk.

"What does the word in the street say?"

"Something I-talian. That's all I know."

"Do you know the Sicilians?"

Hooligan nodded. "Dockworkers, mostly, ain't they?"

"Yes. Have you heard of an organization called the Mafia?"

"Never."

"It's a criminal organization based in Palermo. Very nasty. It is a state of perpetual warfare there. They use weapons—shotguns, knives, whatever comes to hand. They prefer weapons to hand fighting."

"Who wouldn't? So, d'you 'spect my lads to go in empty-handed against these blokes, or will you provide us some protection?"

"What sort of protection would you require?"

"I dunno. A half dozen pistols wouldn't come amiss, for starters."

"I don't wish to provoke a bloodbath, nor would I want to be the means whereby a London gang, even one such as yours, received firearms."

Hooligan shrugged. "Can't blame a man for trying. What about knives, then?"

"I'm sure your lads are well armed, and you'll receive compensation afterward for any knives you purchase."

"Not good enough. I need to see the color of your money first."

"Mr. Llewelyn, give Mr. Hooligan ten pounds."

I pulled out my wallet, which interested the gang leader exceedingly, counted out ten pounds, then handed them over and entered the amount in my accounts book.

"Now, what about the guns? For my own safety, I'd like to know if we have artillery of our own."

"We won't," Barker stated emphatically. "No guns."

Hooligan knocked off his cigar ash. Then he puffed and looked at my employer speculatively through the smoke.

"Who else you got workin' wif us? Will K'ing be there?" he asked.

"Would it bother you if he were? I haven't decided yet."

"It might be a problem. The lads are a bit touchy. We've had a skirmish or three wif his Mongol horde."

"And now you'd be working together. It is a basis for amity."

Hooligan snorted. "Amity? I ain't looking for no bleedin' amity. I'll have to ask my lads if they're willin' to work with the slants. Who else are you bringin' in?"

"It's possible I may engage another group. I haven't formalized my plans."

"But I'm in," Hooligan said.

"If you're willing."

"Always willin'. Now all we 'ave to do is agree on a price. Step into my office."

So saying, the young gang leader stood, pulled off his long coat, and hung it over his arm. Barker reached under the coat and the two haggled silently using the arcane hand signals originated by horse traders in Ireland. Every time I think I've got leverage on what my employment entails, something like this comes along and proves how deluded I am. Where did Barker learn the language of horse traders?

"Done," Hooligan finally said, "providin' I can convince the lads. I'll send word by the end of workin' hours. Pleasure doin' business with you gents as always—Mr. Barker, Mr. Llewelyn. I'll see myself out."

"This entire Sicilian situation reminds me of the condottiere, the mercenaries that the old city-states of Italy hired when they were at war," I said after Hooligan had left.

"They prospered enough from the killing to purchase large villas and become a threat to everybody else."

"Exactly," the Guv replied. "There is nothing more dangerous than a mercenary, trained in the art of war, who is cunning enough to use the political situation to his own economic advantage."

It occurred to me that Cyrus Barker was something of a mercenary himself. Trained in the art of war, yes. A cunning foreigner, aye, laddie. Economic advantage, certainly, the last I looked at our bank account. And as for using the political situation, it was something we did often in our work, though I'll say in his defense that he genuinely had the Empire's best interests at heart. A reformed mercenary, then.

"What are you thinking, lad?" Barker asked gruffly. Sometimes I swear he can read minds.

"I was wondering if there is a Sicilian political group here in London," I went on, "or an Italian one. Is there an Italian newspaper published here?"

"No, there isn't. They're not as large a group as the Jews with their *Chronicle*. It's a good idea about the political group, though. You must ask Gallenga about it when you see him again. How did the blade fighting go?"

"You'd have to ask Mr. Gallenga about that, sir. Do you really think it necessary?"

"Aye. My blade has saved my life half a dozen times. Why? Don't you like the dagger?"

"If you must know, it worries me a little. I can pull out a gun and shoot a man if I know he's trying to kill me, and I have no trouble defending myself with a stick, but a blade . . . to gut a man as if he were a mackerel, it makes me pause."

"Don't pause too long, lad," Barker said, crossing his arms, "or he'll be the one gutting you."

"Being stabbed would be terrible," I went on. "I'd rather be shot. There's something about that sharp blade that sets my teeth on edge, even to think of it."

"There is," he admitted. "I think most would agree with you, even though the gun is more fatal. I've suffered both wounds, and the former is more clearly in my memory than the latter. Let us be off, Thomas. One more stop before we go home. I want to visit Clerkenwell."

13

CLERKENWELL WAS UNEXPLORED TERRITORY FOR me. Most of the buildings were tumbledown, swaybacked old piles of red brick and pantiles, looking like the kind of sentimental paintings of old London one buys from street stalls for a few shillings. Down at ground level, the streets look as Italian as Rome. Street musicians played the violin or the hurdy-gurdy, black-haired children ran about the streets looking nothing like Oliver Twist and the Artful Dodger whom Dickens put there, and men and women sat on steps and balustrades discussing the events of the day in their native tongue. A slum, some might call the area, but flowers bloomed in every window box. Most of the people seemed to be enjoying their lives so far from the shores of their homeland.

I noticed a man we passed wearing a piece of cloth on a cord around his neck, and had not gone another twenty feet before seeing a similar one around the throat of an old woman.

"What do you suppose those charms are?" I asked my employer.

"They are the brown scapulars of Our Lady of Mount Carmel. The Italian Catholics think a lot of this apparition of the Virgin Mary. They hold a festival in midsummer in which they carry a shrine through the district."

"I must say, you have an unusual knowledge of Catholic beliefs for a Baptist."

"I noticed them the last time I was here. This kind of charm is just the sort of thing that caused the formation of the Church of England in the first place. Nothing scares an Englishman more than a powerful organization in London with strong ties to the Continent such as the Roman Catholic Church."

"I thought it was merely old King Henry wanting to be shed of a wife," I said.

"Aye, that, too."

We walked on. It came as no surprise to me that the Italian quarter was dominated by a large church, which was called Saint Peter's. In fact, the street we were on led us directly to it. Barker stopped in front of a large notice board by the entrance, which was plastered with leaflets and handwritten notices, none of which I could read. I hazarded this must be the hub of the community.

"Speak any Italian, lad?"

"I know Latin, and my French isn't too bad. I suppose I could translate something if I had enough time. Do you speak it?"

The Guv gave a sigh. "Not a word, I'm afraid. You see the value of knowing languages in our line of work? Something on this board could be of great use to us and we wouldn't know it. If I were in charge of Scotland Yard—and there's about as much chance of that as my becoming the

Duke of Newington—I would make all my detectives study languages, and I don't mean Latin. Let's go inside."

"In the church, sir?"

Barker gave a thin smile. "I see Methodists are as wary of Catholics as Baptists. Yes, in the church. If anyone knows what's going on around here, it is a priest."

I will admit I stepped in with some degree of trepidation. Coming from a Low Church, Wesleyan upbringing, one can imagine the impressions I received during my childhood about those so-called idolatrous, land-stealing, Protestant-burning Catholics. As far as my minister and my mother were concerned, they still sold indulgences and put non-believers to the rack. The inside of the church, of course, was not much different from others I'd been in, though rather crowded with medieval-looking statuary. To tell the truth, I was a bit disappointed. Not a rack in sight. I'd missed the heyday of the Inquisition by a good few centuries.

We wandered into the sanctuary and watched people enter, pray, and leave, for there was no Mass going on. I recognized a group of booths to one side as being confessionals, and when a priest poked his head out like a mole from its burrow, Barker pounced and held him in conversation for a moment. The priest led us through a maze of hallways to a door and ushered us inside.

Behind the desk in the book-lined study sat a sturdy bulldog of a man of about fifty years in a cassock and skull-cap. He seemed a mild enough inquisitor, though he looked more like a businessman or bureaucrat than a cleric. The priest regarded us from under thick, tufted brows, and over Barker's business card.

"I am Father Amati. What can I do for you gentlemen?"

My employer sat down and over the next fifteen minutes told him everything that had occurred since we were called to the Wapping docks. I was surprised, for he held back only my training with Gallenga and recruiting Hooligan. Father Amati sat back in his worn leather armchair and listened intently without comment and with little movement. Finally, as the Guv finished, the cleric became animated again and nodded solemnly several times.

"What you have said, tragic though it is, I have been expecting for some time. I'll wager a quarter of our Italian citizens here are in the country illegally, although most are not criminals. Families come here to work hard and prosper, and to no longer have their lives threatened by criminals. In fact, I would say the immigration laws in this country exclude the best Italians and Sicilians, while the criminal element has no problem smuggling itself into England."

"I agree with you," Barker rumbled. "But that is a long-term problem and does not address the present one. How do we stop a war between the old established Camorrans and the upstart *mafiusi?*"

"We cannot," the priest said, raising a hand. "It is bound to happen. These criminals are not intelligent. They may be cunning, even brilliant in their planning, but they think on the most traditional level. All slights are to be avenged. All attacks demand retaliation. Every death requires a vendetta."

"You have prayed over this?"

"Until blood stood out on my forehead," Father Amati replied. I assumed he was speaking metaphorically. "I've lived with this situation all my life."

"Where are you from, sir? I hope you do not mind if I refrain from the use of titles."

"Not at all. I am Cumbrian."

"Ah," Barker said. "The 'ndrangheta."

"You know your secret societies, Mr. Barker. My mother wanted me to be a priest to save my life. I've lost two brothers to interfamily warfare and any number of uncles and cousins. When my father died and I was assigned here I brought my mother with me."

All of a sudden, his voice cracked and he put both hands upon the desk to steady himself, as if he were having a convulsion.

"You don't understand. You cannot understand. The members of my parish have all lost relations, been threatened, bullied, and beaten. They—we—thought we had escaped all that. It is England's character and sense of fair play that brought us here. We endure your cold, gloomy climate as the price we must pay for our freedom."

Father Amati stopped and blew his nose in a red silk handkerchief. The last thing I expected upon seeing this pugnacious-looking man was a display of emotion.

"You must forgive me, gentlemen," he said, sniffing once or twice. "This is a spiritual battle that I have fought my entire adult life."

"Not at all, sir," Barker replied. "It does you credit. Tell me, do you have many Sicilians who are members of your parish and come to Mass?"

"Yes, hundreds. We are too small a district to divide ourselves by point of origin."

"Could you speculate upon how they would feel if the Mafia were here?"

Amati gave a grim smile. "You needn't be so circumspect, Mr. Barker. The Mafia *is* here. I know it. I see the signs. We all do. As to your question, the old ones are fearful. They have seen too much. The young are impressionable and idle. They can't find enough work to keep them occupied. These are the same conditions under which the Mafia began. As for the rest, they don't want the Honored Society here, but they have been conditioned to fear and obey; and they, too, struggle to find work. I wish I had something better to tell you, but there you are. You are not Catholic?"

My employer and I glanced at each other.

"No, sir," he replied. "We are both nonconformists."

"But you are men of faith?"

"Aye," Barker replied. "I think we can agree on that term."

"Then I shall renew my prayers and add your names to them, if you don't mind."

"I thank you, but don't mention our names to anyone else. At this point, we don't know for certain whom to trust."

The remark made me think of the Barker clan motto, which was painted on a faded shield on the wall behind my employer's desk. Appropriately enough, it was in Latin. *Fide, sed qui, vide.* "Trust, but be careful in whom."

"That is a difficult thing to know, even in the best of times," the priest replied. "My office is at your disposal. If I can help you in any way, you have but to ask."

We stood and made our way out of the church and then walked several streets in silence. Barker was deep in thought, sometimes coming to a stop in the middle of the pavement. I let him alone, knowing he'd tell me when he was ready to speak.

"I keep thinking that a smarter man than I would find

a better way to flush out the Mafia than the way a beater does partridges. They do beat for partridges, don't they, Thomas?"

"I believe so," I hazarded.

"A smarter man would not use something as obvious as a fight at the docks. There must be a better solution. If only I could think!" The latter remarks were punctuated by my employer smiting his forehead with his fist.

"Perhaps there isn't a better solution," I told him. "If there had been, I'm sure you would have thought of it. They may be common uneducated criminals—"

I never finished my sentence. A cab pulled to the curb, scraping the wheel against it. We both reached into our pockets and grasped our revolver butts. The occupant leaned forward out of the gloom of the cab, and he was the last person I expected to see.

"Inspector Pettigrilli," Barker rumbled. "I thought you were in Liverpool."

"I was," the inspector replied, reaching into the confines of his coat. I had a premonition of what he would give us. "This was waiting for me at my hotel. How did they know? They are dogging my steps even now!"

His hand shaking, he gave Barker the note. From where I stood, I could see that it was marked with the accursed black handprint.

14

I KNEW IT WAS ONLY A MATTER OF TIME BEFORE Faldo found me," said Pettigrilli. It had obviously been penned by the same author as the previous notes. Pettigrilli translated for us: "Your days on this earth are numbered. I am the eraser that will wipe away the chalk marks of your days."

"Poetic," Barker commented, "if a trifle melodramatic. What is your plan?"

Pettigrilli folded it and put it back in his pocket, patting his breast. "I'm taking it to Scotland Yard," he said. "I know a serious threat when I see one."

"Why are you here in Clerkenwell?" I asked. "It is out of your way."

"I leased a flat here last week, but this has changed my mind. London is no safer than Palermo. I have collected my belongings and terminated the lease. I believe I shall return to Paris immediately. Ah! But, forgive my manners. This is Constable Newton, who, he assures me, is no relation to the great philosopher and astronomer. He met me at Euston Station and is to escort me as far as Whitehall."

The constable tugged on the brim of his helmet in greeting.

"Mr. Barker, I wonder if you and your assistant would accompany us back to A Division as well," the inspector went on. "It was a mistake to come back to Clerkenwell. I have noticed the stares from passersby. They know something is afoot."

"Certainly we shall see you back," the Guv said. "There is a cab coming down the street now. We'll follow you."

We snared the hansom and were soon following Pettigrilli and Constable Newton.

"There are certainly a lot of Black Hand notes fluttering about London lately," I commented. "Perhaps whoever is plotting this Sicilian onslaught has engaged the services of a professional scrivener."

"I'll wager that note was posted to Liverpool from here in Clerkenwell," Barker growled.

"If they were Irish instead of Italian, Scotland Yard would have this entire district locked up. Come to think of it, wasn't the very first Irish bombing here in Clerkenwell?"

"Very good, lad," Barker said. "That was in 'sixty-seven, long before my time. This was the Irish district then."

"And before that, it was the setting for *Oliver Twist*."

"Who?"

I keep forgetting Barker doesn't read popular literature. "Dickens, sir. It's another book by Charles Dickens."

"I suppose I shall have to read him, if merely to understand your references. Blast!"

This latter was due to a delivery van that had insinuated itself into the space between our two vehicles. Our cabman cursed loudly and pulled the reins hard, bringing us to a shuddering standstill. The van took its time crossing in front of us, while the deliverymen traded remarks with the cabman in two languages. One of them unlocked the gate to a small courtyard, while the other backed his pair of draft horses into it step by step. Farther down the street ahead of us, there was a loud report, followed a moment later by another.

"Pay him!" Barker cried, struggling through the doors of the cab. I reached into my pocket and tossed up a handful of coins through the trapdoor before jumping down to the pavement. I was under no illusion that the sounds were something innocent. I followed Barker as best I could, noting as I ran that there was no sign of Pettigrilli's cab anywhere ahead of us.

Barker stopped, and when I reached his side, I caught the acrid odor of gunpowder. My employer pointed down to fresh wheel tracks crossing the pavement in front of us leading to a pair of livery stable doors. We both reached into our coats for our pistols, making an elderly gentleman coming toward us turn and scuttle away. Cautiously, we pushed the doors open and stepped forward. The odor was stronger inside the stable.

My eyes took a moment to adjust to the change from sunlight to deep shadow. Motes hung heavily in the air. In the center of the stable was Pettigrilli's cab, its horse pushing and pulling in an effort to get out of the traces. There was no one on the driver's perch and the stable appeared empty. We moved forward cautiously. The windows on either side of the vehicle had been blown out, shattering glass and wood. A pair of limbs extended out under the bat wing doors, unmoving. Gingerly, I leaned in and then wished I hadn't. The cab was awash in gore. Constable Newton and the inspector lay slumped over each other, their heads almost blown apart. Each had received a blast through the windows beside them.

"Lad," Barker said, pointing with his gun. A second pair of doors on the other side of the stable had been left open, and there were wheel tracks in the straw.

"A second vehicle," I conjectured.

The Guv crossed to the second entranceway and stepped out. "They came in through Clerkenwell Road and exited into Clerkenwell Green," he said.

"Should we give chase?" I asked.

"No, they are gone. We must secure the area and alert Scotland Yard. They will not be happy to hear this news, one of their own dead and a guest in our country assassinated."

Barker handed me the police whistle he always kept on the end of his watch chain and nodded me out the front doors. I closed them to discourage onlookers, then stepped out into the street and blew for all I was worth. It instantly drew a crowd, but I refused to answer questions until I saw a constable coming toward me in that steady, reassuring trot they train the men to use in an emergency. I opened the doors with a brief explanation and waved him inside, pushing them shut behind him. The crowd assaulted me with questions, but the most I would say was "police business."

A moment later, Barker stuck his head out and requested that I whistle again. I daren't risk stepping away from the door, so I whistled in the crowd's faces. There are too many people in London these days, I've decided—four million of them in fact—and most of them noisy and inconsiderate. One of the onlookers, seeing how small I was, reasoned that there was little to stop him from satisfying his curiosity. He tried to pick me up and move me aside, and I was forced to use one of the Japanese wrestling tricks Barker had taught me. I stuck my thumbs into the corners of his mouth and tugged outward. He fell back, slurring a curse, and pushed his way out of the crowd, but a second fellow took up his cause, perhaps thinking I'd merely had a bit of luck. He seized my lapel, but a quick poke in his left eye soon disabused him of the notion. I was still blowing the whistle all the while, and was beginning to grow a trifle faint.

Finally, two more constables arrived. One of them stationed himself outside, while the other went in with me, or tried to. The stable door had been barred from within. A knock brought Barker to the door, and we were admitted.

Inside, after being apprised of the facts, the constable volunteered to go to Scotland Yard. Barker gave him Poole's name as the inspector already working on the case, and the P.C. ran out to find a cab. The second constable pulled me over to the other door, which I noted had also been barred, and questioned me thoroughly.

Barker looked about as I was being questioned, and I followed him with my eyes. He studied the damage to the cab and the bodies. The driver was missing, and he might have had something to do with the murders, but I could not recall his appearance. Barker began patting his pockets, and by the time the constable had finished questioning me, he had his pipe going, standing in a cloud of smoke in front of the carriage.

About twenty minutes later, the stable door squeaked open and Poole's thin form slipped through. He came over to us almost casually and stood beside Barker, looking at the corpses inside the vehicle.

"You and the boy are under arrest, Cyrus," he said conversationally.

"I know it," Barker said in his lowland Scots accent. It was more pronounced when he was angry. "'Tis why I've been smoking. It may be hours until I can again."

"How could you let this happen?" Poole asked, waving his hand at the cab. "He was a guest of the Yard, of this country. Commissioner Henderson's on his way. You cannot be here when he arrives. The two of you are going to A Division in bracelets."

"I've got a case," the Guv insisted.

"You had one. Now it's ours. We're going to open Clerkenwell like a tin of smoked kippers."

"It's about time you did."

"Constable!" Inspector Poole barked, as if the fellow and I had been playing marbles together in the corner. The P.C. stepped forward and tugged heavily on the peak of his helmet.

"Yes, sir!"

"Have you taken down both of these gentlemen's statements?"

"I have, sir."

"Then put the little one in darbies and escort him to Scotland Yard."

"Little one?" I sputtered. "You can go—"

"Lad!" Barker thundered.

"Blast it." I held out my wrists for the irons, cursing in my mind the constable; Poole; Henderson; Barker's standards of decorum if not the man himself; and even Mr.

Hiatt for his new, constantly improved, patented wrist restraints.

A half hour later I was cooling my heels in an eight by ten foot holding cell in Scotland Yard. It had taken me less than two years to find myself incarcerated again. Perhaps I was fated to spend my life behind bars. I felt like a football in a celestial game being punted from one angry deity to another.

Time palls in a cell, but eventually a sergeant came and took me to an examination room where Poole went over my testimony several times, as if I was trying to trick him. I'm afraid I snapped. Barker would not have been proud. As I recall, I told him he couldn't find the killer if the two of them had played blindman's bluff in the holding cell I'd just vacated.

"Shut it, Llewelyn!" he finally shouted at me. "I could have gone a great deal harder on you than I have."

"You didn't have to arrest us," I maintained.

"Oh? And how would you know?" he replied. "Are you an expert on criminal procedures? We've just had a guest of Her Majesty's government murdered by the very people he had come here to flee. A hundred inspectors out of a hundred would have arrested you. If I hadn't gotten the two of you out of there, Henderson would have fallen on you like a ton of bricks. If he had his way he'd have hoisted you up in that stable and beaten a confession out of you. He's hated Barker ever since the Limehouse case. I'll speak plainly so you can get it through your thick skull. The two of you have been involved in the deaths of three officers in one year."

"Technically, the constable's not an officer."

"Shut it, I said! You're getting my ulcer up. I'm beginning to think a man can be a friend of Cyrus Barker or a member of the Metropolitan Police, but it is impossible to be both."

"When are you releasing us?" I demanded.

"When I'm ready. And every time you make my ulcer flare, I'll add another half hour to it."

"Perhaps I could speak to Commissioner Henderson myself. He doesn't scare me."

"The commissioner doesn't have time to waste on minnows like you. I'm sending you back to your cell. You can rest at our expense until your employer's fancy solicitor comes to release you."

Back in my cell, I lay on the bed and leaned back on the bit of stained sacking that the Yard dares call a pillow, staring at the ceiling. Barker and I had just been neatly elbowed out of the way, and I for one was not sorry for it. There were too many death threats being handed about lately. As far as I was concerned, Marco Faldo could keep himself occupied sending notes to the various members of A Division. I might even help him write a few.

15

It IS MY HUMBLE OPINION THAT IF ONE HANDS OUT enough money to keep a solicitor on retainer that said solicitor should have the decency to be prompt and not leave a poor fellow wasting away in prison with nothing to do save watch his nails grow. After four hours, I'd managed to dredge up all my old feelings and insecurities about prison life. At least the solicitor Thad Cusp was able to get us off completely, which only went to prove the Yard had had no evidence to hold us in the first place.

"None the worse for wear?" Barker asked when I saw him again. I found him oversolicitous, but then, I was in a foul mood. Did he think I would climb the walls or try to swallow my pillow?

"No, sir," I replied. We were standing in the corridor of the Criminal Investigation Department. "Did you have an interview with Commissioner Henderson?"

"Aye. 'Twas like facing down a nor'easter. But it was all bluff and bounce, nothing he hasn't threatened me with in the past. It was Poole who tried to get under my fingernails.

He wanted me to tell him everything based upon our friendship."

"But you *have* told him everything."

"Precisely. It's all a matter of public record. I didn't give him my private conclusions, of course, which are my own and what I trade upon, but the facts are right there in plain sight."

"Perhaps he recalls the previous cases when you were not so forthcoming."

"I genuinely wish to be of service to Scotland Yard when I can, despite the fact that they shut down my antagonistics classes."

"Technically, sir, they didn't shut them down," I pointed out. "They were blown up. Scotland Yard merely took the opportunity to turn the new rooms into offices. According to *The Times,* they are full to the brim and considering moving somewhere else."

"I must apologize, lad," Barker responded. "Apparently you *have* been reading the newspapers."

"As for your antagonistics classes," I went on, "Inspector Poole is very anxious to have you start them up again."

"If he's trying to get on my good side, he's got an odd way of showing it. Four hours wasted. With four productive hours in Clerkenwell, I might have solved the murder of Inspector Pettigrilli. Let's stop in at our chambers before we go home for dinner."

"I think Mac's run through the larder, sir. We'll have to dine out."

"Damn and blast it, I forgot. I don't have time to waste worrying where my next meal is coming from. Mac will have to get the Elephant and Castle to cater until Etienne returns to work. I shall speak to him on the telephone set. People are being slaughtered left and right by Sicilian assassins and all must grind to a halt while I decide what I find toothsome for dinner."

He was silent and irritable during the short walk back to our offices.

"The last post is on your desk, sir," Jenkins said as we came through the door.

Still in his coat and hat, Barker selected one envelope from the stack, slit it with the Italian dagger he kept in his desk. Absently, he stroked his mustache as he read.

"What is it, sir?" I asked, as I sat down at my desk.

He offered the letter to me. From across the room I could see the large handprint inked in the center of it. Wordlessly, I took it and read.

Il Brutto, you see what has happened to another detective who stood in our way. Sometimes an example must be made. What we are doing here does not concern you. Should you continue, we assure you that you and yours will suffer a fate no less public. You are warned.

"You know what this means, lad. We shall have to leave town."

"Leave town?" I asked. "But why?"

"We must marshal our forces and come in from another angle they're not expecting. Besides, I have responsibilities I must see to. I am not alone in the world."

"Where will we go?"

"Ah, there's the question. It would be best not to take a direct route in case we're followed, though 'twill mean we'll be forced to go miles out of our way. Jenkins!"

Apparently I wasn't going to get an answer just yet, but that was nothing new. Jenkins came shambling around the corner and stopped at the desk.

"Yes, sir," he said.

"We have received a death threat."

"Ah," came the lackadaisical response. "Battle conditions, then. Prepare to repel all boarders."

"Llewelyn and I shall be going out of town for a day or two. Can you alter your routine?"

"It'll be a hardship down at the Sun, sir," he pointed out.

Our clerk reigned at a table at the Rising Sun each night, where I take it his personal conviviality had everything it lacked during the day. I'd never had an audience there, and would not try to do so. He liked to keep his professional and private lives separate.

"If it is not too much trouble," Barker continued, "I'd like to send Thomas along to see you settled."

"As you wish, sir," Jenkins replied a trifle neutrally. *Why send me along?* I wondered.

"Where will you be, sir?" I asked Barker directly.

"I'm going home. Mac must get everything packed and see to the security of the house."

"Will it be shut up?"

"No, it would only encourage the blighters to set it afire or some such nonsense. Mac knows how to take in the sails."

"What about Mr. L., sir? How will he get home?" Jenkins asked. Our routine was utterly changed if our clerk was questioning his master.

Barker looked at me appraisingly. "Mr. Gallenga has trained him," he said. "The lad'll have to make it back to Newington as best he can."

"Your vote of confidence quite chokes me up," I said, wiping an eye.

"Cheek," Barker responded, shaking his head.

At five thirty, Jenkins put a printed sign on the door that said the agency was temporarily closed and suggested another detective within our little court. I saw that all the shutters were securely fastened and the back door locked and barred. It isn't every establishment that requires a three-inch wooden beam to secure a door, I thought, or that has standard "battle conditions." We bade our adieus and left the Guv to lock the front door.

"Where to, Mr. Jenkins?" I asked.

"Right acrost the river, Mr. L., in Lambeth."

Newington is a respectable, if unfashionable, neighborhood across the river in Surrey, but Lambeth, just to its north, was not much different from the East End. In Shakespeare's time, this was where the theatres were located, outside the burgeoning city, as well as where the brothels and other unsavory establishments were allowed to be built. Our century had done its best to suppress such vice, but the district still had a reputation as a dangerous place at night when the shops are closed. As we walked over Westminster Bridge, I reasoned that it was a logical place for Jenkins to live on a clerk's salary, within staggering distance of Whitehall, but I was a little vexed with myself that I had never bothered to ask him where he lived. After all, I worked with the man from one day to the next. I should have tried to take an interest in his life. All I knew of him for certain was that he was a lazy rascal with a taste for cigarettes, a local public house, and the *Police Gazette.*

"Is it far?" I asked.

"Lord, no, sir," he said, stopping to light a cigarette with his back to the river. "It's just on the other side, hard against the embankment."

Jenkins is a long, loose-limbed fellow, whose hands seem to naturally fit into his pockets. He has a hawkish face with a widow's peak and thinning black hair cut straight across his shoulders. He'd once told me he objected to work, but that the world being the harsh place it is he had to suffer his lot like the rest of humanity.

Jenkins suddenly stopped in front of a fish shop that spilled the aroma of hot fish into the street and directed me inside.

"The old gentleman won't be expecting us," he told me. "Perhaps he'll think a bit of crisp fish a real treat."

I had heard that Jenkins lived with his father, but I couldn't quite recall from whom. I gathered the old man was infirm and that the clerk took care of him.

"Will you do the honor of dining with us, Mr. L.?" he asked. "The two of us don't get much company."

"Certainly, but allow me to pay, please."

"Then you wouldn't be a guest, now would you? I insist, though I'm sure it don't matter much. Mr. Barker 'pays for all,' as the old pub sign says."

Loaded with hot parcels of fried fish and chips wrapped in *The Times,* we stepped out into the street again.

"I hope this doesn't throw off your routine too greatly, Mr. Jenkins," I said.

"It's just plain Jeremy after hours, sir, and you'll be

Thomas, if it's not too much of a liberty. As for routine, it's good to be absent from the Sun now and again. It makes them more eager for my return. Here we are, sir. I told you 'twas just acrost the river."

We found ourselves in front of an old clapboard building thrust between two larger ones, like a book pushed casually between companion volumes. It was painted black and had no outward ornamentation, as if it were doing its best not to be noticed. Jenkins pulled a large brass key from his pocket, unlocked the door, and bowed, inviting me in.

"Father!" he cried over my shoulder, making me start. "I am home, and I've brought company!"

From the fireplace corner, a stooped figure looked up at us out of a pair of rheumy gray eyes. In fact, all of Jenkins's father seemed gray, from his hair to his stubbly whiskers to the color of his coat. Mr. Jenkins senior appeared incapable of speech, due to what I took to be apoplexy, which also severely hampered his movements.

"Father, this is Mr. Thomas Llewelyn, Mr. Barker's assistant, who I've told you about. Mr. L., this is my father, Jeremy Jenkins, Senior, the greatest engraver in London as ever was."

I bowed. "I'm very honored, sir."

The man nodded to me. After we'd set down our hot burdens, Jenkins closed the front door, which I saw contained no less than six locks on the inside, including a metal bolt that slid into the stone fireplace. The little house was a fortress.

"I don't know why Mr. Barker wanted me to see you home. It would take an army to break into this place," I said.

"Perhaps he wanted to give you an evening of domesticity before you start traveling about the country," our clerk offered.

"Have you any idea where we're going?"

"Not a clue, and with Mr. B., there's no telling. Is there, Father? No telling with Mr. B., eh?"

Jenkins had a disconcerting habit of trying to bring his silent parent into every conversation. There was no way to judge if the old man understood a word we were saying or if the infirmity had cost him his faculties. I did not envy our clerk the burden of looking after an ill parent; but he bore it lightly, so lightly, in fact, that I had never suspected the old man was in such a poor state.

Jenkins took down some stoneware plates and mugs, a jug of malt vinegar, and cutlery. Then he tied a serviette around his father's neck and began to feed him. It was a tedious and messy process and proved to me how highly he regarded his father. I busied myself with my own food and allowed the old gentleman what dignity he had left.

"Bless my soul!" Jenkins suddenly cried. "If I ain't forgotten the libation. Now don't you trouble yourself, Father, while I see to the drinks."

He rose and went to a corner where a small barrel with a spigot was resting and filled the three mugs full of cider. As I suspected, the drink had the kick of a Surrey mule.

"That's good cider," I said, once I'd gotten my breath back.

"Yes, Mr. Maccabee makes it for us."

"Mac?"

"Oh, yes, he knows his way 'round an apple, that one does."

I looked about the room. It was a cozy bachelor establishment, almost like a public house, very like the Rising Sun, in fact.

"You have a very nice snuggery here, Jeremy."

"Thank you, Thomas. Of course, most of the furnishings were first purchased by my father during the prime of his career, before the tragic affliction overtook him. He was a great man."

"And still is, I'm sure," I said.

"Bless you, sir. You are one of nature's gentlemen."

"So what sort of engraving did your father do?"

"All sorts, sir. In fact, I'm sure you have a few portraits my father did in your pocket right now."

"You mean bank notes?" I asked, astonished.

"I do. He worked with the Treasury for a while, then he worked against it."

"Against it? You don't mean counterfeiting, surely?"

"Oh, yes, there's always been a streak of larceny in the Jenkins blood. I'll show you Father's masterpiece, if the old gentleman will give his permission. What say you, Father? Shall we let Mr. L. in on our little secret?"

Jenkins's parent gave a small convulsion of emotion just then, which caused me to think him not mentally damaged at all, which, if anything, made matters worse for him.

"Very well, then. Mr. L.—er, Thomas. Come with me."

As I stood, I understood why there were so many locks on the front door. I was in a former counterfeiter's den.

Jenkins led me down a long hall to a stout-looking door reinforced with metal studs. He produced a key from his pocket and turned it in the keyhole with a harsh, grating sound. The door opened, and he ushered me into total, airless darkness. I heard the pop of a gas cock coming on as a match was struck, igniting two wall lamps. They framed a mounted object between them, an old and faded document that was the only ornament on the entire side of the room, the other taken up with worktables. I took in the document, stepped closer for a better look, read it to myself, and then stepped back again for another overall assessment.

"I say," I said to our clerk, "that isn't the *real* Magna Carta, is it?"

"You ain't the first to ask that," Jenkins said with a look of pride. "In fact, though Her Majesty's government is certain the real one is still hanging in the House of Lords, they are very interested in owning this one, just in case."

"Oh, no," I said, "I'm not going to let you be cryptic with me. I get enough of that from Barker. Tell me everything."

"Well, sir," he said, eager to impart the story, "the old gent was approached by a couple of former military officers that was trying to make a good retirement. Somehow they'd found a way to get into the House of Lords at night, despite all the precautions. They wanted an exact duplicate, which Father thought would be the ultimate challenge to his work. We visited the old rag a dozen times at least, and he worked well into the nights creating an exact copy. As it turned out, he worked too hard. It was the strain of creating his magnum opus that brought about his attack."

"My word," I said. "So what happened?"

"Well, sir, there was only one man in all England who was up to completing my father's task, and as luck would have it, he lived in the same house."

"I take it you mean yourself!"

"Well, modesty forbids, but I finished the assignment, and the robbery went off as planned, or almost did. You

see, one of the thieves got a bit greedy and just had to take
a walk about Westminster Palace. He tripped and sprained
an ankle in the dark, and that's when the guards caught him
with the framed document in his hands. The other chap escaped. So you tell me: if you were Parliament and you were
wondering if the Magna Carta in your possession was the actual Magna Carta, to who might you turn?"

"Cyrus Barker," I averred.

"Exactly, which was what they did. The Guv chipped
away at the thief for two days before he cracked and
peached on his mate. Mr. B. tracked the fellow to his lair
and recovered the other frame and followed the trail to
our door. You know it meant stir for me and the work-
house for the old gentleman. Well, I'm not afraid to admit
it. I begged him to let us go. Father was not the picture o'
health he is now and if I was in Pentonville or Wormwood
Scrubs, who would look after him proper? I begged Mr. B.
good and appealed to his heart, not knowing him yet, you
understand, not knowing in the least if he was a good man.
He said that to his way of seeing it, we had just one thing
to bargain with: only the old man knew which version was
the original."

"What about you?" I asked. "You finished it."

"Yes, I did, but to tell the truth, I'm not a patch on the
old gentleman. What he did was genius, so good even I
couldn't say for certain.

"Mr. B. went back to the Tower, explained the entire
situation, and then representatives of Her Majesty's government marched over here with both documents, all of them
waiting to find out, and the old man able to communicate
only through me. He let me know which, and I told them

true, after which they gave us both a stern warning about counterfeiting but left us free men. The next day Mr. B. arrives and offers me a position as a clerk, saying he needed a fellow with my skills to make papers and such from time to time in and around my other duties."

"So, the papers he had in the Irish bombing case last year," I began, "the ones that claimed we were a German bomber and his assistant—"

"Oh, those were easy. It's good to keep my hand in now and then."

"Barker seems to have a propensity for hiring felons," I noted.

Jenkins wagged a finger at me. "Now, now," he said. "I wasn't actually arrested, and as for Mr. Maccabee, he was held on suspicion. The only felon in the bunch is you."

I chuckled. I had to admit he had me there. "Knowing the government, I'm surprised they didn't take both."

"Oh, I let them know I'd kick up a fuss. It is my father's property, after all. The last thing they wanted was for it to be made public. This was the price of my silence."

"So you're certain this is the copy you made."

"I certified it in writing. This was the one Father pointed out. However, I must admit he has always had a sardonic sense of humor. Some days, I wonder myself."

Jenkins led me out again and locked the door behind us.

"I was planning to read Mr. Trollope to the old gentleman this evening," he said as we returned to the dining room. "There never was a man as enjoyed Mr. Trollope so much as he. You are welcome to stay if you wish."

"I'd like to, but I should be getting back," I pointed out.

"I'm sure the Guv's got a thousand things for me to do before tomorrow and there is still the journey back. Thank you for your hospitality and a very interesting tale, I must say. Are you certain you will be safe?"

"We've taken on worse than these Sicilian blokes," Jenkins said. "We'll be safe enough. Mind you come out of this in one piece yourself."

"If I don't, it won't be for lack of trying. Thank you, Jeremy." We shook hands. It occurred to me it was the first time we had ever done so.

"See you back in Craig's Court, sir, on more professional terms."

"I will, but I should like to come again some time and buy you both a meal to repay this one. Good evening, Mr. Jenkins. It was an honor meeting you. Thank you for having me in your home."

When I stepped outside, I heard the locks turning on the other side of the door. I had thought our clerk little more than an inebriate, and here he was with a corking story in his life. I sighed and began the long walk to Newington.

Violence is a part of my occupation, whether I like it or not, but for every altercation there is another that fails to materialize. I have no complaint with that, you understand. I chose to walk because in a cab I wouldn't know whether I was leading the Mafia to Barker's door, so I went on foot, using all the skills Gallenga had taught me. I scrutinized every face, window, and vehicle around me. I backtracked and circled and looked behind me in shop windows. No Italian assassins fired upon me with their shotguns, no cloak-and-dagger men stabbed at me with their knives, and no *mafiusu* tried to kidnap me for ransom. As I reached the back gate of our house in the Elephant and Castle district, I reflected that all my efforts to avoid being attacked had been merely practice.

When I stepped into the back passage there was already an assortment of suitcases by the front door.

"Has the Guv said how long we will be out of town?" I asked Mac, who came down the stairs looking harried. For Mac, that meant one of his curls had fallen out from behind one ear; otherwise, he was immaculate and ready at any moment to pose for a statute of Apollo at the Royal Academy of Arts, provided he could be persuaded to remove his yarmulke.

"He has not specified, but I believe it shall be less than a week."

"You've packed for a month. Do you know where we're going?"

"The Guv says south. You're leaving first thing in the morning. That's all you need to know."

I looked up the stairs, where I could hear Barker moving about.

"So, what sort of mood is he in?"

"He's a bit grim tonight. It's like he's playing a game of chess, only with your lives."

I shrugged. "That's nothing new. I find it hard to believe we're actually abandoning London. I suppose I have time at least for a soak."

"Mr. Barker told me not to heat the water. He says it is too dangerous to go out in the garden at night."

Shakespeare says discretion is the better part of valor.

Smart fellow, the noble bard. Rather than beard the lion in his den when he was in a mood, I went upstairs, and seeing that my few possessions had been packed, I decided to read for an hour or two before going to bed. At the same time, however, I made certain there was a loaded pistol on the bedside table within easy reach.

16

THE NEXT MORNING WE BOARDED A TRAIN FOR who knows where. Barker knew, of course, but I might as soon expect a yeoman at the Tower of London to hand me the Crown Jewels in a bag as for the Guv to reveal his personal plans to me. I reasoned that since we were at Victoria Station, we would be heading southeast along the Chatham Railway, but how far? The line ended at Dover, but there was a ferry there for Calais. Did he intend for us to leave the country?

To complicate matters, we were bringing Harm with us, Barker's prized Pekingese dog. The little brute had been placed in a wicker contraption, the better to carry him about, which he considered an affront to his dignity. He stared at us miserably through the small window in the front of the basket; but for once, he did not howl, as he is often given to do.

It was a beautiful morning to escape London, even if one was not being threatened by Sicilian murderers. I glimpsed a fox trotting alongside the railway lines, though we were not yet out of the city. Outside, the air was fresh and invigorating, but that did me little good since, as usual, I was closeted in the smoking compartment with my employer. I always end up near the windows, which I throw open wide, but this only means that Barker's tobacco smoke must eddy around my head before making its way out the window.

My employer had purchased a stack of newspapers at a station stall, and was working his way through them as we passed into the Kentish countryside. The railways really need to do something about the trees that grow along the tracks. They spoil a fine view of the little towns and villages along the way. I supposed the seeds were somehow collected and spread along the line by the moving trains and it is a testament to England's verdant soil that so many trees spring up, but I'd rather have my oil painting views of the small towns and hamlets of rural Kent. Before I knew it we slid into Tunbridge Wells and out again. Barker switched newspapers. I don't believe scenery interests him unless a murder has just been committed in it.

We rolled past tall rows of hops, like overgrown vineyards, being harvested by men with long poles. I understood that many hop pickers were from the East End, and the harvest provides a chance for the workers to get out of the city, as well as the opportunity to lay by some money for the winter. Their lives are hard, but then they haven't been chased out of town with Black Hand notes threatening their lives.

Eventually, my companion's pipe went out and I could smell sea air. The pigeons that had flapped by our train earlier had been replaced by raucous fulmars and gulls, and I knew Dover was not far off. We eased into the station like clockwork, and then immediately, chaos ensued. Two hundred people seemed bent upon catching the next ferry to France. As it turned out, however, we were not among them. Barker merely purchased two fares to Hastings and we boarded another train. Fortunately, it didn't have a smoking compartment this time, and being one of those composite carriages that only has first and third, we found ourselves in a first class carriage. The seats were plush and there were small framed pictures of the countryside behind our heads. The brass overhead racks in which we put our bags shone from much polish.

I would have enjoyed myself fully if it weren't for Antonio Gallenga. Drat the fellow, I couldn't get the "eye" out of my head now. As we waited for the train to leave, I watched the passengers. Were we being followed? Did anyone on the platform look Italian? I studied the faces and postures of the men waiting and developed a list of five possible suspects. I grew concerned because we were in a corridor carriage, where a fellow could walk by our compartment at any time, and I wished we were on the Brighton line with no corridors, all privacy and safety. A fellow could open the door, shoot us both dead, and hop off the train before the next station; and we had not even an exterior door in our compartment by which to escape. Didn't the designers of railway carriages realize how dangerous they could be?

Rolling along the famous cliffs, I could see a thin blue strip across the Channel that was France. It was a cloudless day with crystalline clarity and the horizon seemed but an arm's length away, rather than the twenty miles or so to Calais. Though I jumped every time a guard or passenger passed our compartment, I admitted it was better to be here than scurrying about London watching the victims pile up.

We passed through Rye and Romney Marsh and eventually arrived in Hastings, a collection of houses and buildings, all topped with red roofs, and a haven, I understand, for artists and poets. I didn't see any as we disembarked and changed trains yet again, but neither did I see any of the five men I'd scrutinized in Dover. Perhaps it had all been my imagination. Even better, we changed to the Brighton line, which meant we could travel in a carriage with no corridors.

We passed the old ruins of Pevensey Castle and skirted Eastbourne before crossing the Cuckmere River and coming to a halt in the small coastal village of Seaford where Juno had been sent earlier. As we disembarked, we faced a small esplanade and a shingle beach with the white chalk cliffs known as the Seven Sisters to our left. There were small boats pulled onto the shore, a few scattered net houses, and a stone redoubt built years before to keep Napoleon from landing on our flanks. I doubted there was a cheerier spot in all England that morning, and not a Sicilian in sight.

A dogcart was waiting for us at the station, with a driver that appeared to be acquainted with my employer. We climbed in, with Harm between us, facing backward as the dogcart allowed, and were soon rolling through the quaint streets of the seaside village. Seaford sits at the delta where the Cuckmere pours into the Channel. From there, the land rises north continually, though the bay pulling our vehicle seemed accustomed to the effort. In ten minutes we were in open countryside, with the chalk cliffs to our right and the channel breeze forcing us to clap our hats to our heads.

We finally came up to a gate flanked by a pair of young men resting their arms upon an old stout-timbered fence, reeds sticking out from between their teeth, looking content enough to stand there all day long. I couldn't tell if they were guards or gardeners taking a break from their labors. They plucked at their caps as we passed through, then went back to ruminating on the rise of the South Downs and the chewing of their cuds. Meanwhile, we rolled along a meandering path before finally reaching the house.

It was obvious that part of the building was very old and that it was once a farmhouse. A building of equal size and age stood beside it, and must have been a barn at one time, but further enlargements and extensions had connected the two, and a new barn with stables and other outbuildings had been added over the centuries. It was a wide manor now, of two stories, with plaster sandwiched between old vertical beams and a many-angled roof bristling with chimneys. It was quaint and comfortable, and well tended, with gardens and a pebbled drive. *Lucky is the man,* I thought to myself, *who owns such a comfortable home,* wondering who he might be.

"Here we are," Barker said, hopping down. That was it—no explanation, no hint of why we were there. After releasing Harm from his basket prison, Barker walked to the front door, seized the brass knocker, and gave it two good taps, which I could hear echo inside. Soon a solemn-looking butler opened the door, his countenance brightening when he saw the Guv's weathered features.

"Welcome, sir. It's a pleasure to see you again. Madame is in the conservatory, awaiting your arrival."

My employer stepped past him and led me into the hall, which I thought a very telling action. The butler did not announce us but instead stepped outside to see that our luggage was unloaded. Light finally dawned in the old Llewelyn cranium. This was *her* home, the Widow's home, Barker's mystery woman, whom he disappeared off to see on odd evenings and Sundays when he wasn't involved with a case. I had wondered about her often, questioned the Guv as obliquely as possible, and queried anyone who knew him well, and yet had always found a brick wall before me. Now I found myself about to be ushered into her presence, without a chance to see whether my hair and tie were straight and how much road chalk had managed to end up on my suit.

With Harm at his heels, Barker led me from one chamber to the next, each filled with ornate furniture or paintings the size of a wall in my room in Newington. This was not a farm but an estate, and the Widow must be quite wealthy to own such a large holding. Was it my imagination, or did my employer saunter from chamber to chamber as if the whole pile was his and he lord of the manor?

We finally passed through a pair of glass doors into a conservatory. I had barely enough time to take in the plethora of foliage on all sides, from small pots to grown trees hanging with pineapples, when the owner of all these wonders abruptly rose from a wicker basket chair and came toward us. This was she, the Widow!

"Cyrus, you're late," she scolded, and stepping up, planted a kiss on my employer's cheek. Yes, on Cyrus Barker's cheek. It was astounding. I wanted to pinch myself to be certain I wasn't asleep in my room at home.

"Couldn't be helped, my dear," Barker rumbled. No, no, he didn't rumble. He purred, I'd swear he did. One could hear the affection in it. It took all my training not to stand there dumbfounded, with my jaw hanging open.

Barker cleared his throat. "Philippa, allow me to present my assistant, Thomas Llewelyn. Thomas, this is our hostess for the next day or two, Mrs. Philippa Ashleigh."

Before concentrating on our hostess, I spared a final glance at my employer. While appearing casual, every line of his body was warning me to be on my best behavior. I noted he hadn't explained his relationship with her in any way. Were they friends or, dare I say it, courting? I realized I would have to deduce it for myself. The Guv wasn't going to tell me. If they were in fact involved in a courtship, I would have to add it to the long mental list of contradictions which made up Cyrus Barker. I could no more imagine him as someone's swain than as a grammar school teacher.

"Cyrus has told me so much about you," Mrs. Ashleigh said. She smiled, but her eyes were appraising me from head to toe like a fortune-teller at a fair. If I was hoping for a kiss myself, I'd have been disappointed. I received a cool hand instead.

Three responses entered my head at once and muddled it. The first was, "He's told me absolutely nothing about you," the second, "Where did the two of you meet?" and the third was, "You have the most beautiful blue-green eyes I have ever seen." What came out instead, after my brain ceased to function, was a sort of strangled, "Ahh!"

She was a woman in her late thirties, quite handsome if not in fact beautiful. She certainly seemed beautiful when her face was animated by those luminous eyes. Her hair was a pale red, almost blond where the sun struck it, and was pulled back and pinned in an artfully casual manner. She wore a white day dress with a high collar. She was tall, taller than I, but not nearly as tall as Barker, who was at least six feet. She appeared to have no trouble ordering him about.

"Sit there, Cyrus; and Thomas, you sit over here on my left. How do you take your tea?"

"With a little sugar, please."

She handed each of us a cup, and then a small tray of Barker's favorite shortbread, before pouring a cup for herself. She leaned over gracefully and scratched Harm between the ears. Our lives had become quite civilized all of a sudden, considering we were being hounded by assassins. I munched my biscuit, sipped the steaming tea, and listened to the novel experience of my employer holding converse with his lady.

"Is Peter keeping you safe, my dear?"

"Safe as houses, Cyrus. He moved into the gatehouse with all his crew two days ago. How long shall you have them stay?"

"No more than a week, I'd say. The danger should be contained by then."

"Yes, one way or another," Mrs. Ashleigh said archly. "Have there been any *attempts*?"

"We didn't give them a chance."

"They must be seething, whoever they are."

"Let them seethe. I'm not going to sit by and let them operate in London."

"But, darling, you don't own London; and, last I heard, it hasn't asked for your help."

I wanted to agree but thought it best to remain hidden behind my cup.

"I own property in London—more than one, in fact— and I don't want to see any criminal organization moving in with impunity. You know I wouldn't endanger any of us, unless I believed it was important."

Philippa Ashleigh gave a gentle sigh. "The gardeners have been struggling for most of the week with an old oak stump on the south edge of the estate, but it is not half as stubborn as you."

Barker gave a smile under his bushy mustache. "I am right glad to hear it, ma'am. There are few enough of us old stumps left."

"You know best, Cyrus," she responded sweetly, sipping her tea. It was like watching a match of lawn tennis. Now Barker turned my way and I realized he was looking at me. I knew what he was thinking: never trust a woman when she agrees with you. I quickly took another biscuit and tried to appear occupied with studying the foliage about me, though Barker will tell you I don't know an orchid from a bluebell.

"Cyrus, have you got anything to do?"

"I beg your pardon?"

"To do. Does Mr. Beauchamp require your consultation or advice?"

"I had intended to see him, yes."

"There's no reason why you can't do it now, is there?"

"Well, I suppose not."

"Then run along and leave Mr. Llewelyn to have tea with me."

Barker cleared his throat. "Philippa, I had intended to take the lad with me."

"Oh, bosh," she replied. "You don't need him there. You just like ordering him about. Go see your friend."

Barker cleared his throat a second time. The first had

been to tell Madame that he was in charge. The second was to reassure me of the same. I didn't believe either. "Lad, I'll be back in an hour or so."

"Yes, sir."

"Take your time, Cyrus."

"Aye, ma'am."

Barker picked up his stick, gave her a stern look, and backed out of the room. I didn't think there was anybody on earth who had such control over Cyrus Barker.

17

So," PHILIPPA ASHLEIGH SAID, POURING MORE TEA into a Wedgwood cup, "you are just as I imagined you."

"I am?"

"I don't know if you realize how unusual your presence here really is. He's never brought anyone down before, not even your predecessor, Mr. Quong. I didn't expect to meet you for another year or two at the least, if ever. He's protective of me. I would almost say overprotective."

I was twenty-two, adult enough to realize that everyone has the need for closeness and companionship yet young enough to shake my head in wonder at the thought of the Guv actually courting someone. I had difficulty picturing him playing the swain, with a box of chocolates, a book of poetry, and a bouquet under his arm. It was easier to picture him an ascetic monk, studying his texts at night and bringing his own body into submission with exercise. And yet, the love of his life was sitting here in front of me, pouring more tea into my cup.

"Oh, dear," she said, arresting her hand. "Cyrus told me

you prefer coffee. I've had some brought in specially. Shall I have Genevieve make it for you?"

"Oh, no, ma'am, the tea is perfect. I like Earl Grey. It's so much better than green tea. One sugar please," I said. "You know, he's said almost nothing about you."

"Of course," she said, putting in two. "That's his way, you see. He's rather stern with his assistants. Come to think of it, he's rather stern with everyone. It is part of his character. Even I don't know everything about him. You know the path he built in his garden?"

"The meandering path? Yes."

"I asked him when he was building it if that was his definition of a straight line. He replied that it was as straight as one can come to expect in life."

"It's a metaphor," I said in wonder.

"Yes. Isn't it delicious? I've liked that path ever since. To me it represents Cyrus's life."

"Or all our lives," I pointed out. "One can attempt to make a straight path in life, but it only brings stronger forces to bear."

"He said you were a poet. I suppose it is the Welsh in you. Anyway, I told him it was an inconvenient way to get from the back door to the gate. Do you know what he said?"

"I imagine it was something like 'Only God can make one's path straight.'"

She smiled again. "You know him better than you think. How did you come to be hired? I'd like to hear your version."

I gave her an abbreviated account of my first meeting with Barker, making certain I mentioned that he called me "a black little fellow" to test my patience, which still rankled a bit. Perhaps she would call him to task for it, I thought.

"It's a noble profession you're in," she remarked.

"Is it?" I asked. "The Guv—I mean, Mr. Barker—says we are part of the underworld."

"Do you not provide a necessary service? When people enter your offices, they are often at their wits' ends. Scotland Yard has turned them down and you are their final hope. Frequently, you endanger your lives to help them. I call that noble."

"Well, yes, I suppose we do," I admitted.

"Isn't that better than sitting in some dusty hall of academe, trying to prove a pet theory about Dante or Chaucer?"

"I'm sure it is, but I've often wondered why Barker chose me in the first place."

"Do not sell yourself short, Thomas. Cyrus has his faults, but he has always been an excellent judge of character. He needs to be, for his life often depends upon others. I'm sure this new business might have him a little rattled. It does me, I must admit. When he first told me the two of you were taking on this case, I told him he was mad, though he's heard me say it enough to pay scant attention to it."

"Did he tell you what happened in London, ma'am?" I asked.

"Oh, yes. He tells me everything, though it took me ages to train him to do so. You know how close-mouthed he is."

"But he talks about me."

"Of course he does. You work with him, live with him. He keeps no secrets from me."

I stirred my tea. It didn't need stirring, but I was getting up the courage to ask my next question.

"So, what is his opinion of me, do you think?"

"You're here, are you not? That implies a certain amount of trust. He says you tend to be flippant and a trifle lazy, but then, you must realize you are being compared with an ideal that doesn't actually exist. He commends your intelligence and classical knowledge, and says that sometimes you bring a facet of a case to his attention that he hadn't considered. That's rather high praise, coming from him."

She was revealing my employer's innermost thoughts without so much as a by-your-leave, and I was in danger of having my jaw open again. Didn't she worry she'd reveal too much and thereby anger the Guv? No, I rather thought she didn't. She regarded me with those cool aquamarine eyes of hers, as if nothing on this earth frightened her, least of all Mr. Cyrus Barker. I should have realized it would take more than an ordinary woman to interest him.

"Yes, I suppose it is."

"He told me the first time he saw you, you were leaning against a wall at the end of a long line of applicants, with your collar up, looking dark and moody. He said he knew right then and there he'd hire you. He gets keen moments of insight sometimes. He had intended to hire someone larger than you, but when he saw you he suddenly pictured you questioning a witness or following a suspect."

"Really?" I asked.

"Of course. He says you're coming along, which is the most one can hope for, coming from Cyrus. He's not the most effusive of men, as I'm sure you've come to realize."

"Monosyllabic is the word I'd have used."

"Oh, stop!" she said with a short laugh. "He says you have a devilish tongue and could use an hour a day reading

Spurgeon to improve your character, but then that has nothing to do with your employment."

"It sounds as if he's told you everything about me."

"He has," she admitted. "He's even mentioned your weakness. One bat from a girl's eyelashes and you turn to melted butter."

"That's not fair!" I cried. "He never tells me anything."

"Ah, but you've only known him for a year and a half, while I've known him for far longer. Since China."

"How did you first meet him?"

"My husband brought him home. James was an engineer on Shameen Island in Canton and needed someone to bring in supplies. There was Cyrus in a mandarin tunic with belled sleeves, talking to James in a Scottish brogue."

"Frankly, I have trouble picturing that," I admitted.

"Ah, but you see, he was the son of a missionary. All the missionaries and their families dressed in the Chinese manner. After his parents died when he was eleven, blending in with the Chinese was a matter of survival."

"How long were you in Canton?"

"For several years. My late husband was full of great plans for China's future, but he died and left me with business interests to run. One of them was a small shipping company on the Pearl River. Your employer freighted cargo for us sometimes aboard the *Osprey*."

"Well, he was a ship's captain," I replied.

She'd poured me another cup and was stirring her own. "Is that what he called himself? A ship's captain?"

I nearly choked on my tea. "What do you mean—that he wasn't?"

"Oh, no, he was a ship's captain, I suppose, of sorts."

Here she shrugged and took a dainty sip of tea. "I mean, Blackbeard was a ship's captain, was he not? Drake and Raleigh were ship's captains." She raised an expressive eyebrow, and I wondered if she was toying with me.

"Are you implying that Mr. Barker was a pirate?"

"Oh, the South China Seas can be distinctly unsavory at times. Cyrus and his crew worked in an area bordered roughly by Shanghai, Yokohama, and Sumatra, but his base was Bias Bay, near Canton."

"And exactly what did he do there?"

"Whatever it took to survive, I suppose. He had mouths to feed and repairs to make on the *Osprey*. He must have been a good captain for so many of his crew to follow him back from the East."

"And why did he come to London?" I asked.

"Because I wanted to return home after James was gone. Cyrus made himself invaluable."

I sat quietly with my cup of tea, trying to take it all in.

"What are you thinking, Thomas?" she asked suddenly.

"I beg your pardon. I was just wondering how the congregation at the Baptist Tabernacle would react if they knew there was a former pirate in their midst."

"There's that flippant side Cyrus warned me of," she said archly. "He wasn't a pirate, exactly, more of an adventurer. Anyway, the Reverend Spurgeon already knows. I told him myself."

"Did you really?"

"Yes, I've always been an admirer of his published sermons. I was the one who first took Cyrus there and helped him choose the house in Newington."

Harm came charging into the conservatory in some distress. He leapt into my lap, nearly knocking me out of the basket chair I sat in. A moment later, a tiny white ball of fur appeared at my ankles, hopping up and down. Harm barked at the little creature frantically.

"Is that another Pekingese?" I asked.

"Yes, she's from the litter Harm sired. Fu Ying gave her to me. Her name is Butterfly." She scooped up the little dog and kissed her on the top of the head.

That was one more fact than my overtaxed brain could take in. The woman enjoyed shocking me. Barker, a pirate and adventurer. Barker, introduced to Spurgeon by Mrs. Ashleigh. Mrs. Ashleigh, friendly with Bok Fu Ying, my employer's ward. It was as if I'd fallen down Lewis Carroll's rabbit hole. Curiouser and curiouser. And it wasn't over yet.

"I have something important to ask you," she said, looking at me levelly. "I want you to look after Cyrus for me."

"Me, look after Mr. Barker? Are you serious?"

"Very serious. Cyrus puts honor above everything, even his own safety. I would say *especially* his own safety. I want him to live a good long life. Someday . . . Well, that's enough about that. Just look after him."

"I'll do my best, ma'am."

"Good. Any more questions?"

"Just one. What's behind those dark lenses the Guv wears?"

"That's silly," she said, nuzzling the dog. "Eyes, of course."

18

CYRUS BARKER HAD RETURNED FROM HIS MEETING and was waiting in the hall, a trifle impatiently.

"How was your tea?" he asked.

I searched for an appropriate adjective. "Informative."

The Guv gave me an appraising look, then led me out the door with a wave of his cane. Outside, a man was waiting for us. He had an air of authority about him, in an easygoing, bluff sort of way. He was about forty, tall and thin but muscular, with hair blown by the wind and bleached by the sun. His skin was deeply tanned like leather, and he was without a jacket in the heat, making me itch to remove my own. He wore braces over a white shirt with no collar, and a handkerchief was tied loosely about his neck. By now, I knew the sort of fellow Cyrus Barker would trust and favor, and this was one of them.

"Lad, this is Peter Beauchamp, a former shipmate of mine. Peter, Thomas Llewelyn, my assistant." The man didn't speak, but nodded and turned, heading off toward the Channel. We followed him. Every bird in Sussex was in full throat, and rabbits nibbled on the beds of thyme. The sky overhead was nearly cloudless and so deeply blue that a painting of it might have looked unnatural. The only way I'd find out where we were going, I reasoned, was to get there.

The three of us walked into the town of Seaford and through it. Beauchamp was greeted by some of the villagers and murmured a response. When we reached the water's edge we had a perfect view of the Seven Sisters rising from the town clear up to Beachy Head, the highest point along the entire south coast. The white cliffs were so dazzling they hurt the eyes.

Beauchamp led us to a multicolored group of small dwellings by the Channel's edge. They were coast guard cottages, or at least they once were. Someone must have purchased them all and knocked out walls higgledy-piggledy, turning the entire place into a single dwelling. I almost wanted to call it a warren, for the yard and beach were full of children running and playing and none of them looked over five years of age.

We were met at the door by a cheery, sturdy girl with loose brown hair and a face full of freckles. This, it turned out, was Mrs. Beauchamp, and the brood disporting on the pebble beach was theirs, all seven of them.

"Brought company," Beauchamp said offhandedly. His wife, far from seeming offended, welcomed us warmly.

"Are you gents hungry? I could do a good fry up in a few minutes."

"Thank you, ma'am," Barker said, removing his hat. "We've eaten."

"Ah, yes," came the reply. "Up at the big house. Quite a to-do up there, Peter tells me."

"I'm checking on the fleet," Beauchamp murmured and passed out the back door. He was a man of few words, most of them cryptic. Of what fleet was he speaking, precisely?

The answer was out on the shore. Twenty boats with numbers painted on their sides were drawn up on the shingle with the children running about them. They were sturdy fishing vessels. A larger boat lay out in the water, moored at the end of a long dock. Her deck was of stained teak with whitewashed quarters, and she had both masts and a smokestack. She must have been over a hundred feet in length and all the brass fittings gleamed in the sunshine, but what I noticed first and foremost was the name across the stern.

"The *Osprey*," I murmured with a thrill.

I won't say Cyrus Barker ran—he's not really the running sort—but he easily outstripped me across the beach and dock and was soon climbing the ladder on the side and going aboard. Beauchamp went second; and when I was halfway up the ladder, he laid a hand on me and deposited me on the deck. While my employer plunged below, I looked about the vessel.

Properly, I learned later, it was a lorcha, a Manila-built ship constructed from European plans. It was designed to run with Chinese junk sails as well as European ones, and, of course, had been altered to run on steam as well. No amount of white paint and brass could disguise its piratical appearance, caused by the way the front and back ends were so much higher than the center. I'm no mariner, but it was an odd craft, principally due to a large winch at the stern that must have been used for hauling in nets. It seemed to have gone through so many permutations it could have been turned into anything at a moment's notice.

The captain came on deck. Barker had discarded his jacket and stood in his waistcoat and shirt, the sleeves of which he was already rolling up. In place of his customary bowler he now wore a black cloth cap, already streaked with brine.

"Get up steam. Let's take her out."

"Aye, Cap'n," Beauchamp said, dashing below.

"What should I do, sir?" I asked.

"Sit there and try to stay out of trouble," he said, pointing to the deck.

"Aye, aye, Cap'n," I said, and he frowned.

"Don't worry," he growled. "You'll have plenty to do soon enough."

Getting up steam is a long process. It was nearly an hour before the *Osprey* got under way. During that time, for the most part, we baked in the sun. The Guv tested every knot, caressed every surface, fussed over the mildest rust or warping, and stalked the decks like the captain he was.

"Mr. Llewelyn," Barker called from the helm, once we'd gotten under way. "Go belowdecks and relieve Mr. Beauchamp. Tell him I need him."

"Yes, sir," I told him. I'd worked out by then that Barker couldn't run the entire ship by himself and that his sole crewman could not keep the fire stoked and do his other duties. Boilers run on coal; Welshmen pull coal from the earth; and who better to stoke a fire, any fire, than a Welshman? I was wearing a good suit, but at least I'd decided against my white flannels that day. I'd have been a sight after an hour in the engine room.

"Captain's sent me down to relieve you," I told Beauchamp, who had stripped to boots, trousers, and the kerchief knotted about his neck. His chest was slick with sweat and black with soot. In the red light of the firebox he looked hellish enough.

"Very well," he cried over the roar as he opened the hot doors of the boiler. "Keep the firebox full and the coals evenly distributed. Don't let the fire go out, or you'll regret it."

He went above while I took off my shirt, seized the shovel, and thrust it into the bunker of coal. "Come to sunny Seaford," I growled aloud as I shoveled. "Try the bracing life of a stoker."

While Barker and his old shipmate played pirates above and steamed along on my sweat, I filled that insatiable maw with shovelfuls of coal. No doubt the Guv was congratulating himself on building my character. Now that I knew the *Osprey* had been docked here all along, I was surprised the Guv hadn't brought me down here earlier for a thorough cramming course in nautical training, including deck swabbing, barnacle scraping, and hatch battening, whatever that was.

Doing mindless labor always makes me think, and this was mindless enough. Why had Barker, a man of so many secrets, really brought me down here? Was it to meet Mrs. Ashleigh, the keeper of so many of them? Or should I accept that he was here to protect his interests? Each question was accompanied by a shovelful into the firebox of the steam engine.

"You can stop!" a voice called in my ear.

"What?"

"I said," Peter Beauchamp repeated, "you can stop. No sense killin' yourself down here. You've been at it for half an hour. Go topside and leave this to me."

"Thanks."

"Reckon the *Osprey* has a new stoker."

I had no response to that. I seized my clothes and staggered up the steps to the deck. There was a marvelous breeze coming over it just then, and I stood with a shirt in one hand and a jacket in the other flapping in the breeze like flags as the wind caressed my chest with its wonderful cool fingers. I closed my eyes and threw back my head.

"Are you going to stand there all day, Mr. Llewelyn?" my employer asked. "There's work to be done."

"Yes, sir," I said, struggling into my shirt, which is not easy to do in a stiff breeze.

"Stow your gear below," he ordered. "You'll not be needing it here."

Cyrus Barker now stood with his feet planted widely on the poop deck, the wheel in his hand, steering. His manner had changed subtly since I'd come aboard. There was no more "lad" or "Thomas," but the more formal "Mr. Llewelyn," as if there were a hundred of us at his command instead of two, and he would not play favorites. There was a look of contentment on his face. God was in his heaven; all was right with the world.

"So, where are we?" I asked, after having struggled into my shirt and stowed my gear. One side of the ship faced land a half mile off, but I could not see a coastline on the other.

"Near Newhaven. We took her out as far as Hove and are returning. How's your stomach? Are you seasick?"

"I didn't have time to be, I guess."

"Would you like a treat?" Barker asked.

I hesitated. The Guv's idea of a treat would always differ from mine; perhaps a tot of rum or grog. One could never tell with him, but it would be churlish to refuse.

"Certainly," I said, trying to keep the quaver out of my voice.

"Climb the mainmast there. It's an experience you'll never forget."

It will be, I told myself, *if I happen to fall to the deck from that far up.* The belief that I had any choice in the matter was an illusion, of course. I walked to the mast, seized the first rung, and began to climb. There was no crow's nest at the top of the mast, but presumably, one could stand on the top spar and hold the mast for dear life. I didn't dare look down until I had struggled to the very top.

I could picture it all in my mind—the sudden slip caused by inattention or a bit of grease on the spar; the sudden futile scramble for a finger's purchase on anything; the sudden plunge, knowing that I would probably not survive; and the final, shattering crash upon the hard wood of the deck below.

It was quiet up here, once I'd reached the top spar; I didn't hear the constant complaint of wood creaking against wood. The wind whistled slightly as it broke over the outstretched spars. It was an alien world so far up. I could see the broken line of chalk cliffs and the toylike lighthouse of Belle Tout. On the other side, France had come into view.

Barker changed course; and the mast I stood on dipped from the perpendicular, leaving me scrambling to hold on. I had no wish to be tossed into the sea. When we were upright again, I made my descent to the deck in a sedate manner far better than the way I'd first imagined. The Guv had been right. I would never forget my first time atop a mast.

"That's fantastic," I told him, as soon as my feet landed

on the firm deck. "You can see all the way to France up there."

"I hope you are sufficiently cooled off from your exertions. Now go down and tell Mr. Beauchamp to stop engines. No, wait! I'll tell him. You take the wheel."

"Me, sir?"

"Aye. Try not to crash on any rocks. Captain Beauchamp would not like his ship reduced to kindling."

"I thought it was your ship, sir," I said, tentatively taking the wheel.

"I'm still owner, and may do as I like when I'm here, but he's captain the rest of the time. He runs the fishing fleet here, you see. I can't allow the *Osprey* to lie idle. It has to be worked."

"So he's the fellow you send checks to every month."

"Aye. There's a lot of upkeep on a ship like this. It has to be laid up for the winter, and have the barnacles scraped off the hull. It has to be repainted and polished. Oh, there's a thousand things done to keep a ship afloat year after year."

"It must have taken you years of hard work to buy such a unique vessel, sir."

"Oh, no, lad," he said. "Won her in a game of chance in Manila one evening. Fan-tan, I believe it was. Extraordinary bit of luck."

"I thought you hated gambling and all games of chance."

"Oh, I do. Some people will bet on anything and ruin their families over it. But you know, I haven't always felt that way. Look, there's Seaford ahead. Steady as she goes. I'd better go warn Beauchamp."

Barker called out to Beauchamp, and the ship slowly

came to a standstill, rocking as the waves rolled under it. The Guv moved to the bow and released the anchor with a splash, while Beauchamp came up the stairs again and leaned against a railing, whittling a piece of wood with his jackknife. Barker put his foot up the starboard side of the boat and looked out across the water of the Channel.

"Storm's coming in," he remarked. "The sky was red this morning before we left London."

Beauchamp nodded. I could picture the four of them—Barker, Ho, Dummolard, and Beauchamp—in this boat, not saying much for hours at a time, answering any question put to them with grunts. As much as I was enjoying the trip, if they expected me to endure such conditions for long, they would require a press-gang.

A heavy metal object was suddenly dropped into my lap. It was shaped like a truncheon.

"That, Mr. Llewelyn, is a belaying pin. They go in the holes along the side here, and the lines are tied to them."

"This could cave in a fellow's skull," I noted, hefting it.

"Not a sailor's. They are notoriously thick skulled."

Behind me, I heard Beauchamp chuckle.

"I shall have to practice, then," I said. "Thanks for bringing me along. I know I'm just a landsman."

"Shovels well enough," Peter Beauchamp remarked. He didn't look up, concentrating on his carving, which looked like it would eventually become a toy boat. I thought of his brood of children.

"Thanks," I said.

"Don't let it go to your head."

★ ★ ★

Dinner that evening at Mrs. Ashleigh's estate was almost as fine as one of Etienne's meals, but I was paying more attention to the window behind me. Barker's prediction of a storm was on the mark. In fact, it became a full gale, the kind that buffets the south coast once or twice a year, although it took hours to develop. Soon the rain began, and was quickly followed by thunder.

The wind blew leaves and branches and lashed rain up along the broad South Downs, after gaining force over the tossing waves of the Channel. Inside the old house, most of the shutters had been fastened closed, but the panes shook. Though it was approaching midnight none of us were asleep amid the racket. A steady tattoo of raindrops beat on the glass, and the old structure groaned against the heavy wind. Sometimes, during a lull between the howling wind gusts we heard the plaintive bleat of a sheep or the neighing of a horse in a stable near the house.

Cyrus Barker was restless, which is never a good sign. We were both by an unshuttered window when we saw Beauchamp with a shotgun broken over his arm. He signaled to us, pointing two fingers at his eyes, and away toward the front of the estate. Then he trotted off.

"They're coming," Barker growled.

"How did they find us?" I protested. "Surely they didn't follow us here."

"They found us all the same. Get your pistol. We must prepare to repel all boarders."

Suddenly, there was an exchange of gunfire by the gate. Almost simultaneously, we heard the sound of glass shattering in the conservatory, followed soon by a second crash. Someone had breached the house's defenses.

Barker and I ran to Mrs. Ashleigh's room and flung open the door. Inside, I saw her turn quickly. There was a case on her bed, and she held an old-fashioned ball and powder dueling pistol in each hand.

"They have come," Barker said. "Bolt the door."

The Guv ran down the stairs to the ground floor, and when he arrived pulled a handful of the sharpened coins he always keeps in his pockets. He threw them down the hallway as men stepped out into it from the other side. There were cries of pain and cursing, but when Barker fired his pistol at them, they scattered. I'd counted at least three.

My employer and I moved down the hall shoulder to shoulder, and when we reached the end, stood back to back. The intruders had vanished.

"You take the left, lad, and I'll go right," the Guv said. Before I could suggest that it would be wiser if we stayed together, he was gone. I went into the dining room, where earlier that day I'd been cosseted and cross-examined by the lady of the house. I thought the room was now empty, but as I stepped across to the parlor, I realized it wasn't. There were too many good places to hide. When I reached the rug, I dropped onto it, looking about as the lightning illuminated the room. I could see something between the legs of the couch, and I fired at it. There was a yelp; and as fast as I could, I pulled myself to my feet, sailed over the couch back, and landed on top of him. We were a tangle of arms and legs, and then I hit him with the butt of my Webley.

My assailant looked more like a farm lad than an Italian assassin. He was stocky and unshaven and couldn't have been more than my age. Knowing I'd probably get in trouble for it with Mrs. Ashleigh in the morning, I cut the cording of the curtain behind me with my dagger and tied him up good and tight. Then I proceeded cautiously into the conservatory.

19

THAT WAS HOW I MANAGED TO FIND MYSELF
stepping over the shattered glass door into a darkened conservatory in the teeth of a Sussex gale. Even now it seems a
bucolic place to be set upon by Sicilian assassins, but it was
our presence that had brought them there. Like Barker himself, the Sicilians lived by an inviolable code. Having sent
him the Black Hand note, and found it ignored, they felt
duty bound to go through with the threat.

Less than ten minutes later, I stood in the shattered
greenhouse drenched with rain and bleeding freely from the
face. At my feet lay the Sicilian intruder I had encountered
there, pierced through the heart with a dagger. My dagger.
He had sliced open my cheek but, in doing so, had left himself exposed and I had struck as Gallenga had trained me to
do. When the opening appeared, I'd thrust a knife into his
vitals without thinking and without hesitation. I stood over
him, my heart pounding wildly.

"Thomas!" Barker's rough voice bellowed over the
crashing of the storm.

"Here, sir!" I called.

"Are you all right?"

"I think I've killed one of them."

"Stay there," he called. "I'll come to you."

About a minute later, there was a yellow glow that eventually resolved itself into an oil lantern Barker was holding aloft. My employer bent and rolled the slack body onto its back. The assailant was a thin, hawk-faced fellow with thick stubble. This was no farm boy here. I recognized a true Sicilian by now.

"One blow to the heart dead-on. He's one of the Sicilian dockworkers, by his clothes. Mr. Gallenga would approve, though the fellow seems to have opened your cheek."

"I've got another man tied up behind the sofa, sir," I said.

"Have you, then?" he asked in wonder. "Good work, lad. You've outdone yourself tonight. I've got two of my own. Mrs. Ashleigh will be pleased, though not, I suppose, by the sight of her conservatory glass."

"Not my doing, sir," I said. "It was the Sicilian."

"A good thing, too, for both our sakes."

Barker helped me back into the relative safety of the house. I was shivering and the front of my shirt was covered in blood. Mrs. Ashleigh came down the grand staircase sans pistols, and hurried over to me, touching my shoulder.

"Oh, Thomas," she said gravely.

"Philippa, do you think you can sew his cheek?" the Guv asked. "I doubt we can get a physician in here before the morning. In fact, I prefer not to send a man out for one, conditions being what they are."

"Of course," she said, hurrying back up the staircase, while Barker sat me down in a chair.

"I'm all right," I answered. "A sight better than the blighter in there."

"I did not expect them to actually follow us here," Barker said. "I misjudged them, something I will not do again."

"Perhaps they didn't follow us. Perhaps they followed Juno."

"Take my handkerchief," he said. "Yours is sodden."

Beauchamp came in just then, as soaked as I, though he wore a sailor's cap and pea jacket. He took one look at my cheek and gave a short whistle.

"They broke in, then," he stated.

"Yes, but we're alive," the Guv said. "We've got three men tied up and one dead. How are your men?"

"A few injuries. The gang that tried to break in was the Garrison boys, a family of local ne'er-do-wells that hire themselves out for crimes like this. We're guarding six more."

"I imagine they were the diversion. The one Llewelyn killed in the conservatory is a Sicilian by the look of him. He's got nothing in his pockets."

Beauchamp raised an eyebrow in my direction, and I tried to look as if I dispatched assassins every day. Mrs. Ashleigh returned with a bottle of alcohol, needles, and thread while the Guv poured a tumbler full of whiskey and put it in front of me. I almost preferred the needle to the whiskey.

"Are you sure we shouldn't wait until morning, when Doctor Bales can come?" Mrs. Ashleigh asked.

"Best to get it over with," Barker replied. "Drink up, lad. We haven't got all night."

I tossed the burning liquid down my throat, and then my employer had the nerve to fill the glass again. I hate whiskey and vowed as I downed the second glass that I would never drink the horrid stuff again. Meanwhile, Mrs. Ashleigh was threading the needle. I gritted my teeth as it pricked the skin.

The local inspector, or to be more precise, the inspector for the part of East Sussex from Lewes to the Channel, was named Marsden, a man approaching or retreating from sixty, who looked like a prosperous farmer or a country squire. A square of sheepskin was pinned to his tweed jacket with hooks and fishing flies nestled in it. I expected him to clash with Barker, as nearly every inspector I'd ever met before had done, but he seemed to take Barker in stride. A patient inspector, I thought. The country needed more of them.

"I'll take charge of the Garrison boys, if you don't mind, Mr. Barker," he said. "This is new ground for them. Normally, they deal in nothing more felonious than poaching and smuggling. I suppose they were hired for the work by the dead fellow there. They'd never be brash enough to enter an estate this large on their own. Did you know this person, Mr. Barker?"

"No, sir, but we have recently been threatened by Sicilian criminals. I assume he was sent by them to oversee the operation."

"Did you kill him?" he asked, looking down at the body.

"I killed him," I spoke up. I knew Barker would try to take the blame for it. "He attacked me in the conservatory during the height of the gale. He did this to me."

Marsden nodded. He pushed around the shards of bloody glass until he uncovered the second blade, the first being still in the young man's chest. "Do you always carry a dagger, Mr. . . . . ?"

"Llewelyn. Only since this case began."

"Blood being on both knives, and him being here to break into the house, I'm prepared to consider this self-defense and not arrest you. I'll take the boys with me and question them thoroughly. Would you be good enough to call at the constabulary later, sir?"

"I'll be there," Barker stated.

"Then I'll not detain you further. Do you think Mrs. Ashleigh will mind if we borrow a trap? It's a bit of a walk back to Lewes."

The vehicle was soon fitted out and Marsden left in his own gig while the constables and prisoners filled the other to overflowing.

"I'd have taken the blame, lad," the Guv murmured.

"I am responsible for my own actions, thank you, sir," I said.

Breakfast was a makeshift affair in the kitchen. A large farm table was laden with scones, crumpets, rolls, ham slices, eggs, kippers, tea, and coffee. There was no want of good food down here. Beauchamp's men entered in shifts, jesting with one another while filling gilded plates worth a week's salary. The storm and the danger had passed.

Beauchamp entered last and looked about. He passed the Guv and said a word or two in his ear. Both nodded and went their way. My cheek felt stiff and sore. I contented myself with eggs and coffee, carrying the plate into the dining room, where Mrs. Ashleigh was seated.

"Finally, a bit of excitement last night," she said, putting a brave face on it. "Things are generally deadly dull around here."

"I regret your broken panes, Philippa," Barker said, sitting down beside her.

"I've sent for a glazier. The problem is easily remedied, though if such nightly diversions become a habit, I should consider some reinforced ironwork. I suppose it is rather silly to have only two glass doors between the outside world and all my favorite things."

Around noon, we rode into Lewes on Juno and a chestnut Thoroughbred gelding. Barker did not look as comfortable on horseback as he did at the helm of the *Osprey,* but he did not complain. He looked relieved, however, when we alighted in front of the constabulary.

Inside, Barker shook Marsden's hand and soon each of us was seated in a swaybacked chair with a cup of tea the size of a soup bowl.

"The lads confessed right off," Marsden said. "The Sicilian's name was Venucchi, and he told them he was working for a man in London. The plan was to create a diversion while Venucchi broke in. They received fifty pounds for the work."

"Did he say what would become of us?" my employer asked.

"Venucchi told them he had his instructions, but he didn't say what they were."

"Did you ask them when he arrived?"

"Oh, we talked about a lot of things. The Sicilian arrived three days ago."

The Guv turned his head my way, looking at me. Venucchi had arrived before we had. He could have attacked while we were still in London. It also meant the Sicilians already suspected that Barker wouldn't back down when given the note. In the silence, there was a crackling sound. It was Barker's hand squeezing the armrest of his chair.

"Are we free to return to London, Inspector?" my employer asked.

"I have no objections," Marsden said. "It's been a rare treat for something to happen down here, but t'will be nice to go back to judging marrows at the county fair and tracking down stolen public house signs. Mr. Barker, I know I cannot tell you not to come back. Mrs. Ashleigh is an important part of our community and you've been coming to see her for many years. I ask only, as a favor to me, that you do not bring your work with you. And don't bring this mad killer along with you next time, or I'll arrest him for sure."

It took me a moment to realize he was referring to me. A mad killer? Me? I didn't know whether to be insulted or flattered.

I'm not sure how long Barker had originally intended us to stay, but obviously he had decided to return to London. I overheard our hostess trying to convince the Guv to linger another day or two, but he insisted we get back. The fact that Venucchi had been here before us was more than he could stand. I could tell it by the set of his square jaw.

At Seaford I carried Harm's wicker carrier onto the train and left Barker and Mrs. Ashleigh to say their private good-byes. When he entered the carriage the Guv tried to act nonchalant, as if he was above sentimentalities. I rather envied his having someone, but at the same time I saw all too clearly how much danger his work brought into the lives of those around him.

★   ★   ★

As soon as we arrived in Victoria Station, Barker freed Harm, the empty cage being sent along with our luggage later. We took a hansom to Newington, the dog perched with his little back paws on his owner's knees and the front ones hooked over the doors of the cab, barking at anything he felt required it. The little creature always took great joy in cab rides.

Not being satisfied with only one view, Harm moved to my side; and before I knew it I was in full custody of him. The Guv opened his newspaper like a foldable screen, successfully dividing the cab. The dog and I have a strange relationship: he considers me a servant too addlepated to intuit what he wants, while I consider him to be a burden, though one I've grown accustomed to. I let him share my bed and he lets me share his garden.

London looked the same. Apparently the Mafia had not taken over in our brief absence. We had no sooner begun our journey than it began to drizzle. Harm got down from his perch immediately and attempted to burrow behind my elbow. If there is anything he detests, it is getting wet. Having buried himself in a safe place roughly behind my right kidney he sat comfortably and let me receive the occasional lashing of rain in the face.

Finally we reached the house. I left Barker to deal with his dog, passed the fare through the trap, receiving another face full of rain for my efforts, and then we all hurried down the steps and across the pavement through the familiar front door. Home at last, I thought, and not a moment too soon, as the sky ripped open with a peal of thunder that should have been reserved for Judgment Day, and the rain set to in earnest.

"Welcome home, gentlemen," Mac said, handing each of us a towel. God bless the fellow—he's a competent butler. He even draped one over the dog and rubbed his long fur. He raised an eyebrow at the sight of my cheek but did not ask me about it.

"Thank you, Mac. How has everything been here?" Barker asked. I wondered if he was glad to be back in his bachelor's establishment, which gave him so much more control over everything.

Barker continued questioning Mac about the house and whether anything untoward had occurred. Meanwhile, Harm sniffed the front hallway and made his way to the back door, where his tail went down and he looked my way. I followed him down the hall and opened the door. Harm looked out into the yard and back at me. Apparently, this was one of those times when his servant wouldn't obey. He wanted me to stop the rain.

"Sorry, old fellow," I told him. "You're on your own."

Reluctantly, the dog stepped out into the downpour. I had assumed he would merely accomplish his task and scurry in quickly, but Harm had been away from his domain for a few days, and rain or no rain, was going to inspect it.

"Harm!" I complained, as he waddled over the bridge. I had no wish to get soaked again merely to retrieve a wayward dog. We had played this game too many times before. I crossed over to the hallway stand while Barker and Mac chuntered on about the condition of the garden and what post had arrived, and retrieved an umbrella. This is where human intelligence won out over brute instinct. Gingerly I stepped out into the garden.

Just then something streaked out from behind the potting shed toward Harm. I thought at first it was an animal, but as it scooped up the little creature, it rose up into the form of a man, wearing a black suit with his collar pulled up and a cap. He headed toward the gate, the poor dog's tail hanging limp under his arm. Barker's prized Pekingese was in the arms of a stranger.

I am cursed with a vivid imagination, and here is what I saw in those brief seconds as the man reached the gate. I pictured Harm's pelt, the dried skin of this rare and beloved creature, tossed carelessly over the wall for my employer's edification, to prove to him that he was not invulnerable, that in fact, when it came to the Sicilian brotherhood, no one was.

I yelled something; dropped my umbrella; and then ran as fast as I could, ignoring the crooked path and vaulting the narrow stream that bisected the garden. From the other side of the wall I heard Harm's danger cry, something in between a bark and a howl. For a small dog, he has great volume. *Good boy,* I thought, *tell Uncle Thomas which way he's taking you.*

Reaching the back gate, I squeezed through, then looked both ways. I'd be no good to Barker's dog if I walked into an ambush. There was no one there, but a hundred feet away, the dog thief was having a spot of trouble of his own. Harm had decided he'd had enough of such attacks upon his dignity and had sunk his teeth into his assailant's hand. Now Chinese palace dogs don't visibly have much in the jaw department, but I knew from experience that when he latched onto one, he could hang there until sunset. The man was actually holding the dog out by the hindquarters, trying to break its hold on his wrist.

"Hey!" I cried, being the former classics scholar at Magdalen College that I am. If I'd been given sufficient time I'd have come up with a better remark, something like "I say! Put down that dog!" I'm not always good at coming up with *le mot juste* at *le temps juste*. It was successful, at least. The thief dropped the dog—or possibly the dog dropped the thief—and they parted company to their mutual satisfaction.

Harm ran back down the lane and through the round gate to the safety of his domain, while I pulled the dagger from my sleeve, ready to do battle again. For once, I was spared. The young man took one look at the knife in my hand and the ugly, fresh scar on my cheek and ran in the other direction. I was not inclined to give chase.

I pushed open the gate, then locked it firmly. On the little stone bridge, Cyrus Barker stood in his black macintosh and hat, holding his sturdy umbrella over the shivering dog under his arm. I trotted forward through sheets of water and followed my employer into the house.

It had been a disorganized ruse, a feint, a light dessert to the previous night's meal. There wasn't even a need to speak of it when it was over. Barker and I went our separate ways, and I am happy to report I spent a rather dull evening reading Thomas Hardy. There's a lot to be said for good, calm, dull evenings.

20

HOW SHALL WE START OUR DAY?" I ASKED MY employer the following morning in our offices.

Barker drummed his fingers on the desk. "I want a meeting of the leaders on our side: Gigliotti, Hooligan, Robert Dummolard, and Ben Tillett. There may possibly be others."

"Mr. K'ing?"

"I'd prefer to keep the Chinese out of this, because of Hooligan, unless I have no alternative."

"Where should we meet? Here?"

"No." Barker rose and opened his smoking cabinet. He withdrew a meerschaum and began stuffing it. "It would draw unwanted attention to us, and I doubt any of them wish to be seen so close to Scotland Yard."

"Where then?" I pursued.

"Somewhere private. In fact, the most secure spot in all London. Come."

We took a cab into the City and then crossed over into Houndsditch, where the walled city of London once used to dispose of its dead canines. It was an ugly little place, cheek by jowl with Whitechapel. In fact, the two were like trees that had grown together so it was impossible to tell where one ended and the other began. All the brick here was black. I hazarded they were in fact red underneath, but there were layers of soot and grime shellacked to them. Even the children playing in the street sported a layer.

"You sure you know what you're about, Push?" the cabman asked balefully. Our advent had attracted the attention of the local poor, who stared at us with bold, ravenous eyes, and even came to the curb to watch us pass. Cabs did not come this way often.

"Drop us at the next corner," Barker told him. "We'll make it worth your effort."

We walked down Wentworth Street, past a row of shops to let and abandoned gin palaces where flies batted about the windows. Barker came to a door that was little more than a chink between shop fronts, the narrowest door I'd seen in London, and rapped upon it with his stick so stoutly the faded blue paint fell off in flakes.

Nothing happened for a moment, and Barker turned and surveyed the area with some interest, as if he might consider buying property there. The locals had followed us, hoping for a handout, but no sooner had he knocked upon the door than they scurried away. The door was opened by a bellicose-looking fellow in trousers and braces over a singlet, a bowler atop his head.

"What in hell do you want?" he bellowed. "Take yourself off now, or I'll set my dogs on you!"

"I would speak with Mr. Soft," Barker said calmly.

"Never heard of him. Off with you now. I mean it." He slammed the door in our faces.

The Guv was not daunted in the least. He rapped on the door again with his stick, waiting until it opened a small crack.

"I would speak," Barker demanded, "with Mr. Soft."

"Didn't you hear me the first time? I said there ain't no Mr. Soft here, you ninny. Never was, never will be. Run along afore I wallop you proper." He slammed the door.

Immediately, Barker knocked on the door a third time. The man, now red faced, opened it again.

"I would speak with Mr. Soft."

The man changed in an instant. It was like the Arabian Nights when Ali Baba said *Open sesame.*

"Right this way, sirs. Do follow me. Watch your step."

With his encouragement, Barker and I squeezed through the narrow door and followed him down a corridor. The fellow led us to a door and even knocked on it for us.

"Mr. Soft, you have a couple of visitors."

"Thank you, Cinders," a voice said, and the door opened slowly as the guard departed. A small, mouselike man stood there, blinking at us with nervous, oversized eyes. He had a swath of curling, near colorless hair and a small mustache after the manner of Swinburne, and I noticed one of his arms was withered, the hand folded in his pocket.

"Mr. . . . ah, Mr. Barker, isn't it?" the man said in a high, reedy voice.

"You have a good memory, sir."

"You are difficult to forget, sir. You have need of my property?"

"I do, indeed."

"When will you require it?"

"Tomorrow evening, if it is free. I apologize for the short notice."

Mr. Soft walked over to a writing desk and pulled out a memoranda book. He flipped pages for a moment and then spoke again.

"You are in luck, Mr. Barker. It is free. What are your requirements?"

"I should like to have a table and chairs to seat six or so with lamps enough to see."

"To see or to read?"

"Merely to see, I think. Some food would be in order, as well."

The man was writing down the information in the book with his good hand. "Very good, very good. Is that all?"

"That and complete deniability, of course."

"Of course."

"What is your rate these days?"

"With everything, I'd say twenty pounds would do."

"Then we have an understanding. Half up front, as always?"

"You remembered," the little man said. He was little, even to me, barely reaching five feet tall.

"Pay the man half, lad."

Reluctantly, I pulled out Barker's wallet and handed over ten pounds. As his assistant, I wanted to know exactly what sort of room he was paying for but was too polite to ask.

"Your young gentleman seems fair burning with curiosity," he noted.

"I must admit," Barker said, "that I'd like to see the property again myself."

Mr. Soft pocketed the currency and opened his door. "I say, Cinders! Could you come in here for a moment? Gentlemen, this is Cinders Hardy."

The slovenly guard returned. Soft and Hardy, I thought. They had to be joking.

"These gentlemen wish to see the property."

"Right," Mr. Hardy said blandly. Whatever it was he did, he must do it every day, for his work had obviously lost its mystery. "Come this way."

Mr. Hardy led us down the narrow corridor and into another room. It was a dining room, with a table and four chairs around it, all rather the worse for wear. Surely this was not the most secure spot in London. Tatty perhaps, but not secure.

"If you gentlemen would be so good," Mr. Soft said. With Hardy's aid, we moved the table and chairs off the carpet, which, with practiced ease, the guard proceeded to roll up. There was a large trapdoor, large enough to accommodate the entire table. As I watched, Hardy seized the inset ring and lifted the trap. Below, all I could see was inky darkness and a ladder going down.

As I watched, the guard pulled a farthing from his pocket and flipped it into the hole. Eventually, I heard it strike stone. We were over some sort of chasm.

"What in the—?" I asked.

Mr. Hardy held a fat and none too clean finger to his lips, as if we were about to enter a holy place, then picked up a lantern, lit it, and gripped the handle with his teeth before beginning to descend.

"Your turn," Mr. Soft urged me. "I don't go down, I'm afraid. My affliction."

Reluctantly I stepped onto the ladder. It seemed sturdy enough. In fact, it was bolted to the side. Slowly, I descended, with Hardy below me and the Guv above. There was a feeling of immense space and a damp, musty smell in the air. The rungs seemed to go on forever and my calves began to cramp before I finally put a foot on ground again. The ladder was bolted to the floor as well. Looking up, the opening was a mere square of light, remote in the heavens.

A table much like the one above was here, along with several chairs. Hardy lit two lamps on the table, which provided pools of illumination in the overall gloom.

"What is this place?" I asked, and heard my voice echo in the expanse.

"An abandoned railway tunnel," Barker explained, stepping down onto terra firma. "It's been cut off on both sides. Didn't I say this is the most private place in London?"

"Why was it abandoned?" I asked.

"One railway company buys up another," Mr. Hardy explained, "and makes new plans. The present one felt a line going into the East End was unprofitable and so here we are."

"You own it?"

"Not really. Technically, it is in receivership. However, it was Mr. Soft who thought to burrow down to it and make use of the property and me what done the burrowing."

"It was quite a feat," Barker said. "Mr. Hardy is being modest. Each section of ladder had to be carried down and bolted to the one above it, while hanging upside down."

Hardy attempted to conceal his pride. "The important thing is it got done."

"And what sort of meetings do you have here?" I asked. Both men gave me a condescending look. I shouldn't have asked. "Sorry."

"Will this be suitable for your needs, sir?"

"Admirably, Mr. Hardy. It's always an impressive sight.

I think we'll have privacy here. But what about you, above-ground?"

"I've got three stout bars to put behind the outer door. Her Majesty's Horse Guards couldn't bust their way in. There's a private egress if you require one. You have any persons causing you annoyance, Mr. Barker?"

"Aye. Sicilians."

"They won't get in here, that's a promise."

"I'll take your word for it," Barker said, and began climbing again.

I followed him up the ladder. It was better perhaps that I was surrounded by near perfect darkness. If I'd seen how high I was from the floor I might have frozen to the ladder in fear.

Finally, I reached the top rungs and Barker helped me out. I tried to act nonchalant, but my heart was hammering in my chest.

"What did you think of our little den?" Mr. Soft asked me.

It took a few seconds to realize he was serious. He was very proud of his "property," and I'm sure he and Mr. Hardy lived rather well on the proceeds of their little enterprise. There must be various members of the underworld who required such a secret and impregnable room. I didn't think Mr. Soft and Mr. Hardy were very particular about to whom they rented or for what purpose, as long as the money was paid, half up front, half afterward.

I've been down many a mine shaft in my time, though not as often as my brothers, who became miners, but I was not prepared for the cold, clammy feeling that came over me a minute or two after I'd resurfaced. Perhaps it was the exertion, or the change from open chamber to close, stuffy room, but I broke out in a sweat all over, and couldn't help but jump when it rolled down my spine.

"It always does that the first time," Mr. Soft reassured me.

"Tomorrow, then," Barker said, bowing to the little man.

"We shall have everything at your disposal," he said. "Mr. Hardy, do show these gentlemen to the door."

A minute later we were in the dirty lane again, though this time I was aware we were standing over an immense chasm. Were we to experience a cataclysm such as the one that had occurred in mythological Atlantis, or more recently in Krakatoa, we would be dashed to our deaths a hundred feet below. One shiver of the earth's crust and it would all be over for this little street in the East End, not that it would be much of a loss.

"Do you think the members of our little group shall be impressed?" Barker asked me.

"I don't know about impressed," I replied, "but I doubt they shall forget it."

21

<hr>

"So, EXACTLY HOW MANY *MAFIUSI* ARE IN LONDON, and where are they hiding?"

I can generally be relied upon to ask the most rudimentary question. After I asked it, I pushed a piece of bread around a plate of herbed olive oil and ate it. We were in the Neapolitan again, and Victor Gigliotti felt it was impossible to think on an empty stomach—or do anything else, for that matter. On the table in front of us was the inevitable tray of antipasti. Though it was not yet noon, a flask of Gallo Nero stood at my elbow. I avoided it, for one glass and I'd be no good for the rest of the day.

"At the very minimum, two," Barker said, rolling slices of cheese and ham together and taking a large bite. "It's possible that the two assassins came here together and have planned these assaults themselves, but more likely someone else is telling them what to do and staying in hiding, for whatever purpose. I presume it is Marco Faldo, which makes three. If Faldo is wise—and I believe he must be in order to have come this far—he has either brought along or recruited a handful of underlings, men such as Venucchi who are not as experienced or proficient as his two assassins, to act as bodyguards and lackeys. I don't believe a self-respecting criminal mastermind would allow himself to deliver threatening notes under doors or to attempt to steal small dogs."

"Are you telling me," Gigliotti asked, "that I, with a thousand men at my beck and call, am being harassed by one fellow and a handful of underlings?" He slammed his little coffee cup so hard into its saucer that the handle broke off. "Luigi!" he bawled over his shoulder. "Another cup!"

"I believe he has formed a new organization from among the Sicilian dockworkers."

"Then we know where to look," I put in. "Down by the docks. That must be where they are."

Gigliotti grinned, showing his vulpine teeth. "They would not settle near the docks," he corrected. "Italians always settle near a church, and there is but one Italian church in London, Saint Peter's."

"You yourself live in Clerkenwell, is that not correct?" Barker continued.

"It is."

"Have you moved your family?"

"Yes," he replied. "I have emptied my household, save for guards and servants. You will forgive me if I do not say where they have gone."

"Of course. That is wise. Have you doubled the guard around your ice warehouse?"

"There seemed no need if I have my own guards nearby. It is me they want, me they threaten." He stood and went to the money box by the front door and drew out a shotgun from under the counter. "Forgive me, my friend, but you have been in England too long. You wait upon events. You think too much when you must act. They stabbed your cook, cut your assistant, even tried to steal your dog, yet you wait for all the members of your little coalition to agree when to meet. Let us take this war to them. Hunt them down in Clerkenwell today, I say. I will help you. I'll even call in all my employees to turn over the entire district. You'll have your own private—"

"Down!" I cried.

I'd been facing the front of the restaurant with its elaborate frosted windows and lace curtains threaded on thin rods, not looking at anything in particular, just listening to what the restaurant owner was saying, when I noticed a sudden flutter at either side of the glass, shadows appearing against the panes. Suddenly, that sense that Gallenga had trained in me began jangling.

I kicked over my chair as the glass shattered and buckshot scattered across the room, encountering wood, plaster, cutlery, and human flesh.

Gigliotti turned as the glass shattered. He had been peppered with buckshot and glass but was unhurt, lifting the rifle in his hand. Then a man stepped in front of the windowframe, and before the Camorran could react, fired a second volley into him from ten paces. Victor Gigliotti dropped the shotgun and fell back onto the floor, his body riddled and bleeding. I watched the man turn to leave, and as he did so, the two of us locked eyes. An instant later he was gone.

Belatedly, the bodyguards rose from among the shattered tables screaming curses and ran past us out the door, guns drawn, while I struggled to my feet. What was a well-appointed restaurant a moment before was now a shambles. Tables and chairs were upset, bottles broken and leaking onto the floor, and dishes trampled underfoot.

"Are you all right, sir?" I called from the floor. One of my cuffs was stained red, but I was relieved to see it was only from the Chianti bottle beside me.

"Well enough," Barker said, straightening his tie.

I dared stand. Instead of the intimate restaurant front, there was now a clear view of the street, the buildings opposite, and the dozen or more people surveying the damage in wonder. With the sun streaming down, the street seemed unnaturally bright and colorful, as if it were a stage set and we the audience. Another dozen citizens soon peered in at us. My employer crossed over to Gigliotti and put two fingers to the man's throat, feeling for a pulse, and shook his head. The leader of the Camorrans was dead.

"You're bleeding, sir," I pointed out. "Your forehead."

The Guv dug a tiny ball of shot from his temple with his nail and dabbed at the cut with a serviette.

"Your training with Gallenga seems to have served you in good stead," he remarked.

"Did you see him?" I asked, as I brushed glass from my cutaway coat.

"No, blast it. I knocked over the table to avoid the shot and didn't right it again until after he was gone. What did he look like?"

"Tall and thin, with light-colored hair. Clean shaven, sharp features. I won't forget the look he gave me. I think he regretted wasting all his ammunition on poor Mr. Gigliotti."

"You may be the only witness, then," he said.

Barker shook his head. The waiters stood about, mur-

muring to each other, confounded. The livelihoods of a thousand people had suddenly been put at peril.

"Should we go, sir?" I asked. "I don't relish going back to Scotland Yard."

"You may, if you wish," the Guv replied, "but there's no chance the witnesses outside will not remember me."

He was right, of course. I'm relatively insignificant, and if I slipped out, might go unnoticed, but no one forgets Cyrus Barker, all six feet two and fifteen stone of him, with his fierce mustache and his black-lensed Chinese spectacles. It was his only liability as a private enquiry agent, but then he played upon it often as well. Would I cut and run on him? Of course I wouldn't.

It was in the nature of waiters to want to pick up things and begin restoring the restaurant to some order. It was cathartic for them, and it gave them something to do. A few, I noticed, were crying.

"Touch nothing!" Barker ordered. They all stopped and looked at him. He was not their employer, but it was good to be told what to do, to have someone in charge. They willingly obeyed.

"All of you go back to that table in the corner," he continued, pointing to the large banqueting table at the far back. "Open a bottle of wine, but don't get drunk. Scotland Yard is coming soon."

"You're sure of that?" I asked.

"A window being blown out by shotgun is going to be reported, lad. This is not Palermo yet. Besides, I'm sure Poole is having the restaurant watched. It's what I would do in his shoes."

It took all of five minutes for the first blue helmet to arrive, and another ten before Poole showed his bewhiskered face.

He stepped in and looked about, not saying a word, though there was a spot of color on his cheek. He took in the body laying supine on the black-and-white tiled floor, the scattered glass everywhere, and the upturned tables and chairs. He walked over and regarded the waiters as if they were part of a tableau, and then he finally came to us. The inspector reached into his pocket and put something into his mouth. It was a lozenge for his ulcer. I've heard him say Barker was responsible for it.

"Back in town again, eh, Cyrus?" he asked gruffly.

"As you see."

"You haven't wasted any time."

He went over and spoke to one of the officers in a low voice, who turned and hurried out the door. "Sicilians again, I take it."

"Two men, as before," my employer answered. "Thomas saw one of them."

Poole scrutinized me as if I'd done something clever, or beneath contempt, I'm not certain which. Obviously, I hadn't saved Gigliotti's life, and I'd only locked eyes with the killer unintentionally. It wasn't in my mind, as my chair was falling back and the plate glass window shattering in front of me, to decide to help further this case along by identifying one of the assassins.

"Why do I always find you in the thick of the action, Cyrus?" Poole complained.

"I don't know. Why does Scotland Yard always arrive last? The commissioner should have hired me years ago, when I offered him the chance."

It may have been sunny outside, but there were storm clouds forming in the room just then. It never occurred to me that Barker might have offered his services to Scotland Yard at one time and been refused.

"The C.I.D. is not in the habit of hiring inspectors with shady spectacles and even shadier pasts."

"Your loss," I said.

"I'll have no word out of you," Poole warned.

Barker was glowering at me, but then, he was glowering at everything. "I have been forthcoming, Terry," he said. "I know you wish to bring in the killer of Inspector Pettigrilli, but I cannot help you if you intend to continue locking me up and questioning me. You are impeding my investigation."

Poole removed his hat and ran a hand through his thinning hair. "You were present during two murders in the last week!" he shouted.

"No, only the last one. I was nearby during the other."

"I don't want to talk about it. You've blasted my stomach beyond what it can endure. Pray don't speak to me for ten minutes. In fact, be so good as to step outside but don't go away yet. If you do, I'll only have to come looking for you."

Barker stepped into the street and looked up and down it. I followed. There were close to thirty people watching as the inevitable handcart arrived to transport Victor Gigliotti's body. I had grown heartily sick of handcarts.

Five minutes later, a Black Maria pulled up to the front door, obstructing everyone's view. It was an old vehicle, its paint chipped at the corners, rather dusty from lack of use. It amply shut off the view of the gawkers, but that was not its only use. Poole opened the door and ushered the

Neapolitan's waiters directly into the van. Some of them had not heeded Barker's advice and were clearly drunk, while others gestured and argued all the way into the vehicle. I felt sorry for them, having just lost their employer, their livelihoods, and now, momentarily at least, their freedom. I hoped for their sakes there was a solicitor in London who spoke Italian. Had they been English, I thought, there would have been no need for the van.

"You next," Poole said to me.

"What? Are you serious?" I asked. "Didn't you just hear—"

"In!" The inspector seized my arm and propelled me into the van before closing the door in my face. Cyrus Barker, I noted, was not being arrested, nor was he doing anything to save me. I stood up and peered out the small barred window of the back door.

"Why is he getting special privileges?"

"It's the way of the world," Poole explained. "Get used to it." Behind him, Barker turned and gave one of his sharp whistles for a cab. Under my feet, the vehicle shuddered and began to move.

I heaved a sigh and sat down in what little space there was. There were seven of us in the small vehicle, not counting the driver. It smelled like a vineyard in the close quarters. Someone nearby used too little soap and too much eau de cologne. Beneath it all, I smelled old varnish and the sweat of fear from hundreds of people over the years. Perhaps that included my own. It was hot in there and very close. This was no way to treat witnesses.

Another cell, I told myself. This was definitely becoming a habit. I had to admit that Poole was right. We'd appeared at the wrong place at the wrong time twice now. The Guv should not expect them to simply let him go on the grounds that he had an investigation to run. As a rule, police officers do not respect their private brethren. As Barker said, we are a part of London's underworld, not much better than the criminals we apprehend.

Before I knew it, the van drew to a halt. Looking out the little window, I saw that we were in Whitehall already. The door opened and I hopped down into Great Scotland Yard Street where we were herded inside immediately.

"We're home!" I intoned as we crossed the threshold. "Put the kettle on."

22

ONCE INSIDE DIVISION A, WE WERE TAKEN DOWN a hallway and directed to a bench, where we sat for a good half hour, and then I was called first into one of the interrogation rooms, presumably because my English was better than my compatriots'. However, no sooner had the door opened than I caught the aroma of Barker's tobacco, which I would know anywhere. I stepped in and sat down in the chair provided, and explained to Poole, Barker, and a constable taking notes all that had happened at the Neapolitan, excluding the parts I knew the Guv wanted kept secret, while he sat in a shadowy corner away from the oil lamp in front of me.

"That's it, then," Poole finally said. He'd taken off his hat and coat, and there was a gleam of perspiration on his pate. It was stuffy in the room, and Barker's tobacco hadn't helped anything, save initially to alert me of his presence, which may have been his reason for smoking in the first place.

"That's what?" I asked.

"Don't be flippant. Hop it. I'm tired of looking at you."

I wasn't going to sit there and argue with the man. I stood and left the room. Barker followed, so I assumed he had already been questioned. Something was going on. A half hour before, Poole seemed more than happy to toss me in jail until I rotted. Barker must have made some sort of concession. He had purchased my freedom, but at what cost? I knew better than to ask, and chances are he wouldn't tell me—not yet, anyway. He would merely say something like "All will be revealed in the fullness of time, lad." That really gets up my nose.

I walked with one hand in my pocket and the other swinging my cane, happy to be free. At the same time, however, I considered whether having Barker and Gigliotti together had increased the chance of an attack. Were the Sicilians after Gigliotti or Barker or both? Obviously, Victor had presented a better target and he had been swinging his own shotgun toward them at the time. Were there too many of us protecting the Guv for the killer to risk loading again and stepping into the restaurant? Such an action would have been more than bravado. It would have been suicidal.

I hopped up the steps of our office two at a time, with Barker close behind me. Jenkins was not sitting in his customary chair. I went into the office and called his name, thinking to myself that the assassins could have come in here rather than Gigliotti's restaurant.

"Here, sir," his voice came. I looked about for him and finally spotted his slight figure behind the curtain in the bow window.

"Might have been safer to hide under the Guv's desk," I said.

"Ignore him, Jeremy," Barker rumbled. "He's put out. What has happened?"

"Not sure, sir. There's been a fellow watching the building. He's been all up and down the court for the last hour. Even came up to the door once."

"Describe him."

"Thirtyish, blond hair, wide-brimmed hat. Wears a cape, sir. Thought he might be a messenger, but he could have just put the note through the slot in the front door."

"Is he still there?" Barker asked.

"As far as I could tell, he left twenty minutes ago."

When the Guv went out to take a look, I sat down in my chair, thinking of Victor Gigliotti. I was no friend of his, I'll admit. He was a criminal, for all his pretensions to legitimate business. He'd never been especially civil to me. Perhaps it wasn't Victor himself as much as the thought that each person I knew being killed brought me closer to my own bullet or knife wound or shotgun blast or what have you. Another layer of safety had been stripped away.

Barker walked back into our chambers. "He's no longer there. I've checked the area, and he's gone."

"Do you still intend to supervise a gang war on the docks?" I asked my employer suddenly. "Nothing has changed your mind?"

"Nothing."

"Is it merely a ruse for flushing out Faldo?"

"It is required by his code that he attend such a donnybrook. He must show himself and when he does, I will pounce."

"You make him sound like a wharf rat."

"As far as I'm concerned, that is just what he is. And I intend to get him between my teeth like a good ratter and bite down hard."

I said nothing, but I was thinking, and it showed on my face.

"What is it, lad?"

"He's very close, isn't he? I mean, he had a man in our garden, a man who disappeared. Then, there was the fellow on our corner, the old gentleman who was singing. How do we know that wasn't Faldo?"

"You're rattled," he said. "Gigliotti's murder has gotten to you."

"I'm wondering if we haven't bitten off more than we can chew, sir. I mean, going against the Mafia, an entire Sicilian secret society."

"It may not be as bad as all that," Barker said.

"What do you mean?"

"We have no proof that Faldo arrived as a representative of his brethren. He may have come on a personal vendetta and found London ripe for conquest. I believe he is merely a foot soldier trying to imitate his superiors far from Palermo. He's stretching his muscles, seeing what he can get away with, and trying to make a name for himself."

"If he came all the way here from Sicily to kill Pettigrilli, he must be very determined."

"I'll give him that, lad. He's playing this game for high stakes and has no intention of losing."

"And where does that leave us, sir?"

Barker leaned back in his big chair and crossed his arms. "Well, I'd like to think I have one advantage over him."

"And that is?"

"I don't play games."

★   ★   ★

Several minutes later, Inspector Poole came into our office. I thought we had been shed of him for the day. Granted, there are advantages to living so close to Scotland Yard —one hears news faster, and anyone not satisfied with the way they've been treated can come around the corner and hire an enquiry agent—but there are disadvantages, too. I'd grown heartily sick of Terence Poole and his ulcer.

"We've got him! Two constables in Clerkenwell just arrested a man in a black cape. We need your boy here for an identity parade."

"As a witness or suspect?" I asked.

Poole crossed his thin arms. "Always with the jokes. You really need to learn some respect for the law."

"It was a legitimate question."

"Oh, come along, you."

"He is my assistant, Terry," the Guv pointed out. "I should like to be asked before you take him away."

"You're as touchy as he is these days, Cyrus. I think he's been a bad influence on you."

"I merely think a little professional courtesy is in order."

Poole's cheeks were turning red. Barker and I knew that there must be several people at the Yard waiting for us to arrive.

"Oh, very well, I'm sorry I ordered you about. I'm sorry I tried to take your assistant away without asking you. I'm sorry I decided to become a constable instead of a river keeper. Now, can we get on with it?"

"Since you asked so nicely," I said. "Besides, I've never been to an identity parade."

*   *   *

There's a room in A Division set up solely for this activity, a sort of stage with horizontal lines along the wall, marking heights up to seven feet. The stage is brightly lit with gas jets, but where the witness stands is in heavy shadow, though not heavy enough to suit me.

"Trot them out," Poole ordered as soon as Barker and I were ready. On the way over, the inspector had explained that of all the people in the area of the Neapolitan, only I had gotten a clear look at the assassin. As the suspects slouched in, I considered how often I'd found myself in such a position.

"Take your time; look them over," Poole said, as if it were a patter he had memorized long ago. "Gentlemen in the parade, please turn to the right. Thank you."

I spotted Gigliotti's killer right off, even though he wasn't wearing the cloak and hat. He was second from the right, trying to look like all the others, moving as they did, making the same expressions. It didn't work. I lifted two fingers and Poole nodded in agreement, possibly even relief. He ordered them all to turn to the left and then they shuffled out but not before the fellow looked out past the glare of the gas jets and fixed his eyes on me again, as if it were I in the identity parade and he picking me out of the crowd.

I didn't know then that there could be blond Italians. I never learned what city he came from, but I doubted it could be Palermo. He must be a northerner, from Florence or Milan or Venice, who had come with Faldo to London. His was a bland face, almost pale, with no whiskers or identifying marks, save for a longish nose. Only his eyes gave him away. They were cold as a block of Gigliotti's ice, eyes meant for looking down the barrel of a gun or guiding a blade between a pair of ribs or jamming an ice pick into the ear of a victim. He could pierce your heart and then sit down to a glass of wine and a good meal.

"Now what happens?" I asked Poole.

All the tension had left the inspector's body. He looked almost jubilant. "Now we take his measurements using the latest methods of detective work, the Bertillon system. Inspector Pettigrilli left behind a box of filled-in cards, his own personal rogues' gallery, and your man is in there."

"Who is he?" I asked.

"His name is Vito Moroni. He's from Ravenna. He's had several arrests across Italy. Extortion. Violence. Assault. Finally, he ended up in Palermo where there was steady work for him. Arrested for killing a judge, but he got off. Arrested for killing the chief of police, but got off. Slippery as an eel, this one. Known associates, one Marco Faldo. That should come as no surprise."

"Has he admitted to being Vito Moroni?"

"Of course not. He claims to be Guido Palazzo, an out-of-work carpenter doing casual work on the docks. He even has papers, but I believe they are forged—or he might have killed the real Palazzo for his papers."

By then we were leaving A Division for Poole's office in the C.I.D. building. The sun had gained some strength since noon and was bathing Great Scotland Yard in golden sunlight. We stopped into the next building, and in a few minutes, Poole put a piece of paper into Barker's hand.

"It's the response from the chief of police in Palermo. I think you should see it."

The letter read:

> *Pietro Berruto*
> *Prefecture of Police*
> *Palermo, Italy*

Inspector Poole
A Division
Scotland Yard
London, England

Dear Inspector Poole,
It is with a heavy heart that we learn of the death of our comrade in arms, Inspector Pettigrilli. Alberto was an exemplary officer and will be sorely missed. The government is considering awarding the medal of St. Michael to his widow in his name. All of us here in Palermo have stories of his courage and his strength. He survived no less than three attempts on his life, and so it comes as little surprise that in the end, that life was all too brief. He was a tireless fighter against the organized gangs of Sicily, wishing to rid the country of this plague, for the good of all. It was his greatest wish to provide a way to connect all police agencies around the world through the use of the Bertillon system, and we are glad that before his death he finished training you at the famous Scotland Yard of London, England.

Sincerely,
Pietro Berruto, Commissioner

"Touching," Barker said.

"The question is," Poole said, "whether Moroni will lead us to his boss. He looks like he'll be a tough nut to crack."

"If you could see some way to place him in my custody, I'm sure I can get him to crack open a little," Barker offered.

"I'm sure, Cyrus, but it isn't his skull we want cracked. Or his ribs. Your methods are occasionally heavy-handed."

Barker gave one of his wintry smiles. "Just a trifle enthusiastic."

23

A MAN CAME QUICKLY INTO POOLE'S OFFICE, AND I nearly jumped from my seat when I saw him. He was an Italian in a thick mustache and knit cap, one of the men in the identity parade I'd just attended.

"It ain't him, sir!" he cried in a Cockney accent. This fellow was as Italian as pork pie with chips. Obviously, he was a constable in disguise. "The cards don't match up at all!"

Poole took both cards out of the constable's hands and compared them. The Bertillon card Pettigrilli had brought with him was slightly yellowed with age, but the one the constable had just made was of new buff. The men in the photographs were nearly identical, but now that I saw them together, perhaps not *completely* identical. I supposed one must allow for the vagaries of light and shadow and expression.

Poole exposed the constable to his choicest vocabulary, which one could use to strip paint and barnacles off the hull of a boat.

"Take your pill, Terry," Barker counseled, unruffled by the revelation.

The inspector reached into his drawer and pulled out a small brown bottle. He shook several lozenges into his hand and crunched them in his teeth.

"We can still charge him, can't we?" I asked. "I've identified him as the murderer of Victor Gigliotti, after all. It's him, without a doubt."

"This card says it isn't him, and it was prepared by the very man who trained us. Palazzo claims he was at the East India Docks all morning and he has several witnesses who'll attest to it. His name is even written on the casual labor list, though I suppose it wouldn't be hard for someone to forge it. Damn! I'll have to let the blighter go."

"Did he have a cape?"

"Yes, but no shotgun, no dagger, not so much as a boat hook. Just an innocent dockworker who happens to look exactly like the man who blew a hole in the leader of the Camorra."

"It was him, I tell you!" I insisted. "He even recognized me!"

"I believe you, Thomas, for once," Poole said. "I'll keep him as long as I can, but if a solicitor appears, I'll have no choice but to let him go. Blast Bertillon and his stupid French method!"

"Is there a way the card could have been altered?" I asked. "Could it be a forgery?"

"It looks genuine enough, lad," Barker admitted. "I'm afraid Terence is correct. According to these cards, Guido Palazzo is not Vito Moroni. They merely have similar features."

"Then the cards are wrong, I tell you! I know what I saw!"

"We believe you, lad," Barker murmured.

"You're going to let this fellow go, and the first thing he's going to do is come after me."

"Perhaps we could use that," Poole suggested. "Wait for the fellow to come after Llewelyn here and bring him down."

"After he's used my chest for a pin cushion? No, thank you. I've been sliced enough for one week."

"You're not being particularly helpful to this investigation," Poole complained.

"I'm sorry, Inspector. Shall I walk about Clerkenwell with a big target on my chest? Shall that satisfy?"

"It's a start," he replied archly.

"We want to get this fellow as much as you do," Barker said. "He stabbed Dummolard, after all. But if this charge against him will fail, let it. We'll try again some other way."

"Just once I'd like this to go *my* way, Cyrus. The Yard's way."

"Perhaps it shall," Barker said. "One can never tell about such things. Let's go, lad. I've still got work to do before dinner. Is there any more you need, Terence?"

"The whereabouts of Marco Faldo would be nice," the inspector replied.

"I should think he'd be in Clerkenwell or Soho."

"I've a mind to take Clerkenwell apart. Go on, out you two. I've got to start all over again."

We showed ourselves out. In Whitehall Street, I was using every trick Mr. Gallenga had taught me. Were there any open windows along the way? Was anyone on the roof? What about the cabs? Did anyone in the street look dangerous? Suspicious? Sicilian? Was anyone glancing my way? Were we being followed?

"This eye training is driving me mad," I told the Guv. "I don't know how you can live this way. How can one ever relax one's guard?"

"One can't," Barker replied. "But it gets easier. It becomes second nature. You'll pick it up. Or you won't."

"Such confidence."

"All the confidence in the world, lad. Have you got sixpence?"

"Yes, sir," I said, digging about in my pocket. "Here you go. What do you need sixpence for?"

"For this little fellow," he said, taking a passing street arab by the collar and slipping the coin into his filthy hands. Barker murmured something into his ear, and the boy ran off like Scotland Yard was after him.

"Oh, no—you've asked for Soho Vic, haven't you?" I complained. "Just when I thought today couldn't get any worse."

A half hour later the aforementioned blight upon humanity invaded our quarters in his usual manner—over the back wall and through the back door. I really must counsel Barker to put some broken glass atop the wall for our personal safety. As it stood, just anyone could get in.

"'Ello, Ugly. Cracked your egg, did yer? Afternoon, Mr. Barker, sir."

"Ah, Vic," Cyrus Barker said. He always allowed him liberties. As usual, the young man went to the cigar box on Barker's desk and in a minute, was seated in the visitor's chair attempting to blow a proper smoke ring, one leg wagging negligently over the leather arm.

"I have a message I want delivered to several individuals, some of whom have no fixed abode."

"Got it. What's the message?" he asked. Vic was wearing a collar so loose it hung around his neck, and a rusty coat with his sleeves rolled up at the wrists. As usual, his black hair shot out in each direction, like the spines of a sea anemone, and he displayed his congenital aversion to soap.

"Inform them there is to be a meeting tomorrow at six P.M. sharp. The address is thirty-seven Wentworth Street."

"Meeting tomorrow, six sharp, thirty-seven Wentworth. Got it. Who gets the message?"

"Patrick Hooligan; Robert Dummolard, who can be reached at Le Toison d'Or; and Ben Tillett of the West India Docks."

Vic took a large puff and blew it out again, then listed the receivers in order on his grubby fingers.

"Hooligan, Frenchie in Soho, and the docks. Got it."

"I want you to deliver them yourself, if possible, by noon tomorrow."

"Easy as fallin' off a bridge. I'll need two pounds for my troubles. That's two pounds sterling, turnip face," he said to me, "if you've got the scratch."

With a sigh, I took out two pound notes and started writing the expense in the ledger. Vic reached for the notes and in doing so, managed to flick the ash from his cigar all over the shoulder of my cutaway.

"Oh, I'm so sorry!" he cried, taking the opportunity to rub the ash all over me while appearing to wipe it away. I think he'd been planning it since the moment he'd entered. He's diabolical that way. I bore the insult silently. Barker would take the accident at face value. A businessman like Soho Vic had no time for pranks.

"P'raps if we wipe some ink on it, it'll go black again—" the boy offered helpfully, reaching for the bottle on my desk.

"Never mind," I said, putting the ink out of reach. "You've got your orders and your money. Now go."

"Touchy, he is," Vic said, and tsked. "I'm off, then. Ta for the smoke."

He left, out the back door as always, but a minute later, put his head back in.

"What is it, Vic?" Barker asked with somewhat less patience than he had exhibited the moment before. Vic, I should point out, did not stand for Victor. The boy's real name was Stanislieu Sohovic. He was a transplanted Pole who had buried his origins in a Cockney accent.

"Would you be requiring anyfing else, sir? Anyfing at all?"

"Just the messages. Why do you ask?"

"Well, sir, I know the I-talians are kicking up, and that Mr. Etienne got hisself stabbed. Are you taking 'em on?"

"If I did, 'twould be no concern of yours," the Guv replied coolly.

"I might be concerned if I were part of that list myself. I've got plenty o' boys ready for a scrap anytime. You name it."

"None of them are over fifteen," my employer said dismissively.

"We grow up fast on the streets, sir," Vic continued. "Some of me lads is full growed. We've been in dozens of scraps before. Just say the word, and we're there."

"No, Vic. Do you hear me? No!"

Soho Vic frowned. I don't think Barker had ever spoken to him in such a manner before. He'd always treated Vic as an adult associate, a business partner, but now he was being dismissed as a child.

Vic opened his mouth to speak and then shut it again. Finally he shrugged, affecting that he didn't care. "Suit yourself, then, Push. If you need me, ask around."

He took himself off with less bluster than he had entered with.

"Five thirty, sir," Jenkins announced, coming around the corner as if Big Ben down the street hadn't informed us already. "Dare I risk a return to the Rising Sun?"

"Is your house well fortified?" Barker asked.

"All locked and barricaded, sir."

"If we walk you to the Sun, can you find escorts to see you home?"

"I'm certain I could, Mr. B." It was obvious he was eager to go.

"Would it disturb you if Thomas and I dined there? We would sit at a private table."

"Of course it wouldn't, sir."

"Drat!" I said.

"What is it, lad?" our employer asked, looking my way.

"Nothing, sir. Soho Vic nicked my ledger pen. It must have happened when he destroyed my suit."

"Nonsense. You must have mislaid it. You have several pens."

"It was my favorite nib."

He cleared his throat as if to say that writing instruments were beneath his notice, and returned to the matter at hand.

"You have no objection, Jenkins—you are certain?" Barker pursued.

"Of course not, sir."

"Very well. Let us close up the office for the day."

We were just putting on our hats and extricating our sticks from the hat stand by my desk when something shot in through the postal slot and slid across the polished parquetry of the entranceway. It was an envelope, rather flat. Jenkins opened the door and shouted "Hey!" returning a moment later.

"It was a child, sir. A messenger. He ran off when I called. It's addressed to you, Mr. L.," Jenkins said, lifting it from the floor.

With a dry mouth, I took the envelope and opened it with my dagger. I was clumsy with it, because my fingers were nerveless. Extricating the note, I read the words circling around the black handprint in the center:

We did not wish you to feel left out, Mr. Llewelyn. You have killed a promising young man and are becoming a nuisance. Who will save you when your boss is saving everyone else?

24

OURS IS A SHORT AND NARROW ALLEY, OPENING into a rectangular courtyard where the telephone exchange is located. There are other enquiry agents' offices in the street, as well as a branch of Cox and Company, where Barker does some of his banking. Save a narrow gate at the back of the court, which is generally locked, there is no way of escape. That means that should anyone choose to step in our front door, we would have to go out the back into our private yard and over the wall. Barker is no Soho Vic, however, and would stand and fight rather than escape. During a recent case, a fellow had entered our chambers wielding a saber. I wondered what would happen if someone came in with a loaded shotgun, like the one that killed Victor Gigliotti.

I thought this not because I was in one of my maudlin moods but because a man walked into our offices and I suddenly felt like a rat caught in a trap. It was the hokeypokey man we had seen on the street outside our residence. Were

I a betting man, I would have put money that he was Marco Faldo. Jenkins invited him to wait and came to announce our visitor. Our clerk, who enjoyed proper form as much as Mac, carried a carte de visite on a salver. Did the man have the effrontery to present one that proclaimed "Marco Faldo, late of Palermo"? The Guv scooped it off the tray and scrutinized it. Then he tapped the card against his lower lip as if gathering his thoughts before instructing Jenkins to let the visitor in.

The Italian who had regaled us recently entered in a more somber mood than before. Up close, the lines in his forehead and around his eyes were more evident. His hair was thinner than I had first perceived, and it was possible he dyed it, for the line between the black and the gray of his temples was too severe. He was older than I had thought. Our visitor seemed tired and dispirited and sank down into the chair in front of Barker without a word, and without any display of firearms.

"Good afternoon, sir," Barker said. "This is my assistant, Thomas Llewelyn. Thomas, this is Vincenzo Gigliotti."

"Gigliotti!" I cried.

"At your service," the man replied with quiet dignity.

"Would you care for a cigar, sir?" Barker offered.

He shook his head. "No, thank you. I don't wish to intrude. I understand you are planning a confrontation with the Sicilians."

"Have you come, sir," Barker rumbled, "to claim vendetta against the people who killed your son?"

"I am sixty-eight years old, Mr. Barker, and have retired from the life of secret societies and murder. My son attempted to draw me back into it in order to stop these Sicilians, and look where it got him. His children have no father now, and Concetta is a widow."

"Why were you selling Italian ices outside our home, Mr. Gigliotti?" Barker asked.

"My grandson Alonzo and I were watching you, for your protection. Victor asked me to keep an eye on you. He said you are a good detective, but your weakness is your personal safety. He did not want you to be killed before your plan was carried out."

I thought of Philippa Ashleigh, who had said much the same thing about my employer. I had to admit, he had more scars on his body than any five men I knew combined. He trusted his ability to fight his way out of any situation.

"I had other men in the area if I needed them," the old man continued, "even two watching overnight, should the Sicilians attempt to attack then."

"I thank you for your concern, since I can no longer thank Victor. Was it you who stopped the intruder on my grounds?"

"Yes. We caught the fellow two streets away. That's one less Sicilian to worry about. Your young man here seemed very comfortable with the dagger."

"Maestro Gallenga trained him."

The Italian gave a wan smile. "Ah, Gallenga, yes. He's gone, you know. He got out of town quickly once the bullets began to fly."

"What do you mean?" I asked.

"He and his wife left the city. He wished to spend his remaining years in peace. He never had much of a stomach for violence."

I didn't either, I had to admit, but I didn't have that luxury in my line of work.

"What brings you to my office?" my employer asked.

Vincenzo Gigliotti moved forward in his chair and leaned an elbow on Barker's desk. "I have come to find out what you will do, Mr. Barker. I do not thirst for revenge. That is for young men. Yet even now the Sicilians threaten my family's livelihood. I wish to run my son's business interests until such time as Alonzo is full grown and can assume his rightful position. I don't want to see it driven into the ground by Sicilians. Also, I wish to see the killers of my son brought to justice."

"Our wishes are the same, then," Barker said. "I also want to see the Italians and Sicilians at peace again."

"You go to war in order to make peace? You have an odd way of doing things, Mr. Barker."

"If I crush the serpent's head, Mr. Gigliotti, then I need not crush the whole snake. I need something from you that you will have a hard time giving me."

"You have but to name it."

"What I want from you, sir, is to stay out of it completely. I don't want a single Italian on the dock tomorrow night."

Gigliotti's face grew red, and his eyes nearly bulged from their sockets.

"Do you trust me?" Barker went on. "Do you see that unless the Sicilians face a completely English force, it will only lead to more vendettas? The only way to stop the Mafia is to cut it off from the Italian community, to isolate it like a contagion, and to destroy the germ itself. Then the Sicilians can go back to their normal commerce and begin to make peace with the Italians."

"Are you dictating terms, Mr. Barker?"

"At this time, with Victor's organization in disarray, I could," Barker admitted, "but I have no desire to. You may handle this entire situation yourself if you wish. I would gladly hand it over to you. But if you wish me to do it, I must have a free hand, and I will not make use of the Camorrans. I consider them to be a criminal organization and won't associate this agency with them."

Gigliotti sat tight-lipped for a moment, red to the scalp. It occurred to me that the old man was probably the head of the Camorran secret society in London now and that what Barker said was something of an insult. It also occurred to me that Hooligan's men were as much criminals as the Italian fraternity, but they had passed through Barker's sieve.

"Victor said your word is your bond. Will you kill this man who has murdered my son?"

"I will see him brought to justice," Barker said. "Beyond that, I will not promise. I'm not an assassin."

Gigliotti took a cigar out of the case and bit off the tip.

"You won't kill him. Serafini is dead. There is never an assassin around when you need one." He lit the cigar and puffed a plume of smoke with a sigh. "Very well, if it is the best you can offer. All I wanted was to have a few years of peace before I die. Now this!"

"Most regrettable, sir," Barker agreed.

"My boy," he muttered suddenly. "My wonderful boy." It was as if his mask had slipped and we could see the grief behind it. He cleared his throat and mastered himself once again. "I must get back. I have to plan a funeral for my only son." He stood and began to leave. Hesitating at the door, he turned and frowned at Barker.

"Find him," he ordered.

"I will."

I couldn't help but think it was easier said than done.

25

I SUPPOSE IF THIS WERE A LEGITIMATE ENTERPRISE upon which we were engaged, we would have kept up with what was going on with Mr. Soft. We might have sent a messenger or telegram, and thus would have been in touch with his progress. Instead, we had to trust that all was coming together smoothly. Strange, isn't it, that such matters involving criminals and rampsmen like Mr. Soft and Mr. Hardy should be a matter of trust.

"I don't like this," I admitted aloud, as we rode to Wentworth Street.

"What are you afraid of?"

"I don't know. Of being betrayed, perhaps. How do we know Mr. Soft will not inform the Sicilians or let it become common knowledge on the street? Either way, our goose is cooked."

"No slang, Mr. Llewelyn, please. Let me explain it to you. In legitimate society, honesty and integrity is taken as a matter of course. You don't stand in Oxford Street and try to discern which businesses are honest; but in the underworld, you see, all businesses run on the reputations of the men who own them. Mr. Soft has one and so do I. Part of the money you paid him was for his silence. We are both aware that he could go to the Sicilians, true; but he and his long ladder were established here before the Mafia, and, the Lord willing, shall be here after they are gone. If he double-crossed me, it would come back on him, even if I didn't attempt to avenge myself. My associates would no longer seek his custom. It's all about alliances, and no one allies with a man who is untrustworthy unless the stakes are high."

"Are the stakes high?"

Barker's mustache grew wide, like a bow being stretched. I'd said something he actually thought was funny. "High enough," he admitted.

"I just want to be certain we won't be ambushed. I don't relish being sealed up inside Mr. Soft's tomb. No matter what sort of businessman he is, he's also a criminal."

"You have high principles, Thomas, for someone who spent eight months in Oxford Prison for theft."

"There were extenuating circumstances," I stated.

"Aye, lad, but aren't there always?"

We alighted from the cab in Wentworth Street. When Mr. Hardy came to the door, I noticed he was wearing a shirt and jacket, attempting to look at least somewhat respectable. He nodded us through.

Mr. Soft had undergone a transformation of his own. He wore a green velvet jacket closed with frogs and a soft-collared shirt with an ascot. Atop his downy curls was a tasseled fez. I wondered if he'd purchased the outfit with our ten pounds, and had a good mind to demand our money back on the grounds of poor taste in fashion.

"Welcome, gentlemen, welcome!" he exclaimed. My first impression, that he was a mouse in human form, bore up under a second scrutiny. No doubt he thought he looked cultured, and for all I know, he did. I didn't attend many salons these days.

"Good afternoon, Mr. Soft. Is all in readiness?" my employer asked.

"To the letter, sir, to the very letter. We have not stinted on the plate or the comestibles. All awaits your inspection."

The room in which the trapdoor lay open had been done up with a carpet leading to the very edge and oilcloth lining the rough hole in the floor. It looked vaguely theatrical, as I suppose did Mr. Soft. Perhaps even Mr. Hardy himself was in costume when one considered his everyday attire.

A hundred feet below, the table had been set on a large Persian carpet surrounded by a ring of chairs. Shaded oil lamps had been set on the table at each end, and a sideboard with food and liquors lay behind. It certainly wasn't normal East End fare. The light flickered on the rough tunnel walls, a mixture of natural stone, concrete, brick, and dirt.

At six o'clock, they began to arrive. The first was Patrick Hooligan. Barker nodded when he heard the young man's voice.

"Go down there? Are you barmy? I dunno what's down there!"

"Then leave, Mr. Hooligan." Barker's voice echoed and filled the chamber we were in. "You solicited us, not the other way 'round."

"That you, Barker?" Hooligan called down.

"It is."

"How do I know you don't have a hundred coppers down there?"

"I don't need a hundred coppers, you rascal," the Guv growled, "just a bag to put you in!"

Hooligan chuckled. "Fair enough," he called, and swinging a leg over the side, began to descend. "How many at this church meeting?"

"You'll find out soon enough," Barker responded, and for once the young gang leader agreed, sitting down in one of the chairs.

Our second guest to arrive was Ben Tillett. He alone was not a member of London's underworld, though as a union organizer, I imagine he missed it by only a small margin. He had had to be convinced to join us.

"What is this place?" he demanded. "Why can't we meet at a café or public house like everyone else?"

"This is my get-together, Mr. Tillett," the Guv explained. "My game, my rules. I value my privacy."

"But it must be a hundred feet down. I'm afraid of depths."

"Don't you mean heights?" I asked.

"No, if it's a lookout you want, I'll swarm up to any crow's nest you can name. But I don't like holes in the ground."

"I'm not going to call out everything to you up there," Barker said. "It's here or good night to you."

Tillett grumbled but slowly began to descend. The next I knew, another man was coming down after him. I couldn't see his face from below, merely his wide shoulders. He did not move quickly, but then he couldn't with Tillett going slowly below him. After a moment I could see that it was

Robert Dummolard. He looked tense and alert. Perhaps it was a quality his whole family possessed.

"*Bonsoir, m'sieur,*" Barker said.

"This had better be worth my time," the Frenchman said irritably.

"Here now!" Hooligan objected. "Have you brought the Frenchies in? We got enough lads of our own without bringing in apaches!"

"His brother was injured by the Sicilians," Barker explained. "He and his other brothers have come all this way from France to defend him. I have decided to make use of them. We are all assembled, then. Gentlemen, there is a sideboard stocked with food. We also have water and wine and beer."

"What, no gin?" Hooligan put in. "You really are a nonconformist, Barker."

My employer ignored the gibe. "Pray help yourselves and we shall get down to business in five minutes."

I had to hand it to Mr. Soft: he set a good table. I wondered how many trips it took his associate to bring these items down, one by one. Aside from the sliced beef and cheeses, there was fresh bread and a cold prawn salad I could eat every day of the week.

"Very well, gentlemen—"

"'Scuse me, sir," a voice filtered down from above.

Barker looked up over his head. "Yes, Mr. Hardy?"

"There's a tyke up here what says he's part of the meeting. Shall I send him down?"

"No, sir. He is definitely *not* a part of this meeting. You may toss him into the street and tell him to go home."

A minute later, I heard the indignant voice of Mr. Soho

Vic, Esquire, protesting vehemently. I couldn't help but think the cries he uttered while being tossed out the door were more pleasing to my ear than a concert at Covent Garden.

"Very well, gentlemen, let us begin," Barker said, circling the table. "All of you are aware of a number of deaths in the city recently, which can be put at the door of a Sicilian organization known as the Mafia. It would appear that this group, led by an unknown individual, is attempting to establish itself in London, particularly in the area around the docks, in Soho, and in Clerkenwell. Many Black Hand notes have been issued; I have received one myself and my assistant, Llewelyn, has as well. Two men, Inspector Pettigrilli of Palermo and Victor Gigliotti, ignored these notes at the cost of their lives. My sources inform me that the unknown *mafiusi* leader is organizing some of the Sicilians in the area. In an effort to forestall any further plans this leader might have, I will issue a challenge to his people, a fight at the docks to determine who is the strongest. I do this because I believe the presence of the Sicilian mob would alter crime in London forever."

"Alter in what way?" Hooligan asked. He'd pushed back his plate and was now smoking a villainous cheroot that looked like a piece of tarred rope.

"Escalated violence, extortion, weapons smuggling, murder, and vendettas."

"That doesn't sound so bad," Hooligan said.

"There would be a public outcry, and Scotland Yard must react. How would you like to see twice the present force on the streets and more severe sentences for every crime? And how long before the Italians are against the Irish, and the French against the Chinese, and one man wishing to be head over all London, through murder and intimidation?"

"This must really stick in your craw, Push," Hooligan stated. "A nice gentleman like yourself having to associate with us base criminals. You must want these Sicilians very bad."

"Yes, I do, Mr. Hooligan," the Guv said, refusing to be baited. I imagined that the gang leader had been a disruptive force wherever he was since he first learned to crawl. I wished we had not used his gang and had been in league with the Italians instead, but I understood that Barker did not wish to turn this strictly into a Mafia-Camorran feud.

"How do you intend to accomplish this?" Tillett spoke up. Like me, he wanted to see this meeting firm on its track and trundling along.

"I will issue a challenge in an hour or two for six o'clock tomorrow evening, at the docks. At this point, we have no idea how many men the Sicilians can muster. If we are overwhelmed, we must have reserves. If their force is small, we will have the advantage. This is too important to give them a fair match. They must be brought down, but I don't want a bloodbath if at all possible."

"What if they bring guns?" Tillett continued. I had to admit I was thinking the same thing.

"If they are well armed, we will disperse before anything happens. I don't want a full-scale war, merely the opportunity to discourage the Sicilian Mafia from thinking it can do as it likes here in London."

"What about knives?" Hooligan asked, giving a glance at the stitches in my cheek.

"I'd prefer dock weapons—sticks, belaying pins, staves, boat hooks, monkey's fist knots, and the like—but your men can bring clasp knives for an emergency."

I had to ask. "What's a monkey's-fist knot?"

If I could have seen behind his tinted spectacles, I'm sure the Guv was rolling his eyes. He gave a short sigh.

Tillett spoke for him. "It's a rope with a weighted knot on the end. Useful for thumping noggins."

"Who'll test the waters?" Dummolard interrupted. "Who will see how they fight and what weapons they'll employ? May I have the honor?"

"I would rather Mr. Hooligan and his boys do that," Barker said. "But, remember, it is merely a feint, to pull them out of position. I want you and your brothers to deliver a solid response to their attack from another direction, rather like a right hook to the ear."

"I hope you know what you are about, monsieur," Etienne's brother put in.

"I shall do my best, Mr. Dummolard."

"And where will my brothers and I be stationed?"

"Your men and Mr. Tillett's will be behind Hooligan's. I want the dockworkers to bring up the rear, considering they are untrained."

"I'll do my best to keep them there, sir, but some of them are aching for a scrap," Tillett responded.

"I am certain they'll get one. Are there any other questions?"

"Just one. The same one I asked when I came in here," Hooligan said. "What are you about, Mr. Barker? You're no criminal, and yet you're planning a dock war in the East End.

If the Yard hears of this, you'll be in Wormwood Scrubs till you rot, and some of us with you."

"Let us leave Wormwood Scrubs out of this. I make no apologies for the fact that I am after the assassin and the Sicilian leader, whom I believe is named Marco Faldo. I will challenge him and he must attend as a debt of honor. I'm doing this to flush him out of his hole. It is the only way."

"How do you know it's this Faldo?" Tillett asked. "I don't believe I have heard of him."

"I have the strong feeling that Faldo is in London somewhere, biding his time and sending Black Hand notes. Were there another fellow as dangerous hiding here, I'd like to think he would have reached our collective ear by now. I am in the business of collecting information, after all, and in knowing what dangerous men are in the country."

No one spoke. Apparently, tomorrow's events were going forward as planned. Young Mr. Tillett and Robert Dummolard did not seem inclined to stay and chat and enjoy the food Mr. Soft had provided. If one is not accustomed to being underground, it can be unsettling. Hooligan was not going to be put off, however, pouring himself an ale and putting a thick slice of ham in bread.

"Good victuals, Mr. Barker," he said. "You do know how to throw a party. I'm going to have to rent this place meself sometime."

Our other guests were halfway up the ladder when Mr. Soft's placid voice filtered down to my ear.

"Pardon me, gentlemen, and forgive the intrusion, but there appears to be an altercation at the front door. There is no reason to hurry or panic, but I suggest all of you leave at once. If you would deign to follow me, I can get you safely off the premises. This way, please."

In less than a minute, all of us were on the ladder at once. The metal frame groaned once at the combined weight but showed no signs of giving way. Thank the Lord for good English iron, I say. Barker and I were last, of course. When we reached the top once more, we could hear the disturbance outside. Something was being slammed against the door, perhaps some sort of battering ram. It did not seem to concern Mr. Hardy much, who was sitting in a chair opposite with what I can only describe as an elephant gun over one shoulder and his boot resting against a dog at his feet. The dog was of indeterminate breed and had but one ear and one eye. It seemed to be no more concerned about the pounding at the front door than its master.

"Early stages, gentlemen," Hardy said easily. "There's still plenty of time, yet. Mr. Soft does get the vapors up."

There was a sound of a shot being fired outside and the entire door gave a shudder. The dog put up its head as if mildly curious.

"Ah, now we're gettin' somewheres. Stage two of the assault. I suggest you follow Mr. Soft to the escape room."

So saying, the man pulled a fat cigar from his pocket and scraped a vesta against the wall behind him.

"Hope they tear the whole entrance down," he said conversationally. "I've been meanin' to put in brick. You get ever so much more security with brick. Or stone! Stone would be nice. Granite maybe."

We left Mr. Hardy debating the merits of various types of stone and followed our guests. We went down a narrow hall into a sitting room. All our guests looked a trifle perturbed, but Mr. Soft seemed in no more of a hurry than his associate. He pulled a chair out of a corner and moved a blue and white ceramic pot full of tall grass aside.

"This will only take a minute, gentlemen," he assured us. Taking a small jackknife from his pocket, he cut into the patterned wallpaper and began tearing a straight line. At one point above his head, he stopped and cut horizontally. Then he put the knife away with a fastidiousness that we all found wearing and gave a sudden savage kick to the wall. It gave way with a squeak of rusted hinges. A door had been plastered up inside the wall and papered over. With a bow, he invited us through. We tried to converge upon it at once, propelled by the sound of more shots at the front of the establishment.

"Plenty of time, gentlemen," Mr. Soft assured us. "Just follow the passages to the street. You'll exit in the area of the Jewish synagogue. There should be no trouble finding a cab of a Friday night. Thank you for visiting our establishment. If you ever require such services, I hope you'll think of us. Good evening!"

We squeezed through the small doorway and began to shuffle through a succession of dusty hallways and courtyards. Any moment, I expected to reach the street, only to come upon another abandoned-looking hall. I had heard there were escape passages like this in the warrens of Whitechapel, made by criminals to evade the police. At one point, we went down some steps and through a short tunnel, and at another we found ourselves in a brick alleyway with the stars shining above the roofs three stories overhead. Then, finally, we burst through a door into a courtyard full of Jews in their Sabbath best, the women in dresses adorned with jet and heavy mantles, like Spanish *doñas,* and the men in yarmulkes and long talliths. We made our way through the crowd with apologies, and reaching the street, commandeered some of the vehicles. We all relaxed, I noticed, and were smiling now that the danger had passed, at the novelty of the evening. Tillett tramped off with his hands in his pockets. Hooligan tipped a wink in our direction as his cab rolled by, followed by Robert Dummolard, who gave us a nod.

"Pass me a sixpence, lad," Barker said, taking control of the situation again. I reached into my pocket and handed the coin to him. Part of my duties is always to have at least one of every coin in the realm, as well as every denomination up to and including fifty pounds. Barker held the coin vertically between his thumb and forefinger and then suddenly it vanished like a magic trick. Behind him, a ragged street urchin jogged away as fast as the crowd and his bare feet would allow. That accomplished, we stepped back from the curb and Barker stuffed and lit his pipe. We watched as the well-to-do crowd made its staid leave-taking from the Sabbath services.

I had to admit I was looking for someone, now that I was here. A young Jewess named Rebecca Mocatta had caught my eye a year before, and rarely did I enter the East End without keeping an eye out for her. Alas, she did not pass by, but it was probably for the better. I was not exactly free to speak with her just then.

There was a flutter by my face, and I stepped back involuntarily. Soho Vic had appeared at my elbow and stolen my pocket handkerchief. He blew his nose into it, a honking blast that turned several heads in our direction, then he stuffed the soiled linen back into my breast pocket.

"Quite a scene over in Wentworth Street, gentlemen," he said. "Buncha I-talians tried to break into a certain establishment, with everything short o' dynamite, but it was nuffink doing. They gave up. The door is half stove in and shot to pieces, but it held. The tenant inside discouraged them wif one good shot of his scattergun. Carpet tacks do make wery in'eresting projectiles, don't ya fink?"

26

MAC WOKE ME THE NEXT MORNING WITH THE welcome news that he had located Etienne's baker and purchased *pain au chocolat* for my breakfast, which happened to be my favorite. I've got to hand it to him: Mac's willing to go above and beyond the ordinary, though at the time I recall thinking that this was his subtle way of suggesting this would be my last meal on earth. I sat in the kitchen watching Barker pace about the back garden and reflected on the fact that my fate was in his hands.

After my bun and coffee, I crossed the bridge to the training area and practiced one of my forms, more to please Barker than myself. I didn't want to intrude on his thoughts, which must have been a jumble of plans and concerns.

"Today's the day, then," I said when I was done, which was trite and obvious, but it helped to break the silence.

"Indeed," he rumbled, still half consumed in thought.

"Do you believe we will flush Marco Faldo out from under whatever rock he is hiding?"

"That is in the Lord's hands," he responded, which caused

me to infer that he had been up early praying. A miscalculation on his part could result in more people being killed. If he ever needed divine help, it was now.

Once we were in our offices I found that everything that occurred that day was geared toward the evening's activities. Jenkins sent all new business to one of the detectives nearby, while Barker employed an elaborate system of telephone calls and messages.

"Sir, is there anything I should be doing?"

Barker looked up at me as if aware for the first time that I was in the room. "You want something to do? Go to Charing Cross Hospital and get those stitches looked at. But be careful. Remember the note you received."

There was little chance I could forget. I lifted hat and stick from the stand and headed toward Trafalgar Square, tuning all my senses to what was going on about me. It was another sunny day, and I stopped and reflected on the fact that the weather we were having was almost Mediterranean, as if the Sicilian criminal hiding somewhere in London had brought this weather north with him.

Where was the fellow? I wondered. He was hiding very well; but, then, there were many bolt-holes in London—restaurants like Ho's and abandoned tunnels like Mr. Soft's, basement dwellings, vacant shops, and warehouses. One would assume he was in the Italian quarter, but he could just as easily be in a nice hotel under an assumed name. He might even . . . I stopped in my tracks. He might even be someone we already knew.

Suppose this Sicilian criminal was not Sicilian at all. Perhaps he was Irish: the local criminal leader Seamus O'Muircheartaigh, playing both sides against the middle, or Hooligan, bringing down Gigliotti in order to gain power. Perhaps he was the Chinese Mr. K'ing, in an elaborate charade to enlarge his sphere of influence. Or could it be another Italian? Perhaps someone within the late Victor Gigliotti's organization wanted to be rid of him, someone that Inspector Pettigrilli might have recognized, so that he must be killed, too. I would count it a conjurer's trick were it not for the litter of bodies left behind. So many deaths merely so that one man could stand up and claim himself the ruler of London's underworld? K'ing and O'Muircheartaigh would not allow that, but this fellow seemed bold enough to try anything.

I came to Trafalgar Square and surveyed the area, looking for anything out of the ordinary. No caped assassins stood about, and no one appeared to be following me; but just the same, I detoured through Charing Cross and came to the hospital from another direction.

I sat patiently as the doctor examined my face, his cool fingers inspecting my stitches. He decided since the stitches were already in place, he wouldn't remove them, but he swabbed the wound heavily in iodine and put a sticking plaster on it.

"They're coming along as expected," the doctor said. "I'll need to take them out in another three or four days."

I stepped into a book and cartography shop in Cecil Street to while away half an hour, having convinced myself I deserved a treat for seeing a physician, then arrived back in Craig's Court in time for lunch.

"I like the plaster," Barker judged. "It makes you look more formidable, and you need every advantage you can get."

"I could be cut again at any moment, given the way this case has gone so far."

"It is a corker, isn't it? I don't understand what fellows see in adding accounts or trading in corn."

"You do realize if you are able to solve all the empire's problems, you'll only put yourself out of work."

"Then I shall enjoy my garden. What's that you've got there?"

I'd been trying to hide it, but he missed nothing behind those black spectacles of his.

"A bound Newgate Calendar. Picked it up in Cecil Street for one and six."

Barker picked up the book and grunted his disapproval. Oh, not at the book, of course, but at me. The book, containing records of old crimes from the early part of the century, interested him enough that he started turning pages. "I was unaware there was a clinic in Cecil Street, lad," he said casually, absorbed in the illustrations in the book. I had been caught out. I should have known better.

"The bookstore did beguile me."

Barker sniffed. Mistake number two. "I wish you wouldn't paraphrase verses from the Holy Book for your own ends. Let's get some lunch, then go out to the docks. It's time to choose a location for tonight's events."

Barker was up and out of the office before I even got a remark out of my mouth. I jumped up and just made it to the waiting cab before it started without me.

"You mean you haven't even chosen which dock the fight is going to be at tonight?" I demanded, a trifle out of breath.

"No. That would have been a capital mistake. The Mafia

has eyes and ears everywhere in the docks. If I decided too early, they could get in ahead of us and take the high ground, so to speak. They have a sense of honor, but it is idiosyncratic. If they pledge to fight without guns you may depend upon them, but they are not above stacking the deck. Let's go, lad."

In the East End, my employer and I looked at docks, lots and lots of docks. I had no idea there were so many in the area. East India; West India; London; St. Katherine's; Millwall; and both Royal docks. Some were divided by canals and were two docks together; so actually, there were over a dozen to inspect one by one, which the two of us did. Now, as far as I'm concerned, a dock is a dock. It has boats in it, with warehouses and packing crates of all sorts nearby. They all looked alike, save for the cargo—tea for the East Indian, for example, and coffee for the West Indian—but to Barker they were as different as women. His shaded eyes apparently took in every detail, weighed it as if on a scale, balanced each attribute with a demerit. One might almost think he was buying a property, rather than planning a battle.

That is not to say that the Guv was working while I stood idly by. I counted the Italian faces on the docks and tried to ascertain whether we were being watched or followed. We were not followed perhaps, but we were certainly watched. I saw workers nudging each other and pointing at us with nods of their chins. There were many Italians and Sicilians on the docks—dozens of them, perhaps hundreds. They must have all known one another on an intimate scale, by face and family and personal history, in order to distinguish friend from foe, an ability which we lacked completely. If a stevedore walked up to me, how would I know if he meant to shake my hand or stick a knife into my stomach?

Eventually, Barker narrowed his search and settled upon the South East India Dock, a branch of the East India surrounded on two sides by five-story warehouses that looked dark and menacing. It was a tea dock, and Ben Tillett was working there. Barker stopped dead in the center of it, among the men moving back and forth unloading a newly arrived clipper from Assam. Raising his arm, he tapped the side of his nose and then led me over to some large crates stacked on one side which screened us from view. Once there, he pulled out his pipe, filled and lit it. It was windy on the dock, and lighting it required hunching over between the crates and applying the vesta quickly. Then he sat patiently and waited. Finally, almost ten minutes later, Ben Tillett slipped in beside us.

"All set?" he asked tensely.

"I was about to ask the same of you," Barker said from around his pipe stem.

"My boys are ready. Will it be here, then?"

"Aye. As good a place as any I've seen. You've spoken to Green?"

"Yes, I have, but I'll have used up all his goodwill if tonight's set-to gets out of hand."

"But that isn't fair," I couldn't help saying. "I mean, the Sicilians have been spoiling for a fight for weeks. You're not responsible for them, or even the workers on the dock. You can't control every fight as if it were a boxing match and you the referee."

"Tell that to Green. He doesn't care for Socialist unionizers like me. We cost him money."

"How many men have committed for tonight, Mr. Tillett?" my employer asked.

"I've got close to a hundred promised, but, to be honest, more like seventy-five will show. Some of them will be talked out of it by their wives. You're certain the Sicilians won't bring shotguns or pistols?"

"I shall challenge them with a debt of honor," Barker responded. "Like a duel, I'll choose the weapon. Make sure your lads have clasp knives, just in case."

"They've got them. When and where shall we meet?"

"Five thirty, in the corner of the warehouse there."

"Right. See you then," Tillett said with a nod, and slipped off.

"Fine man," the Guv said when he was gone. "It's good he's on our side."

"He's a Fabian, you know," I said, needling my employer.

"Aye, well, we can't afford to be choosy just now."

"Do we know how many men we'll have altogether?"

"A little over a hundred, I'd say."

"Will it be enough, do you think?"

"I believe so. The number of Sicilian men willing to fight against us is finite."

"You're sure, then."

"Well, lad, we'll find out, won't we?"

"That's what I'm afraid of."

We went back to the office, where Barker sent off another battery of messages. Then he took out his Chinese brushes and ink. He ground the ink and added water, and then made a note in large block letters:

> SOUTH EAST DOCK
> 6:30 TONIGHT
> NO GUNS, ON YOUR HONOR
> C.B.

This note he put into the hands of Soho Vic, who arrived around four. I knew matters were at a head, for the boy did not try to set my shoe afire or call me inappropriate names. He was more serious than I'd ever seen him.

Barker looked at the boy. "You're certain about this, Vic? It's dangerous going into Clerkenwell just now. I could send the lad to deliver it."

Soho Vic gave me a glare but did not insult me for once. "I'll do it, sir. You can count on me."

"Very well. Take it to the kiosk in front of Saint Peter's Church. No histrionics or displays of bravery, now."

"No, sir."

I doubted Vic knew what "histrionics" were, but he had not been allowed to participate in the previous meeting and this was his only chance to get involved. Unfortunately, one look at the note would tell him when and where the battle was going to take place. He would be in attendance and try to get in a blow or two of his own, if only to be able to brag about it afterward.

"Off with you, then. Use the front door and keep a sharp eye out."

Vic was off like a rabbit. Barker stood and stretched, and

then shot his cuffs. I opened a certain drawer in the right-hand corner of my roll-topped desk.

"Should I bring my pistol just in case?" I asked.

"No, lad. We have given our word."

"Did we promise to not bring them or merely not to use them?"

"If you found you needed it, you would use it," he reasoned.

I shrugged and closed the desk drawer with misgivings. "I suppose you're right, though I'll feel rather naked without it. How do you know they are men of honor? They're Sicilian criminals, after all."

"We don't, but if anyone is found to have violated the terms it will not be us. Besides, I thought you detested firearms," Barker said.

"I do, but not as much as I detest dying."

"You're overfond of your own skin. None of us is indispensable, lad."

"Cheery thought, that," I replied.

Barker reached for his hat and stick.

"Are you coming?"

I heaved a sigh. "Yes, sir," I said. There was no getting out of it.

27

THE SUN WAS STARTING TO SET WHEN WE ARRIVED at South East India Dock. We stood on the dock, surrounded on two sides by warehouses and on the other two by the bristling masts of anchored ships. Narrow alleyways separated one warehouse from another, and cargo was stacked in crates or in odd shapes covered with canvas, dotting the terrain like small mountains. A mass of men, mostly young, milled about at the south end, getting to know each other by sight. I estimated there were close to a hundred of us.

"Are they ready?" Barker asked Tillett.

"Ready enough. They're untested, of course, but they're spoiling for a fight."

"Have you seen any pistols?"

"No, but I'm not about to start searching them, especially not Hooligan's men."

"Point them out to me," Barker said in a low voice, appraising the crowd.

"That big one there," Tillett said, pointing out a tall,

gangly man with his head shorn close like a convict. "And him," he continued, indicating a young man with red hair and evil-looking features, who out of sheer fierceness had torn off the sleeves of his coat and shirt. "Those two," he continued, pointing to a pair of sharp-featured persons, apparently siblings, "and him," he finished, indicating a large African in a checked suit and cloth cap who stood apart with the hauteur of a panther.

"Is that all? Just the five?"

"No, there are more, but the rest are dispersed among mine. There are thirty or so."

"How many in all?"

"A hundred fifteen, give or take half a dozen."

Barker nodded. "Not bad. How are they getting along?"

"Well enough, except for your Frenchmen."

"The Dummolard boys? What's the problem?"

"They've chosen a crate over there as their base of operations and won't take orders from me or anyone."

"You've done good work. Let me handle our apache friends."

Barker moved among the crowd, encouraging them as he went. This was a side of him I hadn't seen before, his military side. I knew he'd seen action in China with Gordon during the Taiping Rebellion.

"Messieurs!" he said to the sour-faced quintet of Frenchmen who sat on a large packing crate, sharpening their knives. "I am glad to see you all here."

"This had better not be a trick, Barker," Robert Dummolard spoke for his brothers. "We expect to see Sicilian blood spilt tonight."

"You will get your chance of that, I'm sure. I want you

to know, however, that I will not simply drop a handkerchief and have you all charge at once. This is a game of strategy."

"Strategy," the Frenchman repeated, spitting upon the dock.

"I am sending Hooligan's Irish lads in first. The five of you will lead the second brigade."

"My brothers demand to go first," the Frenchman insisted.

"You must trust me, Robert. I have Etienne's best interests at heart. There will still be plenty of Sicilians for you to fight. But I hope you have no plans to kill anyone. I cannot shield you from a charge of murder. Remember, they cannot regret what they have done to your brother if they are dead."

Robert turned to his brothers and spoke in French too rapidly for me to follow, telling them no doubt what Barker had said. Immediately there was an uproar among them—angry faces and fingers being pointed. Robert silenced them all with an oath, then spoke in a low voice for a minute or two.

"Very well, monsieur," he said. "We agree to your terms. But we lead the second attack."

"We're glad to have you," the Guv told him.

"There they are!" A voice sounded behind us; and on the other side of the dock, the Sicilians appeared. Ben Tillett jumped up on a crate nearby, and I saw him anxiously counting heads from this higher vantage point. Barker surveyed our opponents with one hand on his hip and an elbow resting on the Dummolards' crate. We all leaned forward to watch our opponents.

"No more than ninety," Tillett cried. "I'd bet my life on it."

A cheer rose up, a waving of belaying pins in the air.

"I doubt it'll be that easy," Patrick Hooligan said behind us. "These Sicilians are crafty devils. Shall I reconnoiter the area to make certain there's not a second band of them lurking about?"

"No," my employer replied calmly. "We'll take them as they come. If they are too strong, or too many, don't hesitate to pull back."

"Don't you worry, Push. But, mind you, when this is over, I expect your help in return. I'll be making a bid for the Isle of Dogs."

"You think you can wrest it from Mr. K'ing's grasp?"

"Why not?" he asked. "The Sicilians were going to do it. I'll crowd the Chinaman into Limehouse, so all he can do is smoke on his opium pipey and cry over what he once had."

Barker nodded and deferred answering for the moment, while I wondered if he was going to give the docks over to Hooligan and his grand ambitions. I thought my employer and K'ing had worked out an understanding between them. The Guv turned and pulled out his watch.

"Mr. Tillett," he rumbled.

"Yes, sir?"

"Yours to command. Come, lad."

"All right, boys," the dock foreman shouted. "I want you in lines of ten. Irish first, Frenchmen next, then you dockworkers. Try not to crowd your neighbors!"

"Where are we going, sir?" I asked, as we skirted the armies and walked beside the warehouses.

"To spy out the leader of the opposing force."

"Is he here, do you think? Marco Faldo?"

"He's here. He's bound to be," the Guv muttered. "Step up, lad."

I hoisted myself onto a crate that would offer a commanding view of the proceedings. The sun had almost gone down, bathing us all in a bloodred glow. Our opponents were not as physically large as some of our lads, but they were tough and wiry; and I saw more than one dagger in their hands.

"My word, it's the man in the cape," I cried, pointing across the dock. He stood, shouting orders; and as he looked across at our forces, I recognized him as the man I'd identified at Scotland Yard. "It's the man who shot Gigliotti. The Bertillon card must have been false."

"Or is that the man?" Barker said, pointing a finger of his own. In the rear of the army stood another caped figure, issuing final instructions to the men there.

"Twins!" I cried.

"The Bertillon card was not wrong. Scotland Yard arrested the wrong brother. I suspected there were two of them all along. The measurements were wrong because the twins were born mirror imaged. It's time," he stated, looking at his watch. "Six thirty sharp."

We watched as Ben Tillett crossed the empty dock between the two armies before he came to a stop in the middle. A moment later the first assassin stepped out to meet him. As he approached, he recognized me and gave me a nod.

"Are you ready?" I heard Tillett ask. We had a good

vantage point, with both men almost directly in front of us.

"Very ready, signor," the caped man answered. "The question is, are you ready?"

"We are. May we have your word you have no fire-arms?"

The Sicilian shook his head. "No firearms. We don't need them to teach a few Englishmen a lesson."

The two men turned and walked back to their armies. I could feel the tension in the air. Tillett turned and pointed at the Sicilians with his belaying pin. He bawled a sound, unin-telligible to my ear, and Hooligan's gang bellowed it back. They charged past him, weapons raised. Somewhere in the very middle I saw Patrick Hooligan, looking like he was hav-ing the time of his life.

The Sicilians did not charge, but waited upon events, which worried me. What did they have up their sleeves? I found out as soon as the Irish crashed into the enemy lines. Or didn't crash at all, actually. To a man, they came to a stop and abruptly turned around, with crafty smiles on their faces. Hooligan and his boys had gone with the higher bid-der. They were deserters. I should have remembered my history. If memory serves, the Irish played this same trick against Edward Longshanks six hundred years ago.

"We've been outfoxed, sir," I yelled. "Now what do we do? We're outnumbered by dozens!"

"We accept it and move on," Barker answered. He called to the caped Sicilians, "You may have them, sirs. We have no need of turncoats."

Tillett bellowed again, and a second later the assassins gave answering cries. Our army trotted forward, led by the

Dummolards, who waved daggers in the air. The two sides crashed together in front of us, with the sound of wood against wood and body against body. There were cries and groans. Weapons fell to the ground and were quickly picked up, and knives slashed at human flesh.

"Come, lad," Barker said, jumping off the crate into the thick of the battle. The first *mafiusu* he encountered he spun around and dropped upon the pavement.

I knew better than to think I was going to be merely a spectator. I jumped down, avoided a blade aimed in my direction, and brought the brass ball of my malacca cane down upon the shoulder of my assailant. It wasn't quite enough to stop him, so I tried it again; and when he raised his arm to protect himself, I smote him in the ribs.

Just then a board broke over my left elbow, rendering it momentarily numb. I kicked out at a knee, however, and knocked the fellow down; but there was another to take his place. And another. I was quickly surrounded by fighting men.

As I fought with a Sicilian dockworker armed with a marlinespike, he suddenly tripped beside a large crate, falling heavily to the dock. I was debating whether to give him a kick when he gave a sharp cry and was pulled backward under a side of the crate. Over the fighting, I thought I heard a sound of pounding beneath us. Stepping around the side of the crate, I found a knothole and peered inside. Then I spoke into it.

"Nice factory you've got here, Vic. How many have your boys caught so far?"

"Free," came the response, "but I 'ope to improve if you'll quit discouraging customers by 'angin' 'roun' me box, fathead. Unless you'd like to step in front and investigate the operation first'and. Otherwise, hop it!"

I had to hand it to Soho Vic. He's very resourceful. I couldn't fathom how he knew about the empty crate so quickly after Barker had chosen this dock. Somehow he'd found a way to even the odds for his gang. He didn't go out into their dangerous world. He dragged people into his. I debated informing Barker, knowing he didn't want Soho Vic or his boys on the dock. However, the brawl was far from over yet.

Ahead of me, Barker almost seemed to be enjoying himself, disarming Sicilians and bringing them down. I've always wondered how a man who spends most of his evenings immersed in prayer so well enjoyed a pitched battle against other human beings. He seemed to achieve some sort of release by it.

I'd brought down four men so far, putting them all out of commission. The Guv had not yet trained me in fighting two men at once, as he could; but as long as I took them on one at a time I was doing all right.

Barker suddenly stuffed two fingers under his mustache and blew a shrill whistle. Abruptly, a barge that was standing alongside the dock spewed sailors—dozens of them— out onto the deck. One man rested a long limb against the rail and surveyed the scene with an air of command. It was Peter Beauchamp, here to lend a hand. Barker must have known that Hooligan was not to be trusted days before, and had planned accordingly. I saw relief on the faces of Barker's men and renewed vigor against their opponents.

My employer had almost reached the spot where the Sicilian twins were battering our men to the ground with ebony canes. I was busy knocking the legs out from under a new acquaintance, when a hand seized my collar from behind, and I felt cold metal against the back of my neck. I recognized the barrel of a pistol when I felt one.

"No guns!" I protested hotly, looking over my shoulder. Then I gasped. It took a moment for my brain to verify what my eyes were seeing.

28

⚜

"INSPECTOR PETTIGRILLI?" I ASKED. "YOU'RE ALIVE?"

"No, lad," Barker called behind me. "This is Marco Faldo."

The Sicilian nodded, his pistol barrel still pressed against my neck. "Very good, Mr. Barker. I see you did not fall for my little ruse."

"I did," the Guv admitted, "for a time, at least."

By now the twin killers had fought off other opponents and were standing on either side of my employer, ready to do battle. He looked at them appraisingly.

"Lad, your stick," Barker called.

I tossed him my brass-headed malacca, and he caught it in his left hand, still holding his cane in his right. Barker, I realized, was about to square off against two skilled assassins at once. I wasn't sure if it was possible to defeat them both, even for one as trained as my employer. I dared take one step in his direction.

"Mr. Llewelyn," Faldo warned, "I would not hesitate to blow your brains out through a small hole in the front of your skull."

I stopped. There was nothing I could do—not yet, anyway.

The brothers began to circle Barker, looking for a weak spot to attack. It has been my experience that when it comes to fighting, he doesn't have one, but he's not above giving a false impression in order to bring on an attack. Both brothers closed in at once, raising their sticks to strike, and the fight began.

Cyrus Barker blocked both blows and then attacked, but his reach was not long enough. Caught between them, he could fight only within a limited half circle, whereas they had the full length of their bodies, six feet or so, in which to swing an arc. Barker fended off each new blow, but even as I thought this, the silver ball of a stick struck him on the shoulder, making him wince. It didn't stop him, however, but made him change positions with his back to me.

They attacked again, the exchange coming so swiftly that I couldn't see it. The assassins' sticks were silver arcs in the moonlight, spinning dangerously close to my employer. One of the brothers came too close and received an elbow in the face that drew blood. He wiped it with a handkerchief, and then gave a tug on his stick, pulling out a sword that must have been the weapon used on Etienne Dummolard. His brother followed suit and now, Barker faced not two weapons but four.

"That's not fair!" I cried, but a clap on the head from the butt of Faldo's pistol was all the response I received.

Barker was hard-pressed on both sides as the brothers moved as if they had one mind between them. I thought it likely that they must have trained together for hours every day to be so good. The Guv was defending himself adequately so far, but it could not go on much longer. He would soon be overwhelmed. One of the brothers pressed forward but was rebuffed again. He dared press a second time. Then Barker raised a foot and brought it around behind the other, almost too quickly for my eye to follow. It caught one brother on the knee as he was retreating, and there was an audible snap as it broke. I wouldn't have noticed the move if Barker hadn't once shown it to me and tried to teach me its mechanics. The shadowless kick, it's called, one of those mystical names the Chinese find so attractive. The injured man fell back with a look of pain and consternation; but Barker moved toward him, pulling him forward as a shield, just as his brother drove home his blade. It went through the man's upper chest, possibly puncturing a lung. Then my employer seized the sword from nerveless fingers and lunged forward, driving the blade through the side of the remaining brother, tenting the fabric of his cape behind. The Guv stood as both adversaries fell to the ground at his feet, too injured to fight any longer.

Faldo's pistol came away from my head, and I knew he was about to shoot Barker. I raised my left arm to keep him from aiming, the dagger in my sleeve giving added force to the block. The pistol went off by my ear, but I seized his wrist and we struggled together. I had promised Mrs. Ashleigh that I would look after my employer. I wasn't about to let go. The Sicilian tried to push his weapon toward me so it would discharge in my face, while I tried the same thing with him. I struggled into a position where I could flip him, when something fluttered by my head. A length of rope wrapped around Faldo's wrist, jerking his gun away. I recognized that rope, but it took a few seconds to recall just where. It was part of Ho's rope dart. The Chinaman stood in an alley a few yards away, attempting to control Faldo's arm with his long length of rope.

Marco Faldo was a powerful man, as I soon found out. He strained against both of us, trying to switch his gun to his other hand and fire again. Ho pulled the rope, and I hung onto Faldo's arm for dear life, but the Sicilian was still able to raise both arms over my head and transfer the pistol to his left hand. I leapt for the other arm now, but I was too slow. The pistol went off and Barker grabbed his shoulder with a grunt.

We both had our hands on the pistol now, and it wavered back and forth in an arc with Barker at its center. There were crates nearby, but I realized they were too far away for him to dive behind. I pulled Faldo's hand down hard toward my own stomach, thrusting it into the pocket of my waistcoat. If he wanted to shoot Barker again he was going to have to kill me first. Faldo had untangled himself from Ho's rope and was now using his free hand to tear at my newly plastered cut. Blood trickled down my cheek and into my eye. Clumsily, I tripped over Faldo's foot and staggered to the side. I was going to fail in my mission to save Barker.

Suddenly I felt the Mafia leader jump once, twice, thrice. I heard the shots after, and turned to Barker in wonder as the man I was grappling with sagged, but the Guv had only our sticks in his hands and was looking behind me. I let Faldo fall to the dock and turned awkwardly. Ten feet away, pistol still aimed toward me, stood Terence Poole. It took a moment for my mind to register what had happened. First, Ho had come out of nowhere, then the inspector. Where had they come from? It didn't matter. I was never so glad to see the inspector in my life.

Suddenly police whistles were sounding everywhere, and men on both sides scurried away like rats. Constables were laying about right and left with their truncheons, and I heard the clicks of derbies being applied to wrists.

"It's a good thing you finally moved," Poole commented to me, opening his regulation pistol and shaking out the cartridges. "I was about to think I'd have to shoot through you."

Barker handed me my cane, and we both pulled hand-kerchiefs from our breast pockets, I to stanch my cheek and he his shoulder. "It's just a scratch," he said. "That was a close thing, lad. Why ever did you get in the way?"

"Get in the way?" I shouted. "Get in the way? I was just trying to save your life, is all! I didn't know you and Ho had this set up between you." I turned to Inspector Poole. "Were you in on this as well? Of course you were. Did everyone know what was going to happen but me?"

"He's babbling," Barker commented to Poole. "It's shock."

"Is that Chinaman here?" the inspector asked, looking about. He'd have loved to arrest Ho, whose association with Mr. K'ing made him suspect; but the restaurant owner had vanished, as stealthily as he had come, taking his rope dart with him.

"No," Barker said innocently. "Of course not."

"Do you plan to explain to me how the late Inspector Pettigrilli was suddenly alive again and how I've managed to shoot a guest of this country and a brother officer?"

"You may relax, Terence," the Guv replied. "This is not Alberto Pettigrilli. This, in fact, was the notorious *mafiusu*,

Marco Faldo. You've not only stopped a dispute on the docks but also silenced a dangerous criminal."

Poole wasn't quite buying this pat answer. He crossed his arms and looked at my employer skeptically.

"So, you pulled it off, did you? You and the nipper, here?"

"I have a name, you know," I insisted, "a perfectly good one."

"I'll learn it someday when I can spare the time," Poole said.

Barker reached into his pocket and filled his pipe with tobacco while Poole rolled his eyes. It seemed to me the little meerschaum effigy of its master was smirking at me, but perhaps it was only a shadow. Barker lit a match, not hurrying, and set about properly igniting his pipe before blowing out the match.

"I'm just a citizen who saw a potential dispute at the docks and did his duty by alerting the police. I'd prefer to remain anonymous in this matter, if you don't mind. As far as I'm concerned, the Yard lost Pettigrilli, and the Yard tracked him down again. My agency had nothing to do with the matter."

"You nearly got yourself killed instead," Poole said.

Barker puffed calmly on his pipe. While our backs were turned, most of the dockworkers had melted away. Some had jumped in the river. The South East India Dock was full of constables arresting Sicilians.

" 'Pon my soul, Terry. You're a dour man for someone who's just saved London from being overrun with killers."

"Don't try to play me, Cyrus. You haven't told me everything about this, yet."

"I'll tell you all you need to know," Barker offered, "but

it's thirsty work, and these river vapors are doing no good for the lad's throat."

"Blast the lad's poxy throat," Terence Poole said suspiciously. "What did you have in mind?"

"I've heard that the Bread and Treacle serves a very tolerable porter not two streets from here. It's more comfortable than the interrogation room in A Division."

Poole frowned. His hands were still on his hips as if welded there and his nostrils flared as if he smelled something unpleasant. Finally he licked his lips.

"Done," he relented, "against my better judgment. Let me speak to my sergeant and I'll meet you there. I suppose after an evening like this, a pint of good English porter couldn't hurt anything."

29

⁓⬤⬤⬤⁓

So," TERENCE POOLE SAID, SETTING A HALF PINT of porter in front of Barker and full ones in front of himself and me. The Guv had a reputation once as a villainous drinker and was careful now where alcohol was concerned. "This was your bright idea, was it, to stage a labor battle on the docks?"

"Let us say, it was to coordinate a *staged* labor battle on the docks."

"You tipped the Yard that it was going to take place?" I asked, still irritated at being left out of the plans.

"Oh, aye. They arrived by steam launch, with the aid of the river police," he replied, and took a drink, leaving foam on his mustache.

"But to everyone on the docks it looks like the Metropolitan Police staged a raid instead of you," I said.

"Exactly. I thought it was important that Scotland Yard get the credit for this, to discourage any other *mafiusi* from moving north."

"Well, I'll certainly give them the credit," I said. "Thank you for saving my skin, Inspector."

"It was nothing," Poole said, "but why were you trying to get yourself killed? I swear I saw you jamming that man's pistol barrel into your waistcoat pocket!"

I thought back to a recent sunny day in Sussex. "Keeping a promise I made to a woman," I replied.

"What did she ask—that you sacrifice yourself?"

"Something like that."

Poole put a sudden hand to his stomach and made a sour face. The porter was not doing good things to his ulcer.

"It was a good thing Mr. Barker had the situation under control," I said.

"Here now," Poole objected, "we weren't exactly sitting on our hands. We have an inspector in Clerkenwell who is an expert on Italian culture, and a team of plainclothes C.I.D. officers in the area. We were on top of the situation."

"Did you suspect Pettigrilli was a fake?"

"No," the inspector admitted. "But we had tracked his cohorts to a flat in Clerkenwell Close. Oh, and I deduced that the assassins were twins. It wasn't merely that the measurements were wrong, but they were nearly reversed. We've seen that sort of thing before. So, what exactly did you do to them?" he said, turning to the Guv. "Will they live?"

"They've both been stabbed," Barker said. "And I broke the kneecaps of one."

"You were gentle with them, then."

"I wanted them in good enough condition to be questioned about Faldo. I didn't know you were going to shoot him."

"Who else did you capture?" I asked the inspector.

"Patrick Hooligan, for one. We've had an outstanding warrant for him. He'll see at least a year in jail. The rest are mostly Sicilian."

"Any Frenchmen?" I asked.

"I believe we did catch a few Frenchies, yes."

"Those are Dummolard's brothers."

"No special treatment," Barker said, sipping his half pint.

"How many did you get in all?"

"I don't know. A few dozen. A good many of them jumped into the canal and swam through the basin into the river."

"So there was never to be a full-out fight at all," I said to my employer. "It was a feint to make the Sicilian leader show himself."

"Exactly. Tomorrow, the newspapers will announce that Scotland Yard broke up a fight on the docks between two groups of casual laborers, during which a dangerous Sicilian criminal, Marco Faldo, who had masqueraded as Inspector Pettigrilli of the Palermo police, was shot and killed."

"What of the fact that he killed Sir Alan and the Serafinis?"

"That need not come out, I think. Don't you agree, Inspector?"

"Yes. There's no need to bring Bledsoe's name into a murder investigation. When did you first suspect Pettigrilli was a fake?"

"I suspected when he was found with his head conveniently blown off, but I was not convinced until you showed me that letter from the Palermo police, expressing their regret over the loss of *Alberto* Pettigrilli."

"What did that have to do with anything?"

"He told us at Scotland Yard that his given name was Umberto."

Poole raised a hand to his long, ginger-colored sidewhiskers and looked in danger of pulling them out. "I missed that," he admitted.

"So where is the real Pettigrilli?" I asked.

"Long dead, I'm afraid," Barker said. "I'll wager Faldo assassinated the inspector on the boat to France and assumed his identity. It was an excellent cover, and he must have laughed to himself when the Sûreté took him at face value and began to train him under Alphonse Bertillon himself."

"If his system makes any actual sense, I'll eat my hat," Poole said.

"Sir Francis Galton swears that the markings on the tips of the fingers can be used to identify a criminal," Barker said, "but his theories are often unreliable."

"I certainly don't believe in eugenics," I put in. "No doubt he considers Scots and Welshmen little more advanced than red Indians."

"That makes perfect sense to me," Poole pronounced, looking down his slightly pointed English nose at us.

"It would. So who was found dead in the cab with the constable?"

"The wound was so fresh, the victim must have been one of Faldo's associates, dressed in identical clothing. He'd planned the whole thing down to the last detail, and he was ruthless."

"Why didn't you suspect anyone else of the crimes?"

"I did," Barker said. "I suspected everyone for a time. Give me some examples."

"The Gigliottis."

"Victor Gigliotti didn't want competition from the Sicilians—and he was a reasonable suspect—but he had everything to lose by getting involved with them. His small empire was what Faldo was after in the first place—complete power over the Italian community. Had he succeeded, he'd have taken over the ice factory and the hokeypokey carts, and been producing an income within the week. He would have taken over the other Italian enterprises—the docks and the cafés—and then I imagine he would have purchased influence among the gambling fraternity, both boxing and horse racing. Coming from Palermo, where several families are jockeying for positions of power, he must have felt it would be an easy task with only the Gigliottis to oppose him."

"He was awfully heavy-handed," I said. "All those threatening notes and murders."

"He was not faint of heart," the Guv agreed.

"So what about Hooligan? How was he involved? And how did you know he would become a turncoat?"

"In his position, it made sense. He wanted to control the East End. If he allied himself with Faldo, they could have brought down the Chinese power base together; and as his lieutenant, Hooligan might have been placed in charge of it. Of course, if I know him, his next step would have been to kill Faldo."

"I doubt he would have succeeded there," I said. "Perhaps putting him in jail is more of a kindness than he would have given himself. He'd have been as dead as Gigliotti within the year."

"You'd have a hard time convincing him of that," Poole said. "The Hooley Gang is without a leader now. It will either choose a new one or disband."

"Did you ever suspect Gallenga?" I asked my employer.

"Of course," he replied. "Once one is a member of the Honored Society, one never leaves it."

"Who is this Gallenga fellow?" Poole asked quickly.

"He was a radical in his youth and a supporter of Mazzini's Young Italy party, but his recent years have been spent as a correspondent with *The Times* and an expert on Italian matters. He has recently left London."

Poole finished his pint and called for another, but one was my limit and I was but halfway through it.

"The Sicilian threat is done, then," the inspector finally said. "There are no more criminals among the Italians now, correct?"

"No more so than among any other group of people in London. Their youth are high-spirited and liable to get into trouble, but there is no organized crime."

"What of the Camorra?"

"It is broken," Barker pronounced. "Vincenzo Gigliotti will have his hands full running the factory and the businesses. Unless Palermo sends another would-be Napoleon our way, I suspect Clerkenwell shall be quiet enough for a while."

"I could do with quiet," Poole said.

"So could I," I said, raising my glass. "Here's to quiet."

Our glasses clinked and we each took a long sip, though I wondered exactly what Mr. Anderson would have to say about Scotland Yard getting all the glory.

30

I GAVE A LONG, SHUDDERING SIGH AND LET MY
body float in the bathhouse behind my employer's house.
I lay to the side, my head resting on a towel on the cedar
slats, but my limbs were buoyant due to the Epsom salts
Mac had thoughtfully put in the water. The salts stung a
little, for I had sustained a half dozen cuts and bruises during the last week; but taken altogether, it felt marvelous.
Give me a comfortable bathhouse over a dockside any
day.

Barker suddenly breached like a sperm whale. He didn't
even remove his spectacles when he went underwater. He
stood and waded to the side, where he dried himself, sitting
on the ledge.

"You should get that looked after," I said, regarding the
bullet wound near his shoulder. "It could go septic."

"I'll have Mac disinfect and bandage it in the morning,"
he said, drying his arms. He stretched and gave a yawn.

"It's finally over," I remarked. "Another successful case."

"It's a wee bit early for that, lad. Let's wait to hear from Mr. Anderson."

"To what could he object?" I countered. "True, Scotland Yard got involved at the last minute, but surely the government knows we were working for the Home Office."

"I've never known a Home Office man who was completely satisfied about anything."

I stood up, because I was getting a crick in my neck. "Let them fight their own battles, then. I doubt we shall clear expenses when the check finally arrives."

"It's not always about the money, lad."

"It is for me. I've got a burial to pay for."

Barker soaked his feet in the warm water. "There is a streak of pessimism in you."

"It comes from the Llewelyns having their kingdom taken away, I suppose."

"Aye, well, you don't see me crying over Culloden." He stood and pulled on one of the thick white robes. That's Barker all over. Be optimistic and he cautions you. Be pessimistic and he'll blame your entire race. I got out and threw on my own robe, following him into the garden.

"At least the heat is past," I remarked, as I hopped across the white gravel that the Guv's gardeners were obliged to rake every couple of days. One of the black ornamental stones suddenly moved. I reached down and scratched one of Harm's ears, to stop him from biting my exposed ankles. It was cool enough for me to wish I'd dried myself more thoroughly before venturing outside.

"Are you going down to Sussex tomorrow?" I asked.

"I'll go soon," he said. "She'll expect a report."

I nodded and left it at that. I wouldn't pester him with more questions, nor would I invite myself along. If he wanted me to come, he would ask me.

My employer walked barefoot across the bridge and past the standing rocks to the corner where his potted Pen-jing trees stood on shelves against a slatted wall. It was dark here, but he stuck his fingers into the soil of each. He must have considered them dry because he took up a watering can and plied it thoroughly. Then he gave a low whistle to Harm and led us into the house.

"Nice that the garden is safe again," I said.

"Do you think we should fortify the back gate?" he asked.

It occurred to me that it was the first time he had actually asked my opinion on something. "No," I replied after a moment. "It would ruin the aesthetics. Leave it as it is, I think. We can chase out whatever pests get in."

Barker nodded and went upstairs, the dog tucked under his arm. I locked the door behind us and followed him.

The next morning, our lives had returned to normal, that is, the part of our lives that was like everyone else's. We got up, dressed for church, and walked across the street to the Metropolitan Tabernacle. Or at least we tried. There was an obstacle between us and the tabernacle. It was Vincenzo Gigliotti, resplendent in a morning suit with a white boutonniere. He had not come to sell ice cream that day, but was waiting to speak to Barker. My employer frowned. He does not like to be diverted from a mission, which at that moment was to get to chapel on time and into our accustomed pew.

"Mr. Barker," Gigliotti said, bowing slightly.

"You are not at mass this morning, sir?" the Guv asked, nodding his head.

"I am too occupied with arrangements. I bury my son tomorrow."

"I will miss Victor and our little talks. Will the Neapolitan remain open?"

"For a while, at least. I understand that you have killed the man responsible for Victor's death and that of the Serafinis."

"It was Scotland Yard who killed him," Barker pointed out.

"Oh, come," he objected, as if my employer were merely being modest. "They are but hounds that bite whom you tell them to. I merely wish to inform you that the Camorra is satisfied and our vendetta ended. There will be no reprisal here against any Sicilians, unless they cause a new outrage."

"That is for the best," Barker stated. "Your community is too small to be divided into factions."

"I believe Father Amati is satisfied with the outcome of this situation, save for the loss of my son."

"How is your grandson?"

"He has retreated into himself. His mother is trying to teach him not to nurse anger in his heart, but Victor's death has been a cruel blow to us all. I am glad my wife is not alive to see it."

"And who shall run the Camorra now that Victor is gone?"

"That mantle is on my shoulders now. I gave it to him and now it comes back to me again."

"It was a dangerous business he was in," Barker said.

"It is a dangerous world, Mr. Barker."

"I'll not argue the point, sir. Is there another question I can answer for you? We must get to chapel."

"Just one. These brothers, twins. I understand they actually killed Victor."

"Aye. Both are seriously injured. I understand Scotland Yard is watching them carefully. Do you intend to go against them?"

Gigliotti frowned. "We have not decided. Are you still involved in this?"

"No, my involvement is at an end."

I watched Gigliotti nod in thought. The truce with the Sicilians did not extend to the man who killed his son.

"Give our respects to your family," the Guv said, tugging the brim of his bowler.

We parted company with Mr. Gigliotti. When he was gone, Barker turned to me. "The Camorra is dead, or very nearly. Most of their members joined because of Victor's passion. With him gone, Vincenzo will most likely devote all his energy toward protecting his family."

"Forgive me for asking, sir, but you didn't plan this in any way, did you?"

"No, Victor brought it down upon his own shoulders. You saw him challenge the Sicilians openly on the docks. Why do you ask?"

"Everything worked to our advantage. You didn't just

bring down one criminal organization, you brought down three: the Mafia, the Camorra, and the Hooley Gang, since Patrick is bound for prison."

The Guv gave a wintry smile. "Thomas, sometimes the best defense is simply to step out of the way and wait for the smoke to clear."

31

Monday morning came all too soon. I got out of bed through sheer determination, shaved and dressed, and made my way downstairs. I went into the kitchen, poured myself a cup of coffee, and took it to the deal table.

"You need eggs with that," Etienne Dummolard stated critically. He was leaning against the stove with a cup of his own.

"Etienne! You're back!"

Warmed by my response, Dummolard spat on the floor and lit one of his short French cigarettes. *Now we can have proper meals again,* I thought. No more rubber ham, hard cheese, and pickled onions.

"I'm glad they released you," I told him.

"They didn't. I snook out. That is good English, right? To snook?"

"Perfectly good," I replied.

"I could take no more idiotic doctors and Mireille and Clothilde fussing over me. They buy half the flowers in Covent Garden. I hate flowers to death. What are they for? You cannot eat them. They die in a day. They are a complete waste of money."

"Hear, hear."

"Do you happen to know," he asked, casually cracking eggs against the side of a bowl, "where my brothers are this morning?"

"Well . . ."

"Has your brain stopped working, Thomas?" he snapped. "It is a simple enough question. Where are my brothers?"

"I imagine they are still in jail. I heard they were put in darbies night before last."

Etienne stood with his back to me, mixing the eggs. He stopped suddenly and then started again. He was going to explode any moment, I thought. Really, I had enough troubles of my own. I didn't need the ill humor of my employer's cook right after a harrowing case. Then Dummolard made a sound in his throat that resolved itself into chuckling.

"You're not angry?"

"It is where they belong," he said. "Good riddance. They are criminals. I hope they are deported back to France. I never asked them to come to my rescue, and I did not require their help."

He poured the mixture into a pan already starting to bubble with butter. My stomach rumbled with anticipation. The things Etienne Dummolard can do with a common egg are miraculous. He began chopping chives and herbs from the garden that had been drying on a rack overhead, humming a tune to himself. It must have felt good to return to the work one was destined for.

In two minutes, he slid the plate in front of me. I ate as he watched, and made all the appreciative noises I knew. It was perfect, as always. Who could imagine that an oafish, bearlike Frenchman could produce such delicacies? Dummolard brought us each a fresh cup of coffee and then lit another cigarette.

"What happened the other night?" he asked.

I outlined the entire case. It took me almost twenty minutes. Outside the window, the Guv's Chinese gardeners were discussing the state of the garden, but my employer was not among them. He'd been injured and had worked long hours on this case. If he were having a lie-in, he deserved one.

Dummolard brayed out a laugh. "You, hanging there on the end of his arm with his pistol stuck in the pocket of your waistcoat? Very droll, Thomas."

"I didn't intend it to end that way, it just happened."

"I am sorry I did not get to see it."

Suddenly Mac put his head in the door. "The Guv's got a visitor. They're going into the garden right now."

"Who is it?" I asked.

"It's Mr. Anderson of the Home Office."

Etienne and I looked out the window. My employer and the spymaster were near the back gate, where the standard tour was still in progress. I don't know whether the spymaster had any interest in gardening, but Barker's is certainly unique, at least in this part of the world. By the time I caught up with them, they were stepping into the shade of the pavilion.

"Sorry I'm late, gentlemen," I said. "How is your shoulder today, sir?"

"It's fine, Mr. Llewelyn, little more than a scratch. I've received worse during a sparring match."

"I understand you nearly had it worse," Anderson said to me. "Did you really jam the man's pistol into your waistcoat pocket?"

"Well, sir, I've always found my gun a nuisance, getting caught when I pull it out of my pocket; and waistcoat pockets are a bother, as well. I'm always getting a key caught in the lining. When Faldo shot at Barker, I thought I'd jam the barrel into my pocket before he shot a second time."

"But what was to stop him from shooting you?"

"I knew that shooting me was no guarantee he could get to my employer any more quickly. He would still have to extricate the barrel from my pocket, and by then the Guv would have had him."

"It was still a plucky thing to do. You're a brave little fellow." Everyone thinks that's a compliment, but it only points out my size, as if it's remarkable that any person my height would dare attempt anything.

"I assume, Mr. Anderson," Barker said, "that you had an informant on the dock who witnessed the fight last night."

"Yes, indeed. He said I missed one of the most entertaining events he'd ever seen. He was particularly impressed with how you conjured a ship full of men when you found yourselves outnumbered."

"I thought it likely Mr. Hooligan would double-cross me. It's like him to go with the winning side, having a desire to get ahead and not being burdened with any type of scruple, like the rest of us."

"I noticed that most of the Sicilians were captured, as was your Mr. Hooligan and his men, while few of your men were found to arrest, save a group of Frenchmen who put up a stiff fight. If they can prove that they are legally in the country and are not agitators, they can stay. Hooligan is in jail this morning, and the rest are being questioned. If they are here illegally, however, I'm afraid we'll have to ship them to the Continent."

"Is that fair, do you think?" Barker asked in a neutral tone.

"It is expedient. We don't have time to take each case individually. Some don't speak English and some are obviously criminals. They'll get a fair trial with a barrister to defend them. Both of you know that some will be back in London within the month."

"It is not perfect, but I suppose it's the most they can expect."

"Vito Moroni passed away from his wounds this morning. His brother, Stefano, with the broken leg is still in the infirmary at Wormwood Scrubs. What did you do to his leg, by the way? Our man said he suddenly went down."

"A little method I learned in Canton," Barker said. "It was good to see it's still effective."

"I gather those gents have been sticking those blades of theirs into dozens of poor fellows across Europe. It was a fitting end for Vito, and perhaps his brother will learn something from it. He's still young, barely thirty."

"What about Marco Faldo?"

"His file arrived by the last post Saturday, too late to be of any use to us. It made for excellent reading, but I cannot say it would have been of great help. He had above-average intelligence, but he was still a brute. He grew up on the streets of Palermo after his father died and was arrested half a dozen times for extortion and assault. His reputation for ruthlessness helped him rise through the ranks. It's believed he beat a policeman to death with the butt of his pistol, and he would have swung for it if the principal witness hadn't recanted his testimony. Since then, he's had several arrests but no convictions for the same reason. There's a lot in there about Pettigrilli's attempts to incarcerate him, poor chap."

"Have you wired the Palermo police about the inspector's fate?"

"I have. So far, there's been no response. I'm certain it must be a cruel blow for the department, let alone his wife and family."

"What's to become of the bodies?" I asked.

"They'll be buried here at government expense."

"A better fate than Pettigrilli's," Barker growled. "His body was probably tossed overboard."

"I imagine the police there will hold a memorial service for him," Anderson said. "The city needs its heroes to carry on the fight. To think that could have been London. Would you say there will be more men like Marco Faldo, exporting crime from Sicily?"

"It seems inevitable. If Faldo had not been a criminal, he could have challenged Gigliotti in business and brought him down that way. His methods will be picked up by someone else and exported elsewhere. Given the right conditions, it will flourish."

"Heaven help the world, then," Anderson said.

"I hope you don't mind taking joint credit with Scotland Yard over this matter," Barker said. "It was the only way to keep us from remaining in custody."

"When my superiors read my report, there will be no

question over who actually pulled this thing off," the Home Office man replied. "A check will be sent to you very shortly."

Presumably he found our performance satisfactory. The remuneration from the government probably wouldn't begin to pay for all our expenses, let alone the personal debt Barker owed to men like Tillett and Beauchamp, but it would recompense our efforts, at least. Barker walked Anderson to the front door and returned.

"That's it, then," I said. "He went for it."

"You make it sound as if we were trying to trick him," he said, pulling his walking stick out of the hall stand. "We accomplished all he asked of us, though not necessarily in the manner he might have imagined."

We hailed a cab and rode to our office in Whitehall. I feel curiously deflated after a case is done.

Barker chose a pipe from the cabinet, stuffed it full from the jar that bore the legend *Tabac,* and lit it with a match from the small ceramic striker. He hooked his ankles on a corner of his desk and looked out the window, which was flooding the chamber with light. There was nothing to see but a bare, brick wall opposite, unless one stepped to the window, but he continued staring, as he filled the chamber with his tobacco smoke. I gathered my notes from the case and began putting them in some semblance of order prior to typing a full report for our files.

"Lad," the Guv rumbled, "I wish to speak with you."

"Sir?" I asked, putting down my notes. I had no idea what he would say. He could have spoken with me in the cab but preferred the formality of our chambers.

"Thomas, I wish to tell you that your apprenticeship is now over. As far as I am concerned, and my judgment is the only one required, you are now a journeyman in the field. I believe you've shown yourself knowledgeable and proficient in the skills of the profession."

I have to admit I was taken aback. I suppose I should have realized that my apprenticeship would not last forever, but I wasn't expecting this.

"Thank you, sir," I said. "Is there some sort of test to take or license needed in order to become a journeyman?"

"No, lad," Barker said. "Her Majesty's government does not recognize our profession. Even when you have become an enquiry agent, there will be no license, no letters after your name. If you wish, Mr. Jenkins could make up a diploma for you, but we both know it's just a piece of paper. We among the enquiry profession regulate ourselves, and I am able to say that you have completed the first leg of your training successfully."

I wanted to say something brilliant and professional just then but couldn't think of anything. It was just as well, for Barker went on.

"You will still have the position of assistant, of course. When you're completely trained, have some seasoning, and have accrued enough money in your account, we may discuss the subject of your buying into partnership with me, but that is still many years from now. However, I have a question for you."

What was he going to ask? He puffed a time or two on that dratted pipe of his. If I moved forward another half inch on my chair, I'd fall off.

Barker cleared his throat. "Mr. Llewelyn, I understand fully the circumstances of your hire—that you were going to throw yourself into the Thames if you were not gainfully employed, that you considered yourself a failed scholar, and that this was the only position available to someone with a criminal background such as yours. In short, you came here out of desperation. Now you are desperate no longer. You have earned enough to move your late wife's remains to a proper site; you could if you so chose send money to your family in Wales and still live well here. I provide your room and board and training. I would be content to continue training you as my assistant, Thomas, but I would not have you here against your will. If you wish to become a clerk or private secretary, or even a poet, now is the time to do so. I can offer a letter of recommendation that should offset your criminal record, in certain circles, at least. I could even get you an interview or two. Your skills in shorthand, typing, orthography, and organization are exemplary; and you don't have to be prompted to do anything. If you wish to leave my employment, now is the time. Of course, if you go, I shall miss our conversations and training together, but we shall both move on. However, if you stay, I shall rely on you more fully; and were you to leave then, or grow dissatisfied with your work, you would throw this agency into turmoil. Do you understand?"

"Yes, sir," I said, though my tongue felt as if it were stuck in my mouth.

"So, what's it to be, then? Will you be signing on for another voyage?"

I didn't hesitate or even consider. "I will, sir. I'm afraid I'm ruined for any other kind of work now. I don't want to sit in an office and fill out forms on a chancery case that has been going on for decades when I could be saving some person's life or helping stop a crime from occurring. Two weeks with nothing but accounts in front of me and I would run mad."

Barker actually chuckled. "Very well. I'm giving you a raise of five pounds a month. Also, if we open this school of which you and Terry Poole are so enamored, I expect you to run the operations and act as junior instructor. That is, if we stay open very long. You shall be paid for that as well, but you must sacrifice some of that free time you cherish so. Do you understand?"

"Yes, sir."

"Good. That's settled. How are you coming along with the notes on the Sicilian case?"

"I'm just getting started," I said.

Barker tsked me. Now that I was in his clutches completely, I could expect no more panegyrics on my exemplary performance.

"Really, you had a full day of idleness yesterday to work on it."

"Sorry, sir. I don't know what I was thinking. I won't let it happen again." One of the good points about working for Cyrus Barker is that sarcasm soars right over his head.

"See that it doesn't. I suggest you— Yes, Jeremy?"

Jenkins came into the room.

"A visitor for you, sir," he said. "Rather impatient, too."

My employer and I looked at each other, and we both gave a short sigh. We no sooner finish a case than another one crops up. There is no peace for the wicked, as Spurgeon is fond of quoting.

"Show him in," Barker said, putting his pipe in the ashtray.

And so it began again.

ACKNOWLEDGMENTS

As always, I have been aided and abetted by my wife, Julia, and daughters, Caitlin and Heather. I also appreciate the staff of the Tulsa City-County Library who tracked down information on the early methods of the Sicilian Mafia.

I owe a special debt to the late Pat Berry of the Seaford Historical Society, Sussex. She provided me with more information on the south coast than I could possibly use, and encouraged me, over a decade ago, to first attempt writing a novel. She will be sorely missed.

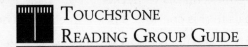
The Black Hand

1. The following quotation from Machiavelli is used as the book's epigraph: "I'm not interested in the status quo; I want to overthrow it." What is the significance of this statement? Why do you think the author chose a Machiavelli quote, and this one in particular?

2. The prologue to *The Black Hand* is set at the seaside estate of Barker's lady love, though "the Widow" herself is not actually introduced until midway through the story. What effect did this opening setting have on your reading experience, especially if you have read previous novels in the Barker & Llewelyn series? Do you think that introducing the novel at Philippa's home emphasizes an element of romance? If the story had begun with a scene involving the battle at the docks, how would that change the tone of this novel?

3. Barker relates the history of the Mafia to Llewelyn as they become more involved in their investigation. Were you surprised to discover that the Mafia was actually conceived in London by a member of the Freemason society (p. 55) as a movement to overthrow the French occupation in Sicily? Did you find that the historical references throughout the novel enriched your reading experience? Are there any particular historical elements in the book that you might further explore and research?

4. Inspector Pettigrilli remarks to Barker, "You make it very easy for criminals in this country. They come and go quite freely, if I may say it. England is very indulgent" (p. 66). Consider what you may know about modern immigration laws in England. How different do you think the situation is today from the way it is portrayed in the Victorian London of *The Black Hand*? How do Barker and Llewelyn regard the various immigrant communities featured in this story? Do these immigrants consider themselves true Londoners? Do you think that crime is a result of illegal immigration, or are the two primarily unrelated? Discuss your feelings with the group.

5. Barker explains to Llewelyn, "There is nothing more dangerous than a mercenary, trained in the art of war, who is cunning enough to use the political situation to his own economic advantage" (p. 118). As Llewelyn points out, Barker, too, can be defined as a mercenary of sorts. How does Barker regard his occupation?

6. Were you surprised by Llewelyn's decision to continue working with Barker after he was given the option to find new employment? Or did you expect it? Do you think his decision was affected by the fact that so much of Barker's personal life was revealed to him while the two worked on this case? How did your feelings about Barker evolve after you learned about his life as a pirate, his relationship with Philippa, and his atypical praise for Llewelyn?

7. As Barker and Llewelyn wrap up the details of the case, Barker reveals that at some point throughout the investigation he suspected almost everyone involved (p. 272). As the reader, who did you believe was guilty? Did you guess

that Hooligan would defect and help the Sicilians during the dock battle? Did you think that Marco Faldo was actually masquerading as another character? What methods did Will Thomas employ to maintain the mystery in *The Black Hand*?

8. How does *The Black Hand* compare to other mob and Mafia stories that you're familiar with? If this book were to become a movie, whom would you cast as its characters?

Enhance Your Book Club

Research the secret societies or organizations mentioned in the book, such as the Camorra, the Mafia, and the Freemasons. Find a surprising fact, such as an unexpected member of such societies or an episode in which such societies were involved. Share your research with the group.

Play a game using the *L'occhio* skills (p. 75) that Llewelyn learned from Mr. Gallenga. Have one member of the group create a setting with various target objects. Pass out flyers with the target objects listed, and allow the group members to have thirty seconds to survey the room and record where the objects are located. The person who successfully spies the most objects from the list should win a prize.

Host your book club meeting at an Italian restaurant or, if possible, one serving Sicilian-style dishes.

A Conversation with Will Thomas

What was your inspiration for the plot of The Black Hand?

My inspiration came from various books I've read about the founding of the Mafia and the methods they used during the nineteenth century, before getaway cars and tommy guns were invented. Secret societies always fascinate us, don't you think?

What kind of research did you do in advance of writing the novel? Are any of your characters based on historical figures?

I did research on the Mafia and Sicily back to the days of the Crusades, and on the Camorra back to the time of Cervantes, mostly through books long out of print. It is amazing what horrible deeds are recorded in old tomes buried in college libraries. Antonio Gallenga was a historical person, but the others have come from my overactive imagination.

Do Italian organized crime groups still exist in modern England? Has the Black Hand technique been employed by such groups since the nineteenth century?

Like *Some Danger Involved*, *The Black Hand* is a what-if novel. In this case, what if the Mafia had tried to set up shop in the British Empire's capital city? Instead, they went to New Orleans and eventually to Chicago and New York. As for Black Hand notes, yes, they were used often, and are more historically accurate than the "kiss of death" shown in many movies.

You've integrated martial arts and stick fighting into previous Barker & Llewelyn novels. The Black Hand *features Sicilian dagger fighting. Did you know anything about this form of combat prior to writing this novel?*

Writing gives me the opportunity to study various historical arts under private tutors, and *The Black Hand* is no exception. At the same time, there's something very unsettling about knife fighting. That's why I have Barker and

Llewelyn discussing the question "Is it worse to be shot or stabbed?"

Are you a fan of The Sopranos *or of contemporary mob movies such as* The Godfather *and* Goodfellas?

The Godfather is a classic. Like most men, I have to see it once a year. When watching a movie like that, however, I always ask myself, "What would this have been like in 1885?"

Now that you've written five novels in a series, how do you come up with new adventures for Barker and Llewelyn?

Sometimes I focus on particular people in London. Other times I follow historical events that still resonate today. Or I will simply ask my characters, "What comes next?" Before I know it, Llewelyn is spinning me another tale.

Every novel in the Barker & Llewelyn series thus far has been told from Llewelyn's perspective. Would you ever consider writing from Barker's point of view?

Never! Cyrus Barker keeps his secrets and hasn't the ego to set down his own cases. It is Llewelyn, the frustrated storyteller, who cannot help but pick up the pen and try to make sense of the world.

Your books are all set in Victorian London; are there any other time periods that particularly interest you? Would you want to explore those periods through historical fiction?

I'm more interested in exploring the Victorian era around the world—in Japan, perhaps, or colonial Hawaii, even the Old West. But I'd like to write a contemporary novel with a protagonist who has Victorian sensibilities. That idea has prospects.